The Literary Construction of the Other in the Acts of the Apostles

Princeton Theological Monograph Series

K. C. Hanson, Charles M. Collier, D. Christopher Spinks,
and Robin Parry, Series Editors

The Literary Construction of the Other in the Acts of the Apostles

Charismatics, the Jews, and Women

Mitzi J. Smith

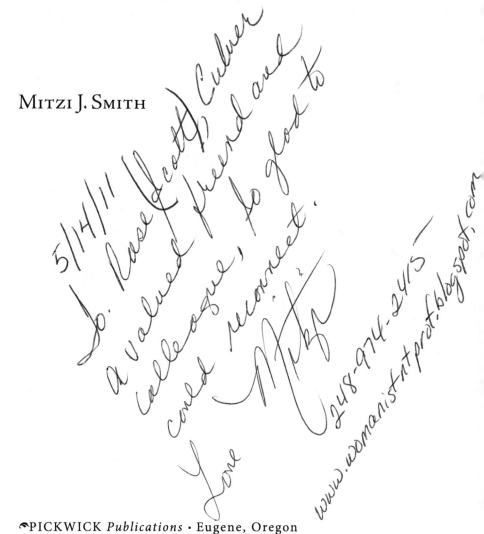

5/14/11

To. Rose Scott Culver

a valued friend and colleague, so good to

could uneconnect.

Love Mitzi

248-974-2415

www.womanistprof.blogspot.com

PICKWICK *Publications* · Eugene, Oregon

THE LITERARY CONSTRUCTION OF THE OTHER
IN THE ACTS OF THE APOSTLES
Charismatics, the Jews, and Women

Princeton Theological Monograph Series 154

Pickwick Publications
An Imprint of Wipf and Stock Publishers
199 W. 8th Ave., Suite 3
Eugene, OR 97401

www.wipfandstock.com

ISBN 13: 978-1-60899-384-0

Cataloging-in-Publication data:

Smith, Mitzi J.

The literary construction of the other in the acts of the Apostles : charismatics, the Jews, and women / Mitzi J. Smith.

Princeton Theological Monograph Series 154

xiv + 172 p. ; 23 cm. Includes bibliographical references.

ISBN 13: 978-1-60899-384-0

1. Bible. N.T. Acts—Criticism, interpretation, etc. 2. Narration in the Bible. I. Title. II. Series.

BS2589 S55 2011

Manufactured in the U.S.A.

To my late mother

Flora Opheila Carson Smith

(February 4, 1929—March 14, 2009)

whom I loved fiercely and miss daily.

Thank you for loving, guiding, mentoring,

and always believing in me.

Contents

Acknowledgments

This book lay dormant in me waiting for the moment of its birth. In fact on my Facebook page I likened its creation to the birth of a child. I was in labor for quite some time. This book is based on my Harvard doctoral dissertation, which I completed in October 2005. In March 2006 I accepted a teaching position. Shortly thereafter I became Executive Minister at the Oak Grove A.M.E. Church in Detroit. Needless to say, the two positions combined left little time for writing and research. In addition, one night I returned from a church meeting to find that my apartment had been burglarized. My laptop and my new memory drive were stolen and both contained the only copies of the latest revisions to my dissertation manuscript. The novelty of owning a "jump drive" created a false sense of security. And I failed to email copies of revised chapters to myself as I had done when working on the dissertation. Therefore, all that remained was the bound dissertation and partial copies of revisions.

I returned to the manuscript after experiencing a vocational revival of sorts. I attended the Wabash Center's 2008–09 Workshop for Pre-tenured Faculty at Theological Schools. That program afforded me the opportunity to work on another writing project in the summer of 2009. That project renewed and reawakened in me a sense of vocation that had slowly seeped from my soul. The Spirit (I prefer to believe) reminded me of all of my hard work and of the support and time my dissertation advisor, Professor François Bovon, invested in my project and in me. I am thankful to Prof. Bovon for his willingness to share with me his expertise and his time. I am equally grateful for the confidence he demonstrated in me and in my project. I thank Lawrence Wills, Allen Callahan, and Laura Nashrallah for serving on my dissertation committee and for the helpful counsel that they provided.

I greatly appreciate and value my friends and colleagues Naomi Jacobs and Sheila Winborne for reading parts of the manuscript at various stages. I am grateful to my colleagues and students at Ashland

Theological Seminary in Detroit and Ohio for their support and encouragement. I truly appreciate the proofreading and citation checking provided by Ashland Theological Seminary/Detroit master's students Dr. K. C. Lazzara, Marshondra Lawrence, Lisa Mayowa Reynolds, Sheyonna Watson, and Judith West.

I am most eternally indebted to my late mother, Flora O. Smith, who knew I would earn a PhD long before I decided what I would do with my call and life. My mother was my first mentor, from whom I learned to pray without ceasing, to trust in the promises of God, to have confidence in the God in me, to persevere even when I seem to be standing alone, and to know that God is "no respecter of persons." I dedicate this work to her memory. She was truly my shero.

Abbreviations

Ancient Sources

1 Apol.	Justin Martyr, *First Apology*
Act Andr.	*Acts of Andrew*
Act Pet.	*Acts of Peter*
Act Thom.	*Acts of Thomas*
Ag. Ap.	Josephus, *Against Apion*
Alex.	Lucian, *Alexander the False Prophet*
Ant.	Josephus, *Antiquities of the Jews*
Ascen. Isa.	*Ascension of Isaiah*
Aus.	Suetonius, *Life of Augustus*
Chaer.	Chariton, *Chaereas and Callirhoe*
Civ.	Augustine, *De civitate Dei*
Eccl. Hist.	Eusebius, *Ecclesiastical History*
Flacc.	Philo, *In Flaccum*, translated by Andre Pelletier, in *Les Oeuvres de Philon d'Alexandrie*, edited by Roger Arnaldez et al. (Paris: Moubourge, 1967)
Gos. Pet.	*Gospel of Peter*
Gos. Phil.	*Gospel of Philip*
Herm. Mand.	*Shepherd of Hermas, Mandate*
J.W.	Josephus, *Jewish War*
Mos. 1, 2	Philo, *De Vita Moses* I, II, in *Les Oeuvres de Philon d'Alexandrie*, translated by Roger Arnaldez et al. (Paris: Maubourge, 1967)
Prot. Jas.	*Protoevangelium of James*
Ps.-Clem.	*Clementinorum Epitomae* [*Pseudo-Clementines*] *Duae*, edited by Alberti Dressel and Friderici Wieselerie (Lipsiae: Henrichs, 1873)
Test.	Cyprian, "ΔΙΑΘΑΚΗ ΝΕΦΘΑΛΙΜ ΠΕΡΙ ΦΥΣΙΚΗΣ ΑΓΑΘΟΤΗΤΟΞ," in *Testaments of the Twelve Patriarchs: A Critical Edition of Greek Text*, edited

by Marinus de Jonge; Pseudepigrapha Veteris
Testamenti Graece 1/2 (Leiden: Brill, 1978)

Secondary Sources

AB	Anchor Bible
AJSR	*American Journal for the Study of Religion*
ANRW	*Aufstief und Niedergang der römischen Welt: Geschichte und Kultur Roms in Spiegel der neueren Forschung*
AusJL	*Australian Journal of Linguistics*
BETL	Bibliotheca Ephemeridum Theologicarum Lovaniensium
Bib	*Biblica*
BibInt	*Biblical Interpretation*
BibRes	*Biblical Research*
BibT	*The Bible Today*
BTB	*Biblical Theology Bulletin*
CBQ	*Catholic Biblical Quarterly*
ChH	*Church History*
CTM	*Currents in Theology and Mission*
DiscSoc	*Discourse & Society*
DownRev	*Downside Review*
ExpT	*Expository Times*
FF	Foundations and Facets
FPNT	*Feminist Perspectives on the New Testament*
HTS	Harvard Theological Studies
ICC	International Critical Commentary
Int	*Interpretation*
JAAC	*Journal of Aesthetics and Art Criticism*
JBL	*Journal of Biblical Literature*
JES	*Journal of Ecumenical Studies*
JHS	*Journal of Hellenic Studies*
JRS	*Journal of Roman Studies*
JSNT	*Journal for the Study of the New Testament*
JSNTSup	Journal for the Study of the New Testament: Supplement Series
JSoc	*Journal of Sociolinguistics*

JSOTSup	Journal for the Study of the Old Testament: Supplement Series
JTC	*Journal for Theology and the Church*
JTS	*Journal of Theological Studies*
LL	*Language and Literature*
NIBC	New Interpreter's Bible Commentary
NIDB	*New International Dictionary of the Bible*
NLH	*New Literary History*
NovT	*Novum Testamentum*
NTApoc	*New Testament Apocrypha*, edited by E. Hennecke and W. Schneemelcher, translated by R. McL Wilson; 2 vols. (Louisville: Westminster/John Knox, 1963–65)
NTS	*New Testament Studies*
PRS	*Perspectives in Religious Studies*
PT	*Poetics Today*
RevExp	*Review and Expositor*
RHR	*Revue de l'Histoire des Religions*
RSPT	*Revue des sciences philosophiques et théologiques*
RSR	*Recherches de science religieuse*
RTP	*Revue de théologie et de philosophie*
SBLDS	Society of Biblical Literature Dissertation Series
SBLMS	Society of Biblical Literature Monograph Series
SBLSP	*Society of Biblical Literature Seminar Papers*
SEA	*Svensk exegetisk arsbok*
SLJT	*St. Luke's Journal of Theology*
SNTSMS	Society for New Testament Studies Monograph Series
SocRel	*Sociology of Religion*
SP	Sacra pagina
TDNT	*Theological Dictionary of the New Testament*, translated and edited by G. W. Bromiley; 10 vols (Grand Rapids: Eerdmans, 1964–76)
ThT	*Theology Today*
ThZ	*Theologische Literaturzeitung*
TynB	*Tyndale Bulletin*
VC	*Vigiliae Christianae*
WW	*Word & World*
ZNW	*Zeitschrift für die neutestamentliche Wissenschaft und die Kunde der älteren Kirche*
ZTK	*Zeitschrift für Theologie und Kirche*

Introduction

IN THE 2008 PRESIDENTIAL ELECTIONS, CANDIDATES FROM BOTH PAR-
ties struggled to demonstrate the differences in their positions on the
pertinent issues in order to distinguish themselves from their opponents. To win votes and elections they discursively demonstrated that
their positions on issues aligned with voters' opinions. Candidates constructed and capitalized on differences between themselves and their
opponents in order to minimize similarities. Candidates discursively
constructed their opposition as the other. This othering was manifested
in the categorizing, name calling, and demonization of others with similar convictions in order to portray them as absolutely other. Candidates
represented their opponents as immoral, uncaring, lacking the talents
and/or experience for the job, unsafe, palling around with terrorists,
inter alia.

Of course, this othering continues beyond the election season.
And with the election of the first African-American U.S. President
and the seating of a Democratic majority in the house and senate, the
public and discursive construction of otherness among opponents has
ratcheted up. For example, during the health care debate, the discursive
construction of otherness cluttered the mediasphere, the blogosphere,
the Twittersphere, and other social network sites with intensity. Some
Democrats, the president and his administration, and supporters of
health care reform have become the immoral and annihilating enemy
who want to kill grandma and invade the lives of Americans. They are
described as anti-American, Hitler-like, socialists, baby killers, com-
munists, and ultimately demonic. Likewise, some Republicans and
teapartyers were labeled as categorically racist, self-serving, greedy,
"Republican Rhinos," hate mongers, and satanic as well.

This othering takes place within the larger context of the worst re-
cession since the Great Depression and the Iraq and Afghanistan wars.
In this context, people are trying to preserve for themselves a sense
of identity (or shape a new and viable one) amidst these global and

I

mundane challenges affecting our lives (i.e., job losses, foreclosures, threat of terrorism [domestic and foreign], and an uncertain future). People want to know how their lives might change for better or worse in this uncertain and threatening climate. Some people are experiencing an identity crisis, and certainly our nation is at a decisive and redefining moment, and the choices made will determine our place in the world and how we are perceived globally. Within this context, a redefining of self takes place over against a demon within and a demon without; us against them.

Othering in politics is often theologically framed, and othering among Christians is inherently political. One day after the earthquake in Haiti and before the ground had stopped trembling and the dust could settle, some Christian leaders hastened to demonize the Haitian people while many still lay trapped and buried alive under ruble and concrete and singing the praises of God. Even as the Haitians expressed their hope in God amidst devastation upon devastation, some Christians in America were accusing them of being devil worshippers. One blogger stated that the four apocalyptic horsemen had been unleashed over Haiti and that, through the practice of "voodoo" and witchcraft,[1] the devil is strategically subduing Haiti.[2] And that same day, January 13, 2010, of course, Televangelist Pat Robertson declared that Haiti had made a "pact with the devil" years ago. To which the Honorable Raymond Joseph, Haitian Ambassador to the U.S., rebuffed that one of the greatest beneficiaries of Haiti's so-called pact with the devil was the U.S., which consequently purchased the Louisiana territories for fifteen cents an acre.[3] Jonathan Z. Smith argues that "[t]he issue of problematic similarity or identity seems to be particularly prevalent in religious discourse and imagination."[4] Smith further asserts that the demonization of someone against her/his will who is considered as estranged is restricted to "Christian texts [and contexts] that represent a unique attempt to overcome similarity rather than the perception of dissimilarity."[5]

1. For an informative and brief article on Vodou in response to the demonization of Haitian religious practices, see Diakité, "Myth of 'Voodoo.'"

2. Kaylania, "Earthquake in Haiti."

3. Maddow, "Haitian Ambassador."

4. Smith, "Differential Equations," 245.

5. Smith, "Towards Interpreting Demonic Powers," 428.

Too often we resort to constructing difference between those who are like us but whom we do not understand and cannot control. Otherness is "a description of interaction" according to Smith. He argues that a project of otherness, othering, is more often than not about proximity and not about absolute difference. Otherness is about proximity and not alterity; the other who is most like us is most threatening and most problematic. Rarely is the radically, absolute other of concern to us, but we are most concerned with the other who is too similar.[6] Difference is constructed in order to distinguish ourselves from proximate others. Our constructions of the other generally function to subordinate the other to us. Projects of othering are linguistic or discursive, evaluative, hierarchical, and they are "essentially political and economic."[7]

When we construct images of ourselves over against an other, we will go to great lengths to preserve our constructed self-identities as well as our representations of others, since in a project of othering we create our identities on the backs of or in opposition to our representations of others. This construction of otherness occurs in written texts as well as in public discourse. Otherness gets inscribed in both fictional and nonfictional texts. We more expect or readily accept how characters are represented in fictional works as synthetic or constructed. But we do not expect, or we find it difficult to accept, that characterizations in sacred texts might be synthetic constructions and mimetic representations of real people. Sacred texts produced by fallible humans, mediated through human language and culture, and arising out of human situatedness, are no less likely to represent projects of othering or to construct otherness, consciously or unconsciously. Often otherness gets reinscribed and fossilized or codified in texts, especially sacred texts. And we tend to uncritically imbibe those literary and discursive constructions of stereotyped and politicized others. Those images likely become foundations for how we view others in the real world. We impose or reinscribe the stereotyped and demonized other upon our world and the world of others, many times unwittingly and sometimes consciously.

When we read a text, we enter the constructed world of the text. The world of the text is a constructed literary cosmos that reflects and reflects upon a real world. In the beginning, God gave humans the power to re-create or to contribute to the continued construction of

6. Smith, "Differential Equations," 256, 259.
7. Smith, "What a Difference," 253, 259, 275.

our world—to till, to plant, and to multiply. This power to construct our worlds did not cease with the entrance of sin, and thus our fallibility is imprinted upon the worlds we construct. No less in the world of a text, even in the biblical text, we find the imprint of human fallibility on the world constructed within the text. When we read, we enter into a fallible world, and we are confronted with fallible characters; the only infallible one is God who precedes and transcends the text. "Doubtless God is by no means man [or woman]. He is the other, the absolutely other. . . . Human language can only ever speak of him in approximate terms or by homonymy."[8]

In the Acts of the Apostles, Luke[9] constructs a world. The world that Luke constructs centers on the story of how the eleven apostles and other disciples continued the Jesus movement after his ascension. It is the story of how that nucleus of believers gathered in an upper room to wait on the Holy Spirit that the Father promised would be poured upon them to empower them as God's witnesses. It is the story of how after the Holy Spirit anointed them, they witnessed about how God raised Jesus, they baptized believers who accepted Jesus as the Messiah, and they gathered the new believers into a community/communities that became known as the *ekklēsias* (usually translated "church," but throughout this book I will primarily use this term to represent the early assembly of believers who later became an institutional church).[10] Acts is the story of the beginnings of the Christian church; it is about how the early believers became a unified koinonia; it is about how they constituted themselves and began shaping a self-identity. And this self-identity was formed over against others, beginning with the selection of Judas' replacement, if not sooner. Judas' replacement had to be a male who accompanied the eleven and Jesus from the event of his baptism by John until his ascension (1:21–25).

Historically, some church fathers and others have used passages and images from the book of Acts to distinguish orthodox Christians from heretical others. François Bovon notes that in the third century Tertullian (ca. 160–220) used the canonical book of Acts polemically in

---

8. Benbassa and Attias, *Jew and the Other*, 10.

9. Throughout the book I refer to the author of Luke-Acts as Luke.

10. See Acts 19:32–40 where *ekklēsia* is translated "assembly" in the NRSV and refers to a formal and informal secular gathering. Schüssler Fiorenza (*Power of the Word*, 10) notes that *ekklēsia* is primarily a political and not a religious term.

his opus *Against Marcion*. Bovon further notes that Acts was less useful among early Christian communities but "only became important later, when it was necessary to base correct doctrine on the teaching and career of some of the apostles."[11] And Cyprian (third-century North African bishop), Bovon asserts, mined the quarry of Acts for the multiple quotations that supported his *Testimonia against the Jews* (*Test.* 1.21 quotes from 13:46b–47 Paul's exclamation of turning to the Gentiles).[12] Cyprian refers to Acts as a "scriptural authority" when he uses it in a doctrinal controversy over the (in)validity of baptism received by heretics wanting to join the catholic church.[13] It is likely because of Luke's construction of the Jews as the other that Arator, the sixth-century orator and subdeacon in Rome, referred to the Jews as "savage men" in his commentary on Acts.[14] Many interpreters of the biblical text, ancient and modern, have reinscribed and appropriated characterizations of groups such as *the Jews* or the Pharisees in polemical, didactic, and kerygmatic discourses unchallenged and without qualification.

Again, othering has to do with interaction among groups, and it is about constructing ourselves over against others. In Acts, interaction is inherent to the story of the dissemination of the gospel. Othering in Acts is exacerbated by the fact that the primary plot of the narrative takes place within the framework of expansionism ("to Jerusalem, Judea, Samaria and to the end of the earth," 1:8) both in familiar and unfamiliar territory, among peoples who are similar or proximate even in the diaspora (i.e., in synagogues, where Paul dialogues with both Jews and Godfearing Gentiles). The construction of the other has to do with the drawing of boundaries in order to clearly distinguish between them and us. The drawing of boundaries becomes necessary because of any fluidity or similarity that exists between them and us. Othering involves the obliteration of sameness and the foregrounding and/or construction of difference.

---

11. Bovon, "Reception of Acts, " 74. While Cyprian (middle third century), following Tertullian, uses the phrase "in the Acts of the Apostles," he only once considers an Acts quotation as an excerpt from "Scripture" (ibid., 75).

12. Ibid., 74

13. Ibid., 76. Cyprian favored (re)baptism since the first baptism was not a true baptism (Cyprian, *Epist.* 72).

14. Arator, *On Acts*, 43.

In the prologue of Luke's Gospel (1:1–4), he inscribes in the text a dichotomy of otherness between the "many" and himself ("me"). Both Luke and the "many" have written narratives about Jesus' deeds based on eyewitness accounts. Luke's project of othering is prompted by the existence of other accounts on the same subject. Luke further evaluates his narrative as "more accurate," and this evaluation gives Luke's readers the impression that his Gospel constitutes objective truth and is therefore superior to other accounts. Thus, the motivation given for writing Luke's narrative is based on sameness and the need to distinguish his Gospel from the narratives of the "many." This evaluation applies to both Luke and Acts. The reference to the *first* book at Acts 1:1 connects Acts to Luke's Gospel as its sequel. Thus, the inscribed audience in Acts (Theophilus) and some contemporary readers should apply Luke's evaluation of his Gospel as objective truth ("more accurate") to Acts as well. By contending that Luke-Acts is objective truth in the sense of being more accurate and able to transmit "truthfulness," Luke rhetorically constructs, communicates, and inscribes otherness. As stated above, a theory of otherness is political in that it creates hierarchical relationships. In this case the hierarchical relationship is between "many" other narratives and Luke-Acts. This othering project extends beyond the prologue.

In addition to the boundaries drawn between proximate others who are differentiated and identified as outside of the collective, a second boundary is marked. Jonathan Boyarin asserts that the second boundary lies "between the collective with which one is conventionally identified and the presumably alien collective Other."[15] For example, most named women in Acts are identified with the collective *ekklēsia* as believers, but their gender also identifies them as the "alien collective Other," or the internal other.[16] My goal is to demonstrate how characters are constructed as internal and external others in the book of Acts. Characters who are considered or who become insiders, acknowledged believers, and/or members of the Jesus movement but who are in some way marginalized constitute *internal others*. Internal others are generally passive in relation to the apostles; but external others act more aggressively when compared to the apostles. *External others* consist of characters that remain fully or partially outside of the Jesus

---

15. Boyarin, "Other Within," 433.

16. See Wills, *Insiders and Outsiders*, 205.

movement and who are stereotypically depicted as hostile others in relation to the apostles despite their religious and functional proximity.
Both external and internal others function as a foil for the construction of self-identity for the apostles and other approved intermediaries.
Stereotypical images of proximate others are weaved into the fabric of
Acts. Readers encounter a constructed or represented world of character interaction. The witnesses of the gospel mission, as approved
intermediaries, interact with other characters, their proximate others.
As characters interact, Luke constructs and foregrounds difference between the approved intermediaries and three groups: charismatics, the
Jews, and women. Constructions of otherness are inscribed in the text,
and if we are not careful we accept constructions of others, of otherness,
as infallible and pure. Consequently we reinscribe that otherness, the
constructed stereotypical and demonized other, into our worlds. This
has been particularly true in the case of women and Jewish persons.
Women whose lives and actions do not fully coincide with literary and
discursive constructions of women in the biblical text as submissive,
silent, or subordinate are considered as walking outside of God's will.
Jewish persons who do not accept their collective blame for the death of
Jesus and opposition to the apostolic mission are in denial and continue
to be blamed and damned.

Too often our self-identity as Christians relies upon our readings
of the inscription of otherness in the biblical text. If that foundation is
shaken, if the other is deconstructed so that she is no longer the reliable foil against whom we understand ourselves, our whole theological
and ontological house, we fret, might crumble. We find it difficult, if not
impossible, to communicate about ourselves without talking about others whom we have determined are nothing like us. We are not like the
Pharisees, the Sadducees, the Jews, the Romans, the Philistines, or the
Jezebels. And as Virginia Domínguez argues, our representation of the
other belongs to us; we author them.[17] The other we have constructed
is our creation, and no one else, not even the other herself, can redefine
her; she is exactly how we have constructed her, and what she has to say
about her own identity is irrelevant and false. We do not want anyone to
tamper with what we have constructed because in so doing they meddle
with the identity we have constructed for ourselves. I once had a stu-
dent in an Acts class assert that anyone who refused to sign her pro-life

17. Domínguez, *People as Subject*, 157–58.

petition was not a Christian. Many Christians, black and white, voted for Bush's second term as president solely on the grounds of the abortion issue. It became the defining factor of their Christianity over against the pro-choice advocates, and little else mattered.

In this book, I employ Smith's theory of otherness as a framework for analyzing Luke's literary and discursive construction of character in Acts. In chapter 1 I examine how Luke has constructed charismatic others (so-called magicians) over against the approved intermediaries of the gospel mission. Charismatic others are proximate others who function like approved intermediaries but whom Luke constructs as external others in order to demonstrate the superiority of the approved intermediates and to form a self-identity for the *ekklēsia* and its leadership. In chapter 2 I continue to explore how Luke constructs an identity for the approved intermediaries, but this chapter focuses on the characterization of *the Jews* as the external other. I also demonstrate how Paul's three declarations about turning toward the Gentiles constitute a dialectic of abandonment and remaining, and create a narrative tension that is unresolved when the narrative ends. Chapters 3 and 4 focus on Luke's construction of women in relation to apostles Peter and Paul, respectively. I continue to use a theory of otherness as a framework for examining how Luke constructs women as the internal other to enhance the identity of apostles as approved intermediaries and to redeem Peter from negative portrayals of him in Luke's Gospel. Women are primarily situated in narrative instabilities involving disorder, but they never have a say in the restoration of order. The ordering of the community and the restoration of order remains the privilege of approved intermediaries, and they are male.

In this study I generally bracket attempts at historical reconstruction, but I employ extra-biblical sources comparatively and dialogically. In other words, extra-biblical sources sometimes provide analogs for insightful dialogue with the book of Acts. I am concerned primarily with a close narrative or literary reading of Acts as a unified text. This study does not concern itself with source-critical questions, even though I engage scholarly interpretations that are based on source criticism.

In addition to a theory of otherness, I also employ ergative-based transitivity analysis to highlight transitive agency. An ergative-based transitivity analysis differs from a simple transitivity analysis, primarily in terms of perspective.[18] A simple transitivity analysis concerns whether or not an action extends to an object beyond the acting subject. For example, in the sentence "Napria threw the ball," the verb "threw" extends to the object/noun "ball." The verb is therefore transitive and the action extends to someone or something. We identify "Napria" as the participant-actor and "the ball" as an inanimate participant-object. The action is a material process, namely, doing something to someone or something beyond the subject-actor.

Both ergative and simply transitivity models are concerned with whether or not there are one or two participants (participant-actor and/ or participant-object) in the clause. However, the primary issue in the ergative-based transitivity model is whether the participant involved in the process is the same one who engenders the process or whether the process is caused by another entity. An ergative-based transitivity model focuses on causation.[19] For example, in the sentence "The boat set sail," the grammar does not tell us who caused the boat to sail. In the sentence "*The Jews* aroused the crowd," we can say that *the Jews* as participant-actor caused *the crowd* as participant-object to be aroused; *the Jews* acted in a material way upon *the crowd* as participant-object. Ergative material processes express the highest degree of transitive agency. Causative agency can be obscured by passive constructions, by circumstantial elements, or by embedded speech acts. Transitivity analysis can aid in answering more precisely these questions: Who does what and to whom? What kind and degree of agency do the characters portray? And how do these depictions contribute to the structure and resolution of the narrative instabilities?[20] Transitivity analysis shows that when the apostles are inserted into narrative instabilities with external others, the apostles are passive displaying the lowest level of transitive agency when compared to *the Jews* and charismatic others. The apostles are primarily the participant-objects, while the external others are the participant-actors. More often the apostles' agency is expressed in performative speech acts. While speech is central to the agency of approved intermediaries, speech or the muting of speech contributes to women's marginalization.

---

18. Halliday, *Introduction*, 154–59.

19. Ibid., 145, 149; also Halliday, *Explorations*, 36–44.

20. Phelan, *Reading People*, 15, 91.

I hope that this study will at least provoke critical thinking about how character is constructed in Acts and how those constructions might become reinscribed into contemporary discourse about Christian identity and in our public theological discourse in non-liberating ways.

1

The Construction of Charismatics as External Other

IN THE MIDST OF THE DEVASTATION AND UNIMAGINABLE SUFFERING of the Haitian people exacerbated by the recent earthquake, too many religious leaders chose to interpret the event in the framework of a self-serving theodicy. Christian pontifications that the practice of voodoo religion among Haitians is derivatively demonic and constitutes devil worship functioned to construct the Haitians as the external others in need of salvation. Some religious leaders concluded that the Haitians brought this destruction on themselves; that God was punishing the Haitians because of their so-called practices of witchcraft, magic, and voodoo. Haitian men, women, and children sang and testified of God's goodness while trapped under the rubble. They praised God because they escaped death's grip; they sang even though their mothers, fathers, sons, and daughters died before their eyes. They sang God's praises when the sky was the only roof over their heads and when hope alone cradled their grief and succored their hunger. Yet, some Christian leaders persisted in using this catastrophe as an opportunity to distinguish between themselves and the other. Such leaders would proclaim that their own misfortune is primarily because the devil is after them. But others' misfortunes are because they *are* the devil or children of the devil.

Few contexts and texts are free from projects of othering, including the contextual world inscribed in the biblical text. In this chapter I employ a theory of otherness as a conceptual framework for examining the relationship between the apostles and other charismatics in the world Luke constructs in the book of Acts. The construction of otherness has to do with proximity. Proximity allows one to see one's self or likeness in the other and to view one's self differently from others. In a construction of self, we attempt to overcome or transcend proximity— to distinguish the self from others that are most like us. Proximity can constitute a barrier to the construction of self-identity. To construct a self-identity, which includes claims to authority, power, or space, we distance ourselves from others like us. As noted above, a theory of otherness concerns sameness rather than difference or alterity.[1] The proximate other is problematic and rarely considered an object of indifference. A group or individual considered radically other remains simply other and of little consequence. The other becomes most problematic when she appears too-much-like-us; and thus hinders construction of a clear self-identity.[2] Otherness is predicated upon distinguishing between entities that are proximate. This proximity manifests itself in several ways. Proximity may be based on ethnicity, social status, geography, religion, or vocational activities.

The charismatic others that I examine are Simon (Acts 8), Bar-Jesus (Acts 13), the Pythian slave girl (Acts 16), and the seven sons of High Priest Sceva (Acts 19).[3] I argue that these charismatics are at least spatially and functionally or vocationally proximate to the apostles. This proximity to the apostles is the impetus for Luke's othering of non-apostolic charismatics. Functional proximity refers to the charismatic others' possession of capabilities and/or powers similar to the apostles (and the seven Hellenists). These capabilities include the performance of miraculous acts, exorcisms, and/or prophetic oracles. The charismatic others perform miracles and exercise influence that often results in the amassing of disciples or devoted followers whom the apostles also seek to affect. Similar to the apostles, charismatic others either claim divine power and/or authority or persons attribute power and/or authority to them.[4]

1. Smith, "Towards Interpreting Demonic Powers," 428.

2. Smith, "What a Difference," 10–16, 45–47.

3. Reimer (*Miracle and Magic*, 47) considers these four characters as negatively portrayed intermediaries. Peter, Paul, Philip, the Twelve, Ananias, and the prophets and teachers in Antioch are key intermediaries. Negatively portrayed or illegitimate intermediaries are unsuccessful at managing "the tension of gaining power without appearing to be ambitious."

4. Sanders (*Charisma, Converts*) employs Max Weber's sociological framework to show that Jesus was a charismatic leader similar to prophets in Millenarian movements. The framework for deciding whether one is a charismatic leader includes:

The spatial and temporal proximity of charismatics to the apostles refers to how the charismatics occupy the same geographical space as the apostles, either simultaneously or successively. This sharing of space by the charismatic others and the apostles is not accidental. Luke creates situations in which the charismatic others converge with the apostles, spatially and temporally. These situations introduce instabilities and opportunities for the forward movement of the story. Narrative instabilities revolve around conflict between characters. Authors produce instabilities by introducing situations between characters that are complicated and/or resolved through further actions. In other words, instabilities develop from narrative situations. An author can create instabilities by introducing an event or someone that alters (or potentially alters) in some way relationships between characters.[5]

In the narratives I shall analyze, the conflicts center on the convergence of proximate characters that perform similar activities and interact within the same space. The narrative instability is resolved through further action or inaction. The resolution is the marginalization and discursive othering of the charismatic others who are ultimately rendered impotent.

Luke attempts to present a dynamic overtaking and overcoming of proximity by constructing difference and drawing boundaries between the apostles and other charismatics. As the book of Acts unfolds, the narrative progresses toward constructing a clear self-identity for the apostles (particularly for Peter and Paul, who metonymically represent the gospel mission and or the *ekklēsia*) as superior to indigenous charismatics. The apostles' identity as the superior charismatics metonymically translates into a representation of the gospel mission as triumphant.

Simon—Acts 8:4–24

The Simon narrative deserves special attention as the most extensive narrative of the four. Acts 8:4–24 serves as the basis for extra-biblical ancient traditions about Simon Magus, including the Christian apocryphal *Acts of Peter*, works of later heresiologists, and some church

(1) a call, (2) performance of wonders or miracles, (3) teachings, (4) emerges in distressful circumstances, (5) randomness—not always predictable, and (6) hated by others.

5. Phelan, *Reading People*, 15.

fathers.[6] Modern scholars have chiefly attempted to (a) disentangle hypothetical sources or traditions Luke might have relied on to construct the Simon narrative,[7] (b) excavate the text for vestiges of the historical Simon, and/or (c) clarify the relationship, if any, between Luke's Simon and the Simon of later ancient traditions.[8] Recently, scholars have examined Luke's story of Simon to discern distinctions the ancients may have made between magic and miracle.[9]

Ancient traditions constitute polemical and political constructions that categorically distinguish between magic and miracles. But many contemporary scholars disregard the polemical and political character of literary or rhetorical constructions of so-called magicians in Acts. Instead, some scholars uncritically impose on Acts the same absolute ideas about magic and miracle inscribed in ancient texts. Consequently, scholars identify Simon and other non-apostolic characters collectively as magicians under the influence of the demonic. Luke's construction of charismatic others does not betray a systematic, unambiguous, or universal conceptualization of magic or magicians as opposed to miracles and miracle workers.

Like Florent Heintz, I am interested in *how* Luke constructs character.[10] Heintz identifies the stereotypical motifs for accusations of magic

6 Justin Martyr, *1 Apol* 26.1–4; Irenaeus, *Against Heresies* 1.2; Hippolytus, *Refutation* 6.4–15; Epiphanius, *Panarion* 21.3.1–6; Ps.-Clem., *True Prophet* 17.3—35.5; also Eusebius, *Eccl. Hist.* 2.1.13.

7. For example, Waitz, "Die Quelle"; Haenchen, "Gab es seine vorchristliche Gnosis?"; Koch, "Geistbesitz, Geistverleihung." Derrett ("Simon Magus") appears to presume the historicity of Simon Magus. On the source critical question, Derrett argues that Luke interjected a Peter source into the middle of a Philip source. Matthews, "Philip and Simon."

8. For example, Cerfaux, "La gnose simonienne"; van Unnik, "Die Apostelgeschichte"; Beyschlag, *Simon Magus*; Wilson, "Simon and Gnostic Origins"; Bergmeier, "Die Gestalt des Simon Magus"; Lüdemann, "Acts."

9. Tuzlak, "Magician and the Heretic"; Haar, *Simon Magus*.

10. Heintz (*Simon*, 27–28) argues that the proper historical context for examining accusations of magic in Acts, particularly the Simon narrative, is Graeco-Roman invective against "thaumaturgical prophets" (a functional phrase): "The accusation of sorcery and of charlatanism charged against one or more thaumaturgical prophets constitutes, in fact, a extremely polemical genre shared with the ancients. Like many other charismatic personages in antiquity (Moses, Pythagoras, Jesus, Apollonius, et al.), Simon is the subject in Acts 8 of an accusation of magic in due and true form." ("L'accusation de sorcellerie et de charlatanisme portée contre un ou plusieurs prophètes thaumaturges constitue, en effet, un genre polémique extrêmement répandu chez les anciens. Comme

employed in invectives against thaumaturgical prophets, and he shows how Luke constructs these motifs to characterize Simon. Heintz departs from the traditional apologetic argument that contends Luke defends the apostles against accusations of sorcery leveled against Christians. Yet, he argues for an apologetic function that serves both "to legitimize their thaumaturgical power and to establish their spiritual authority" (*à légitimer leur pouvoir de thaumaturges et à établir leur authorité spiri-tuelle*). Conversely, Luke constructs a portrait of Simon that encourages his ancient readers to recognize him as "a sorcerer who casts a spell on his audience in order for them to admire and attach themselves to him as one who has been endowed with supernatural power" (*un sorcier qui a jeté un charme sur ses auditeurs pour les amener à l'admirer et à s'attacher à lui comme à un être dote d'une puissance surnaturelle*).[11] But Luke likewise constructs the apostles with a similar and superior su-pernatural power. Luke does so to shape an identity for the apostles as "approved intermediaries" over against charismatic others and to dem-onstrate the priority and success of the gospel mission. "Approved in-termediaries [i.e., the apostles] meet with success where non-approved intermediaries [i.e., Simon, Bar-Jesus, the Pythian slave girl, and sons of Sceva] have previously met with success as well."[12]

First Encounter between a Charismatic Other and Approved Intermediaries

The Other Across the Border: The Convergence of Philip and Simon

The first approved intermediary we encounter in the Simon narrative is Philip (one of the seven men that the apostles consecrated for table

---

beaucoup d'autres personages charismatiques de l'Antiquité (Moïse, Pythagore, Jésus, Apollonius, et al.), Simon fait l'objet en Actes 8 d'une accusation de magie en bonne et due forme"). Here and throughout, all translations are mine unless otherwise noted.

11. Ibid., 28–29, 36–40, 107, 144–45. Heintz (*Simon*) ultimately reconstructs a por-trait of historical Simon. Simon was perhaps a Samaritan thaumaturgical prophet who rendered some oracles, performed some signs, accumulated disciples, and was attached to a religious tradition. Heintz argues that invective begins with actual reported or known miracles (*wundergeschichte*) or skills, onto which are superimposed an accusa-tory framework.

12. Reimer, *Miracle and Magic*, 160.

ministry in response to the conflict concerning the neglected Hellenist widows; 6:1–7). The narrative situation featuring Simon and Philip (and later between Simon and the apostles Peter and John) constitutes the first instability beyond Judea. Philip arrives in Samaria after fleeing the persecution in Jerusalem (8:1–4). His border crossing or geographical transition from Jerusalem to Samaria is foretold at 1:8 (cf. 8:1).[13] It is in the context of border crossing that the reader meets the first named active charismatic other who is contemporary with the apostles.[14] Simon had already established himself in this Samaritan city where Philip flees from persecution. Philip's preaching and miracle working resemble Jesus' activities in Luke's Gospel. But Philip "goes beyond the bounds of Jesus' missionary territory when he does these things in Samaria." In Luke's Gospel the Samaritans generally do not accept Jesus, and he avoids crossing their borders (9:51–53; 17:11).[15]

Philip's border crossing into Samaria occasions the meeting of two charismatic figures who inhabit and function simultaneously in the same geographical area. This narrative instability involving the convergence of these two charismatics may prompt some readers to ask the following question: What happens as the gospel spreads outside of Jerusalem/Judea and the consecrated emissaries encounter other influential charismatic persons who possess capabilities similar to those of the approved intermediaries?

---

13. The Samaritans did not receive Jesus in Luke's Gospel because Jesus was determined to go to Jerusalem (9:51–56). This allows for the depiction of Samaria in Acts as virgin territory for the proclamation about Jesus.

14. This does not include Theudas and Judas the Galilean whom Gamaliel mentions at 5:34–37, although I would likewise categorize them as charismatic others.

15. Matthews (*Philip*, 48) further argues that Luke likely possessed a tradition about Philip's activities in Samaria. "Although it is quite schematic, it is clear that Philip follows directly in the line of Jesus with respect to the kinds of signs that he performs and the success that he enjoys. Further, his wonder-working activities put him on a par with the apostles and Paul, while at the same time the description of his deeds is suggestive of his particular contribution. Such a carefully constructed positive portrait of Philip calls into question Haenchen's contention that Luke viewed Philip as a 'subordinate outsider' and did everything possible to suppress traditions connected with him," 49–50. Matthews argues that the "transparent connection between Philip and Simon" is Samaria. Luke discovered a tradition that reported Philip's successes in Samaria including the conversion of a rival sect leader, 63.

THE PROXIMATE OTHER AND THE CONSTRUCTION OF OTHERNESS

After crossing the border, Philip wasted no time amassing adherents by proclaiming the word and performing signs (*sēmeia*), including exorcising unclean spirits and healing the lame (8:4–8). Thus, the Greek phrase *ekērussen autois ton Christon* ("he preached Christ to them [the people]," 8:5; cf. 8:4, 12)[16] only partially reflects Philip's activities in Samaria. Luke provides no direct speech for Philip (as compared to Peter and Stephen), but "the characterization of the manner and content of his speaking is comparable to Lukan descriptions of the preaching of Jesus, the apostles, and Paul."[17]

The signs (*sēmeia*) and great miracles (*dunameis megalas*) Philip performs win the people's undivided devotion. The Greek adverb *homothymadon* (of one accord) signifies the unified people's attachment to Philip (8:6, 7, 13). In Acts, *homothymadon* occurs similarly in the major summaries, where it depicts the unity of the new believers and their devotedness to the apostles' leadership and to their new community (2:42–47; 4:32–35; 5:12–16; cf. 7:57). Perhaps, similar to Peter and Paul, Philip could be credited with forming an *ekklēsia* in Samaria. Possibly, the same could be said for Simon.[18]

After the narrator describes Philip's success in Samaria, he flashes back to Simon. The interaction between Simon and the people and between Philip and the people are similar. Simon had been practicing magic (*mageuō*) in the city before Philip's arrival, amazing the people, and referring to himself as someone great (8:9; cf. 5:36; Luke 1:32, where the angel tells Mary her son "will be great"). Although Simon practiced magic, Luke does not use the Greek noun *magos* (magus/magician) for Simon (cf. 13:4–6; he uses it later as a title for Bar-Jesus).[19] Luke underscores the types of acts Simon performed in relation to Philip. The use of the Greek verb *mageuō* (to practice magic) would have been sufficient to plant a negative and/or suspicious seed in the minds of some

16. Unless otherwise noted, all Scripture translations are mine.

17. Matthews, *Philip*, 42.

18. An *ekklēsia* constituted a broad secular term that referred to a civic gathering of like-minded people for a particular purpose under the direction of a magistrate or other city leader (see Acts 19:32, 35, 39, where *ekklēsia* refers to both an unofficial and official gathering of the Ephesians.)

19. Luke's Simon is not characterized as a magus in the sense of a priest or royal court advisor as is Bar-Jesus.

readers. If Luke had called Simon a magician, the ancient reader would have had a broad ideational field of meaning to draw from, as noted below in my discussion of Bar-Jesus.

But the use of the verb *mageuō* limits the semantic field to powerful *acts*. The focus is actions. The foregrounding of the *practice of magic* by Simon is a part of Luke's othering project. Nevertheless, Kimberly Stratton asserts that the term *magic* was used discursively to construct otherness since the fifth century BCE. The term was combined with other vices to form a "semantic constellation" that inconspicuously signified "un-Greek, antisocial, effeminate and dangerous" activities. Magic as a discourse of alterity also arises in early Christian writings as a means of marking boundaries and forming identity.[20]

Luke's project of otherness manifests itself as well in the depiction of the relationship between the people and Simon. People from *all* social classes know Simon as a performer of magical deeds worthy of their admiration. The breadth of Simon's impact in Samaria across social class ("from small to great"; 8:10) indicates evaluatively the magnitude of Simon's influence. Simon amazed (*existēmi*) Samaritans from every socioeconomic background.[21] Luke employs the absolute adjective *all* to describe the extent of Simon's influence on the people. Heintz argues that the Lukan vignette of the massive "bewitchment" of the Samaritans constitutes a distortion of the extent of Simon's influence. And Simon's influence on the crowd (and not on any one individual), like that of a conjurer in a marketplace, is totally abstract, dehumanized, and estranged. Simon has not one singularly identifiable disciple, only an anonymous, faceless mass of people captivated by *des prodiges suspects* ("some suspicious miracles").[22] But the same can be said about Philip but for Simon's conversion. By magnifying the pervasiveness of

20. Stratton, "Rhetoric of 'Magic,'" 90, 97–104. Stratton includes the Apocalypse of John and the Acts of the Apostles among the earliest Christian writings containing this discursive use of magic. She is particularly interested in how ideology shapes Christian depictions of magic and gender.

21. In his Gospel, Luke uses the Greek word *thaumazō* most often (4:22, 9:43b, 11:38, 20:26) to describe reaction to Jesus' words and/or deeds, amazement at someone else's words or deeds (e.g., Joseph was amazed at Simeon's prophecy, 2:33; 2:18), or even Jesus' amazement at, for example, the Centurion's faith (7:9//Matt 8:10). Luke also uses *existēmi* (2:47; 8:56//Mark 5:42; 24:22), *ekplēssō* (2:48; 4:32//Mark 1:22//Matt 7:28–29; 9:43a), and *thambos*.

22. Heintz, *Simon*, 138. Luke habitually uses absolutes and hyperbolic numbers (2:41; 13:9–10; 19:10).

Simon's influence, Luke emphasizes Philip's superiority since he supersedes Simon and his magnanimous impact on the people. The contrast between Philip's mission and Simon's pre-baptism activity in Samaria is by no means absolute.[23]

Just as Simon previously amazed the people with his magic practices, he himself is amazed (*existēmi*) after witnessing the great miracles Philip performs (8:13). The same Greek verb *existēmi* (to amaze) that illustrates Simon's reaction to the great signs and miracles Philip performs also describes the Samaritans' reaction to Simon.[24] The people were amazed by Simon's practice of magic; Simon is amazed by Philip's performance of miracles. But Heintz argues that, in Simon's case, the phrase *the people* is the object for both Greek verbs *existēmi* and *mageuō*. Thus, Luke constructed his invective to show that Simon practiced magic directly on the people thereby plunging them into a stupor.[25] Grammatically and semantically, the two masculine singular participles separated by the conjunction, *mageuōn kai existanōn to ethnos* ("practicing magic and amazing the people"), represents a sequential and cause-effect relationship: the noun *the people* is the object of the second participle, *amazing*, but not of the first participle, *practicing magic*; the people were amazed because of the magic Simon performed.

Existēmi (to amaze) is predominantly associated with reactions to divine, miraculous, or extraordinary encounters. It describes the Pentecostal crowd's amazement at the outpouring of the Holy Spirit (2:7, 12),[26] the circumcised believers' astonishment when the Gentiles receive the Holy Spirit (10:45), and the disciples' response when Peter is

23. According to Heintz (*Simon*, 110), Luke constructed the text of Acts so as to establish "an absolute contrast between Philip's mission and Simon's activities in Samaria before his conversion" ("un contraste absolu entre la mission de Philipe et l'activité de Simon en Samarie avant sa conversion").

24. Heintz (*Simon*, 112, 115) argues that *existēmi* in Acts 8 reflects a stereotyped motif about the accusation of magic, which is used to depreciate the psychological effect that exalts the activities of the prophet in the mind of his disciples. Heintz further notes that Luke employs the verb only in the intransitive form ("he was astounded," "we were astonished") when he depicts the stupor that originates from the encounter with the divine. In the case of Simon, Heintz argues, the spectators are not astonished at what Simon has done, they are hypnotically bewitched.

25. Heintz, *Simon*, 106–8. Luke does not mention the actual miracles Simon performs so as to concentrate on the illegitimate means by which he produces them.

26. At 2:7, Luke uses both *existēmi* and *thaumazō* to express the crowd's astonishment and amazement when they hear the people speak in their distinctive languages.

unexpectedly released from prison and appears at Mary's door (12:16).[27] I propose that Luke's use of *existēmi* signifies, linguistically and semantically, the similarity and/or proximity of Simon and Philip's activities. Both Simon's and Philip's activities have a similar effect. But the more powerful Simon's activities are, the more significant are Philip's, since he displaces Simon. This is reminiscent of the contest between Moses and Pharaoh (Exod 7:8—8:18).

The people's amazement at Simon's practice of magic (*mageuō*) lasts for an extended time period (*dia to hikanō chronō*; 8:10-11). Similarly, the Pythian girl (as noted below), the other charismatic at a border crossing, practiced her oracles for many days (*epi pollas hēmeras*; 16:17). Luke's emphasis on the length of time that these charismatics function in their areas heightens the significance of the subsequent, and seemingly quick, success of the approved intermediaries. The apostles (and Philip) do not supersede some fly-by-night or transient novitiates. Luke demonstrates how Simon's magic practices were consistently efficacious and comparable to Philip's.

The Samaritans' perception of Simon differs slightly from Simon's view of himself (8:9, 10). Simon identified himself as "someone great" (cf. 19:27–34), whereas the people identify Simon as "the power of god called great."[28] Simon esteems himself highly; but the people, it seems, view him as a deity. The people (and Philip) do not consider Simon as demonic but as divine. Humans often deify other humans in Acts. The Samaritans' deification of Simon resembles responses to the apostles elsewhere in Acts. At Malta the people assume that Paul is a god after a viper wrapped itself around his arm without biting him (28:6). In Lystra, Paul heals a crippled man, and the crowds conclude that he and Barnabas are Hermes and Zeus, respectively, descended from heaven (14:8-13). Subsequently, Paul and Barnabas ripped off their clothing and begged the Lystrians to stop worshipping them. Additionally, people

---

27. Elsewhere in Acts, Luke employs semantically similar words: *thaumazō* (3:12; 4:13; 7:31), *ekplessō* (13:12), *ekthambos* (3:11), *thamos* (3:10a), or *eksasis* (3:10b). These words primarily describe reaction to miracles the apostles perform (or to the apostles themselves) or to the teaching of the Lord.

28. Based on later sources (e.g., Justin Martyr), Haenchen (*Acts*, 303–7) argues that this phrase should be "the great power," which is the Samaritan term for the supreme deity. Luke includes the gloss "of God"; "great power" is not "*a* power of God," but it is the "highest divinity itself." Simon claimed to be more than a "pseudo-Messiah." "This however is not discernable in the present episode."

associate miraculous acts with some known and innocuous power. The rulers in Jerusalem inquire by what power and name Peter and John healed a lame man (4:7).

Even if Simon's magic practices had been considered harmful, the Ananias and Sapphira punishment miracle (5:1–11) demonstrates that the positive or negative use or effect of miraculous power is not necessarily a "decisive criterion for distinguishing miracle-workers from magicians,"[29] even in Acts.[30] Extra-biblical sources show that it was not sufficient to simply accuse someone of being a magician or of practicing magic; one had to provide distinguishing details, "since the practices being defended were often indistinguishable from forbidden ones."[31]

By attributing to Simon the title "the *power* [*dunamis*] of god called *Great*" and by describing the activities Philip performs as "signs and great powers [*dunameis megalas*]" Luke engages in word play. When Simon submits to baptism, he becomes one of God's (or Philip's) miraculous or powerful acts (*dunameis*) performed by Philip, so to speak. In his Pentecost speech, Peter described Jesus' transformative activities as "powers [*dunameis*], wonders [*terata*] and signs [*sēmeia*]" (2:22).[32] Luke does not use the Greek noun *dunameis* again to characterize the apostles' activities until Paul performs miracles just before the emergence of the charismatic seven sons of Sceva (19:11; cf. 2:43, 4:30; 7:36).

Philip demonstrably claims divine authority when he preaches about the *basileia* of God and the name of Jesus (8:5, 12). He is the first approved intermediary to do so in Acts.[33] As noted above, the only statement Luke attributes to Simon is that he is *someone great*! (8:9). Both Philip and Simon invoke an epithet or name (*great* for Simon; and *Jesus Christ* for Philip) associated with their powerful acts.

29. Reimer, *Miracle and Magic*, 107–8.

30. Because Peter determines that the couple has lied to the Holy Spirit, each immediately dies.

31. Janowitz, *Magic*, 18.

32. The Hellenists and the apostles perform signs (*sēmeia*) and wonders (*terata*) (5:12; 6:8; 14:3; 15:12). Matthews, *Philip*, 45. The Greek word *sēmeia* "stands alone and unqualified only in the addition to Joel 3:3 at Acts 2:19 and here at [Acts] 8:6 where it describes Philip's activity."

33. Ibid., 44. Matthews also notes the distinctive use of the Greek infinitive *kērussein* for Philip's preaching. The only other person this Greek verb applies is Paul who preaches and testifies about the Basileia of God (19:8; 20:25).

That the people listened (*proseîchon*) to Simon implies that he both *said* and performed some significant things (8:10).[34] This same Greek verb *proseîchon* (listened) also describes the people's response to Philip's preaching (8:10; 8:6); the difference is that the people are referred to as "crowds" (*hoi ochloi*) in Philip's case. As Pervo has noted, the Greek verb *proseîchon* "establishes a precise comparison between Simon and Philip."[35]

The ultimate show of transfer of allegiance from Simon to Philip is Philip's baptism of the people based on his preaching *and* miracles (8:12). The Samaritans are no longer Simon's disciples, but they become Philip's disciples. Philip supplants Simon with his preaching and his superior miracles, which function to distinguish him from Simon. And the transfer of allegiance shows that the people themselves perceive of Philip's activities and powers as superior to Simon's.

After Simon's baptism and displacement by Philip, Simon devotes (*proskartereō*) himself to Philip (v. 13). One charismatic yields to the powers and expertise of another charismatic. Thus, Luke demonstrates that Simon himself recognizes the superiority of Philip's words and deeds above his own. The Greek verb *proskartereō*, expressing Simon's devotion to Philip, generally denotes the commitment of individuals to something or someone superior to themselves. Such devotion usually anticipates an efficacious benefit or outcome for the devotee(s), which may serve to linguistically and semantically anticipate Simon's later attempt to purchase the power to disseminate the Holy Spirit. *Proskartereō* characterizes the attitude of the inner circle of women and men gathered in the upper room harmoniously committed (*proskarterountes*) to prayer (1:14), as Jesus had instructed. Their devotion is an obedient response to the promised and expected outpouring of the Holy Spirit. But in Simon's story, his loyalty to Philip and the bestowal of the Holy Spirit on the Samaritan believers are temporally and semantically disconnected. In the first Lukan summary, the new believers dedicated themselves to (*proskarterountes*) "the teaching of the apostles, fellowship, breaking bread, and prayer" (2:42, 46). Their devotion engenders unity and

---

34. Garrett (*Demise of the Devil*, 68) and Heintz (*Simon*) argue that Luke's description of Simon warrants labeling him as a (false) prophet, even though he is not explicitly called one (a connection that Garrett also acknowledges cannot be made with certainty).

35. Pervo, *Acts*, 209.

growth. The word also describes the commitment (*proskarterēsomen*) of the Twelve to the ministry of the word as opposed to the ministry of tables (6:4). The Twelve anticipated that their singular devotion to the ministry of the word would demonstrably please God. Luke employs this same Greek verb to express the loyalty (*proskarterountōn*) that Cornelius's two slaves (*oiketoi*) exhibit toward him (10:7).[36]

MORE BORDER CROSSINGS: THE CONVERGENCE OF PETER AND SIMON

Luke resolves the narrative conflict that arises when Simon and Philip converge through Simon's acquiescence to Philip's superiority. But a new conflict occurs when Peter and John arrive in Samaria because of the Samaritans' acceptance of the "word of God" (8:14).[37] At their arrival in Samaria, Peter and John inquire whether Philip's converts had received the Holy Spirit (8:15). Simon is, of course, among the new converts, but he temporarily blends in with the anonymous others. Peter and John confer the Holy Spirit on the new believers by placing their hands on them (8:17).[38] The conclusion that Simon, along with the other believers, did not receive the Spirit's empowerment has no textual basis.[39] The text mentions no concrete manifestation of the Holy Spirit, such as glossalalia (speaking in other languages) (cf. 2:4–6; 10:44–46; 19:6). But Simon witnesses the pneumatic transfer, and he expresses a desire to imitate what he saw. Simon is willing to purchase the authority (*exousia*) to imitate how Peter and John anointed the believers with the Holy Spirit. Although Simon's attempt to purchase the apostles' power to anoint others with the Holy Spirit is denounced, his effort indicates that he recognized the apostles' authority as approved intermediaries (8:18, 19).

Nothing in the narrative implies that Simon profited from his previous practice of magic in spite of his effect on an entire city; such

---

36. Cf. Rom 13:6; Mark 3:9.

37. Conzelmann, *Acts*, 65. Although Luke mentions both Peter and John, "John's role is peripheral."

38. Koch, "Geistbesitz, Geistverleihung," 70. The conception of Spirit transmission exclusively through the Jerusalem Apostles is unhistorical, and an *ad hoc* construction especially in light of Acts 11:22–24.

39. Wall, "Acts," 139.

massive success would have yielded a considerable profit.[40] Nor does Luke mention that Simon intended to profit from the authority he sought to buy.[41] "To impute to [Simon] the intention to use such a gift for his own exclusive profit" is gratuitous.[42] Yet, certainly Luke is familiar with the motif of "trafficking [le commerce] in the sacred" since he employs it adeptly in the story of the encounter between Paul and the Pythian slave girl at 16:16; her masters gained a substantial profit from her prophesies. The persons who risk being placed in the role of a magician by Simon's offer are the apostles themselves; they bear the responsibility to accept or to refuse the money.[43]

Simon did not offer to buy Philip's power to perform signs and miracles, even though "Philip's miracle-working is much more impressive than Simon's."[44] But Philip's inability to bestow the Holy Spirit on his converts minimizes his capabilities and authority relative to Peter and John's.[45] In Acts, lack of membership among the Twelve does not pre-

40. Kolenkow ("Problem of Power," 105–110) lists the use of miracle for monetary or socio-political gain as one of three types of accusations leveled against miracle/ magic workers. The other two types of accusations are (1) subversion and (2) the use of magical power for evil purposes. She makes no distinction between magic and miracles, possibly intentionally.

41. Wall ("Acts," 138) argues that Simon wants the same "authority to rule that Jesus had given only to his apostolic successors." According to Derrett ("Simon Magus," 61–62) "Simon was not offering Peter a bribe to be co-opted as Matthias was. . . . But simply a price for a 'priesthood' subordinated to Peter, who as the steward of the 'kingdom' evidently had subordinate 'priesthoods' (e.g., Philip's!) under his control." Spencer (Portrait of Philip, 19, 198–99, 215) argues that "throughout the book of Acts a non-hierarchical, democratic process characterizes church government in general and the appointment of ministers in particular. Peter and the apostles play a leading role but do not lord their authority over fellow-believers in Jerusalem or elsewhere. Persons chosen and commissioned to specific tasks—such as Philip and the other table-servants—are not so much placed under the Twelve as alongside them and the larger community of disciples, all of whom work together as partners in the service of the church's sovereign Lord." Spencer does acknowledge that Peter sometimes assumes a leading role.

42. Derrett, "Simon Magus," 55; contra Reimer, Miracles and Magic, 134.

43. Heintz (Simon, 123–27, 133) argues that the motif of trafficking in the sacred does not apply to Simon. In this instance, Luke portrays Simon not as the object but as the subject of the stereotype. Thus, the proposition of buying (v.18b), as it references a more widespread stereotype in the accusation of magic, is eliminated from Heintz's reconstruction. Heintz also eliminates the motif of boasting, which Luke applies to Herod (12:23).

44. Reimer, Miracle and Magic, 94–95.

45. Haenchen, Acts, 304.

clude one from conferring the Holy Spirit (9:17; 19:6). But Acts denies Philip this authority requiring Peter (and John) to visit from Jerusalem to christen Philip's converts, which functionally subordinates Philip and Simon to Peter's (or Jerusalem's) authority. Perhaps, by limiting Philip's ministry, Luke shows how the Acts 6 decision pragmatically restrains the ministry of the Seven. This restriction also signifies proximity between Philip and Simon since neither has the authority to confer the Spirit. Conversely, this limitation functions as a basis for distinguishing between Simon and Peter (and John), as well as between Philip and the Twelve. Pervo argues that Luke's primary concern is "to show that Christianity has nothing in common with magic."[46] Christianity did not yet exist as an institution, but in Acts we see a nascent *ekklēsia* attempting to create a self-identity over against proximate others. Othering is a discursive project that requires distinguishing the apostolic leaders of the *ekklēsia* from others who are demonstrably similar to them.

The ultimate distancing of Simon occurs when Peter performs speech acts condemning Simon's offer to purchase the authority to administer the Holy Spirit. A performative speech act is an utterance that does something.[47] Peter's speech act places a curse on Simon that he can only avert through prayer. Simon desperately wanted to participate in the apostolic ministry (8:21; cf. 1:25, 26), but Peter's curse leaves him struggling to survive. Further Peter's discursive evaluation of Simon as not right (*eutheia*) before God seals his future as external other. The critical language of divine condemnation and personal culpability (i.e., *cursed* and *not right*) discursively constructs Simon as spiritually alienated and defective. Peter's "curse" and judgment against Simon applies only to his post-baptism attempt to purchase the authority to confer the Holy Spirit and not to his pre-baptismal magical practices.

Peter's discursive condemnation of Simon's post-conversion actions estranges him from and subordinates him to his fellow Samaritan converts, as well as the larger *ekklēsia*. A discursive construction of self-identity assigns value to and subjugates the other. Evaluative and subordinating discourses create hierarchical relationships while constructing or preserving self-identity over against the other. These hierarchical relationships are predicated upon the subordination of one set of behaviors and discourses to other behaviors and discourses by judgments

46. Pervo, *Acts*, 214.
47. Austin, *How to Do Things*; Searle, *Speech Acts*.

and evaluations. This concern with relationships and hierarchy betrays the political nature of the construction of otherness.[48]

The language of repentance and forgiveness that Peter applies to Simon post-baptism also reinforces Simon's status as external other (cf. 5:1–11). Simon's repentance will not restore him to his previous position among the Samaritans, nor will it guarantee him a position alongside the apostles. Simon is permanently displaced as an influential charismatic figure among the people of Samaria. If Simon repents and prays to the Lord, as Peter demands, he thereby acknowledges his guilt and his subordination to the Lord, and by extension he submits to Peter as the Lord's representative. The efficacy of Peter's speech act cursing Simon is evidenced by Simon's response: "You [please] pray in my behalf to the Lord so that nothing that you have spoken should happen to me" (8:24)[49] Domínguez asserts that the subject's construction of otherness shapes the others' views of themselves.[50]

Simon's remorse portrays him as submissive to the apostles and is an acknowledgement of the apostles' authority as the sole *ad hoc* approved intermediaries for conferring the Holy Spirit. And the narrative infers that the very Lord to whom Simon must appeal his sentence can only be accessed through Peter! And the Lukan Jesus taught, if "your brother" should sin, he should be rebuked;[51] but if anyone should repent, forgive that one regardless of how many times he should repent and seek forgiveness (17:1–4).

However, Luke characterizes Peter as having divine insight, foresight, and moral authority. Peter makes several prophetic and evaluative assertions: "You think you can purchase the gift of God with money," "Your heart is not right before God," "I see you in a gall of bitterness and a bond of unrighteousness" (cf. Ps 78:37; 77:37 LXX; Dan 2:5; 3:19; Deut 29:18; Trito-Isa 58:6; Heb 12:15–17). Peter also performs two speech acts: "You have no part or share in this ministry" and "May you and your silver be destroyed." These assertions and speech acts have the force of

48. Smith, "What a Difference," 45–47.

49. In the Bezan text (D), Simon asks Peter to pray to "god" rather than to "the Lord." Simon pleads that none of "these wicked (*kakōn*) things" happen to him. Then D adds "who did not cease weeping profusely." This addition emphasizes the intensity of Simon's repentance.

50. Domínguez, *People as Subject,* 164.

51. NRSV translates "a disciple" for *adelphos.*

objective truths. Marginalization and othering are generated and per-petuated through "regimes of truth."[52]

Readers cannot (would not) *know* Simon's motives absent Peter's assertions. The narrator expects readers to rely on Peter's judgment. By placing these assertions in Peter's mouth, Luke attributes to Peter moral authority and superiority. The optative statement expressed with "may" shows deference to someone exterior to Peter.[53] Although Peter expresses what he thinks should happen to Simon, the option of com-mitting Simon to eternal destruction is implicitly deferred to God but exercised through Peter as the visible representative of God.

Peter's prophecy about Simon's impending doom further destabi-lizes Simon's status as the great power of God in the eyes of the people. Historically, a successful practitioner of magic or miraculous feats might hope to achieve divination. Instructively, Smith notes that the vision the magician Thessalos received in the context of an oracle had three parts, one of which was "a promise of divinization: '[T]oday a god greets you . . . later men will greet you as a god.'"[54] If Acts implies that Simon had some hope for future divinization, Peter spoiled any such expectation.

Peter knows Simon's thoughts, the content of his heart, and what his future holds should he fail to repent. Thus Peter's knowledge exceeds Simon's (1:24; cf. 15:8). This prescience implies that God has gifted Peter with special revelation. In Thessalos's same oracular vision, the god re-veals to him that although King Nechepso possessed natural wisdom and "great magical powers," the King had *not* previously received se-crets from the divine voice, which is what Thessalos had requested for himself. When Thessalos is granted his request to receive the "divine voice," it is said that he had "made the pilgrimage from natural wisdom to revealed knowledge."[55] In the end, it is Peter, not Simon, who displays a revealed knowledge.

52. Silberstein, "Others Within," 7.

53. See, Lee, "Embedded Performatives," 105–8.

54. Smith, "Temple and the Magician," 236.

55. Smith (ibid., 238) argues that the holy man was present before the end of the classical era in the person of "entrepreneurial figures as early as the second century (B.C.)." In the Thessalos text we can witness a shift away from a temple/wisdom/priest-clergy–centered cult. "The ancient books of Wisdom, the authority of the priest-king, the faith of the clergy in the efficacy of their rituals, the temple as the chief locus of revelation—all of these have been relativized in favor of a direct experience of a mobile magician with his equally mobile divinity," 239. Contra Brown, "Rise and Function."

Transitivity Analysis

An ergative-based transitivity analysis highlights Simon's transformation from one who mastered his environment to one who submits to outsiders who enter the space he inhabits. Luke depicts Simon with less agency post-conversion than pre-baptism. Before his baptism, Simon exercises agency over people rather than inanimate things, and he is a participant-actor in three ergative material process clauses, which express the highest degree of transitive agency. Pre-baptism, Simon participates in one ergative relational process clause (he previously existed in the city, 8:9a) and three ergative material process clauses affecting persons or things beyond himself (he was practicing magic in the city, 8:9b; and twice he was amazing the people, 8:9c, 11).[56] Pre-baptism, Simon was a participant-actor in one verbal clause (he was saying that he is someone great, 8:9c).

Post-baptism, Simon does not have any real impact on people or things. He unsuccessfully attempts to purchase the authority and/or power to impart the Holy Spirit. Post-baptism, Simon is a participant-actor in two ergative clauses: one is a material process (he offered money, 8:18c) and the other is a relational process (he I constantly devoted himself to Philip, 8:13b). Simon is a participant-actor in three ergative mental process clauses (he believed [in Philip who had preached], 8:13a; he saw the signs and great deeds, 8:13c; and he sees the laying on of hands, 8:18a). Of these three mental process clauses, one is cognitive (he believed, 8:13a); and two are perceptive or non-cognitive (he saw, 8:13c; he sees, 8:18b), and hence demonstrate a much lesser degree of agency on Simon's part. Simon is also a participant-actor in two verbal clauses (he says give me this authority, 8:19a; he responds pray for me, 8:24).

This transitivity analysis highlights Simon's transformation or status reversal. Simon has morphed from an effective practitioner of magic to a loyal disciple of Philip and ultimately to a discredited external other. He has transitioned from a free agent in a thriving market to a disappointed potential consumer of a monopolized "commodity." It appears that Simon accepted the apostles' representation him as

---

56. At 8:9b, the circumstantial element "in the city" is considered as a participant-object.

external other. Transitivity analysis can uncover "subtle changes in the inner world of a character."[57]

Philip is more active and influences people more often in Samaria than do Peter and John. An ergative-based transitivity analysis shows that Philip is a participant-actor in three ergative material process clauses affecting other persons (he baptizes men and women, 8:12c; he baptizes Simon, 8:13a; and he performs signs, 8:6). In the first two instances, the agency is implicit in passive verbs. Philip is a participant-actor in two ergative verbal process clauses (he preached to them, 8:5b; and he preached the gospel about the *basileia* of God, 8:12b). He is a participant-actor in one ergative relational process clause (he went down to a city of Samaria, 8:5a).

Peter and John together are participant-actors in one ergative verbal process (they questioned [the people of Samaria], 8:15b; two ergative relational clauses (they went down to Samaria, 8:15a; they placed their hands on them, 8:17a). Thus, Philip is more active and influences more people more often in Samaria than do Peter and John. Peter is a participant-actor in one ergative verbal process clause (he said [to Simon], 8:20–23). Several assertions are embedded in the secondary projected clause of this verbal process. The speech acts embedded in the verbal clause attribute prescience, moral authority, and superiority to Peter with regard to Simon's character, as noted above.

The crowds in Samaria, similar to the crowds *the Jews* incite, are the least active participants in the narrative episode. They are participant-actors in no material process clauses. Four out of the seven clauses in which they are participant-actors involve mental processes (they paid attention to Simon, twice at 8:10b, 11; they believed Philip, 8:12a; they received the Holy Spirit, 8:17b). One other clause in which the crowd is a participant-actor is a verbal process (they say he is the power of god called great, 8:10b). After Peter and John, the crowd or Samaritan people are the least active participants in the narrative.

---

57. Ji and Shen ("Transitivity and Mental Transformation," 337) document the mental transformation of the protagonist as reflected in the author's adept "manipulation of transitivity patterns as part of an overall stylistic strategy of the novella" (336). See also, Wills, *Jewish Novel*, ch. 4. Status reversal is a significant theme in Luke's Gospel (1:46–51; 3:4–5; 14:11; 18:14).

Summary and Conclusion

In summary, narrative conflicts occur between Simon and Philip and between Simon and Peter (and John) when the second geographical stage of the apostolic mission crosses the border into Samaria after the dispersion of the *ekklēsia*. This convergence of the proximate charismatic figures creates a dilemma in the story. The situation begs the question of how the two charismatic individuals will be able to operate simultaneously in the same space or sphere of influence. The narrative instability between Simon and Philip is resolved when Philip is demonstrated to be superior to Simon, and subsequently Simon submits to Philip. Luke demonstrates no denunciation of Simon's magic practices, but only of Simon's attempt to buy the authority to transmit the Holy Spirit.[58] Luke does not attack Simon's magical practices, as is the custom in ancient texts when magic is viewed negatively, but he could easily have done so. Any negativity is directed at Simon's post-baptismal behavior. Luke does not accuse the Samaritans of being deceived—a charge often accompanying accusations of magic. For example, in the apocryphal *Acts of Thomas*, Charisius refers to Thomas as a magician and warns Mygdonia not to be deceived by the words and "works of magic" that Thomas performs in the name of the Trinity.[59] As Janowitz argues, one cannot separate the different uses of "magic in antiquity from broader rhetorical goals of the writer."[60]

The second narrative instability between Peter and Simon is solved when Simon submits to Peter's authority. Some commentators argue that the narrator leaves Simon's fate open, but this is not the case. Luke's narrative renders Simon functionally impotent, dismantles any authority he had previously exercised over the people of Samaria, and discursively constructs him as external other, despite his recent baptism. Fitzmyer asserts that Luke's story of Simon "ends on a favorable note."[61] If Simon could speak, he might disagree.

---

58. Contra Heintz (*Simon*, 127–29) who argues that Peter's reprimand includes motifs for the stereotypical accusation of magic—wickedness and perversity—which Luke applies to Simon as a magician and not just to the attempt to buy the authority to bestow the Holy Spirit.

59. *Act Thom.* 96.10.

60. Janowitz, *Magic*, 17.

61. Fitzmyer, *Acts*, 407.

Bar-Jesus—Acts 13:6–12

Second Encounter between a Charismatic Other and Approved Intermediaries

FROM ONE PROPHET TO ANOTHER: THE CONVERGENCE OF PAUL AND BAR-JESUS

Paul and Barnabas' encounter with Bar-Jesus, a magus and Jewish false prophet, constitutes the first extended episode between Paul and another charismatic since the Syrian Antioch *ekklēsia* commissioned them (13:4–6). Like Philip, Paul meets Bar-Jesus as he begins his Gentile mission in the diaspora (8:1–5; 13:1–3).[62] Similarly, the outbreak of persecution forced Philip into the diaspora where he embarked upon a new evangelistic effort in Samaria.

The narrator counts Paul and Barnabas among the prophets and teachers in the Antiochene *ekklēsia* (together with Simeon, Niger, Lucius the Cyrenian, and Manaen; 13:1). Similar to Paul and Barnabas, Luke identifies Bar-Jesus as a prophet, albeit a false one. Thus Bar-Jesus is functionally or vocationally proximate to Paul and Barnabas. The proximity of a false prophet to other prophets in the immediate literary context invites readers to infer that the latter are true prophets. Again, it is the proximate other who is of crucial concern and whose closeness drives a project of differentiation for the sake of constructing self-identity.

With Paul's entrance into Cyprus, Bar-Jesus and Paul become spatially and temporally proximate. Bar-Jesus has already influenced the proconsul Sergius Paulus. And now at the proconsul's request, Paul attempts to convince the proconsul about the "word of God." Luke identifies Bar-Jesus as a magus, but he does not explain the term. Although Luke does not clarify the relationship between Bar-Jesus and the proconsul, we can assume Bar-Jesus functions in an advisory capacity. Historically, a *magus* could refer to (a) one belonging to the Persian priestly class who sometimes performed signs and was influenced by

---

62. The *ekklēsia* at Antioch laid hands on Paul and Barnabas as the Holy Spirit instructed and consecrated them as emissaries of the gospel. The Jerusalem *ekklēsia* had previously commissioned Barnabas to Antioch, and Barnabas would subsequently recruit Paul to minister at Antioch (11:25–26). Thus, Johnson (*Acts*, 225) asserts that Luke signaled his readers that by proxy "Saul was acceptable to the Jerusalem leadership."

philosophical ideas closely linked with religion; (b) a magician, with various connotations; (c) someone who possessed supernatural abilities or knowledge; and/or (d) a deceptive person with no real power.[63] Nothing in the story indicates that Bar-Jesus performed magical acts, but he is portrayed as deceptive.

Luke's emphasis on the proconsul's intelligence together with the evaluation of Bar-Jesus' as a false prophet anticipates an epistemic dissonance between the two. The proconsul's intelligence signifies his ability to discern between truth and deceptions and more particularly between true and false prophecies or teachings. That Sergius summons Paul and Barnabas indicates he believes they can help him with his theological strivings to know the "word of God" (13:7). We might infer that either the proconsul has suspicions as to whether Bar-Jesus would supply reliable knowledge or that Bar-Jesus' counsel has proved in some way inadequate or unreliable. Or maybe the proconsul just wants a second opinion. The proconsul's request may constitute a precautionary measure that would shield him from potential deception. Magi are sometimes depicted in ancient texts as persons willing to sacrifice truth to please officials who solicit their services.[64]

Hearing that the proconsul has summoned the apostles, Bar-Jesus opposes (*anthistēmi*) Paul and Barnabas (13:8a).[65] It is instructive that Luke uses semantically similar Greek verbs to describe both Bar-Jesus' and *the Jews'* opposition to Paul's mission to the Gentiles (i.e., *antilegō*, "to speak against," 13:45; 28:19; *antitassō*, "to set oneself against," 18:6). In fact, Bar-Jesus' opposition to Paul immediately precedes the beginning of opposition to the Gentile mission by *the Jews*.

Bar-Jesus attempts to block Paul and Barnabas from testifying before the proconsul about the "word of God" (13:8c). What is at issue in this conflict between Bar-Jesus and the apostles is epistemic superior-

---

63. Delling, "magos, mageia," *TDNT* 356–59. In Xenophon's *Cyropaedia* (4.5.13; 4.5.51; 5.3.4; 7.3.1) the magi are primarily portrayed as the guardians of the gods. After successful military campaigns Cyprus summons the magi so that they can select the spoils they deem appropriate for the gods.

64. Plutarch, *Alexander* 18.6.4.

65. Bar-Jesus is also known as Elymas. In Codex Bezae (D) we find *Et[ ]imas* and not Elymas. Metzger (*Textual Commentary*, 355) states that the Latin side of the manuscript that reads *Etoemas* shows that D should read *hetoimas*. See also Josephus, *Ant.* 1.6.4; Johnson, *Acts*, 223. Luke could be using the phrase "is translated" in a general, "non-technical sense" here and in the case of Barnabas/"Son of consolation" (4:36).

ity. This narrative instability invites some readers to ask the following questions: Whose knowledge will the proconsul accept as truthful? And by extension, which prophet will be validated as the superior source of knowledge? Will the proconsul be convinced by Paul and Barnabas's presentation about the "word of God"? What will happen to Bar-Jesus if Paul and Barnabas succeed in persuading the proconsul about the "word of God"? Will the proconsul become aware that Bar-Jesus is a false prophet, as the narrator has informed his readers?

The proximity between Bar-Jesus and the apostles is obfuscated for some readers when, for example, Luke characterizes Paul as full of the Holy Spirit. The same is true when Paul attacks Bar-Jesus' character, demonizes him, and accuses him of perverting their mission: "Oh [you] full of all deceit and of all villainy! Oh son of the devil and enemy of all righteousness! You do not cease making the straight ways of the Lord crooked" (13:10; cf. 8:21–22). Instructively, in the Epistle of Barnabas (ca. 70–135 CE) magic is listed along with other practices, such as double-mindedness, deceit, and wickedness that destroy people's souls.[66]

Written more than a half-century after Acts, the *Shepherd of Hermas* distinguishes between true and false church members. The author of the *Shepherd of Hermas* compares the false prophet with the wizard (*mantis*), to whom double-minded persons appeal. By contrast, Luke describes Sergius Paulus as an intelligent man and not as a double-minded person. *Hermas* further asserts that the false prophet has "no power of the divine spirit in him."[67] The false prophet is duplicitous since he "speaks some true words, for the devil fills him with his spirit" (*tina de kai rhēmata alēthē lalei ho gar diabolos plēroi auton tōi autou pneumati*). Here, the idea that the Spirit of God does not fill the false prophet (some other spirit fills him) is the same notion implied when Paul is described as full of the Spirit (by implication Bar-Jesus is not). The author of *Hermas* argues that anyone who appeals to a false prophet is an idolater.[68] However in Acts, Luke provides no explicit or implicit

66. Barnabas, *Epistle* 20.1c.3. Ignatius (*Epistulae interpolatae and epistulae supposititiciae* 11.19.3) attacks sorcery (*goēteia*) as idle talk (*huthlos*), and magic (*mageia*) is a joke (*gelōs*). In the *Ascen. Isa.* 2.5.2 (the Amherst Papyrus I Greek fragment contains the text of 2.4—4.4, NTApoc, 604) (second century CE) magic is listed with sorcery (*pharmakeia*), divination, sexual immorality (*porneia*), and the persecution of the righteous.

67. *Herm. Mand.* 11.2.

68. Ibid., 11.3–4.

link between false prophecy and idolatry.[69] In *Hermas* the true prophet is meek, gentle, abstains from wickedness and evil worldly desires, does not seek wealth, speaks only when God permits, and possesses power; whereas the false prophet exalts himself, is loquacious, deceitful, prophesies only for remuneration, and has no power, for his spirit derives from the devil.[70] Perhaps the reason that Bar-Jesus performs no powerful acts is because of a shared cultural notion about false prophets lacking power. Yet in both Acts and *Hermas*, false prophets function as agents of the devil and are full of deceit and wickedness. But agents of the devil are not generally understood to be powerless. And this contradiction betrays the polemical and political nature of the paradigm. Luke resorts to polemical claims of false prophecy and/or collaboration between the devil and Bar-Jesus to discredit him before the proconsul and before his readers.[71] Although we treat the other as the stranger among us, as the representative of a distinct species, "the most crucial point is that we treat him as a *threat*."[72]

But by connecting the false prophet with the devil, Acts stands within a broader shared biblical tradition that also links the two. The author of the New Testament Apocalypse connects the false prophet with the devil; and demonic spirits perform signs (*sēmeia*) (Rev 16:13–14; 19:20; 20:10). The book of Matthew, more than any other New Testament text except for the Apocalypse, warns against false prophets as deceivers (7:15; 24:11; and 24:24 following Mark 13:22; cf. 2 Peter 2:1; 1 John 4:1).[73]

The title *son of the devil* (*huie diabolou*) does not point to some demonic origin for Bar-Jesus as a magician, but Paul directs his vitriolic

69. Derrett ("Simon Magus," 63) looks to the Mishnah for evidence of the relationship between magic and idolatry and then to Gal 5:20 where Paul lists "sorcery" immediately after "idolatry."

70. *Herm. Mand.* 11.6–16.

71. Johnson (*Acts*, 226) proposes three literary functions for the Bar-Jesus narrative: (1) to evince that in continuity with Jesus and Peter, Paul is an authentic prophet: he is filled with the Holy Spirit; he can read Bar-Jesus' heart; he is capable of pronouncing a curse in the Lord's name, (2) to illustrate the word of God has spread to new territories, conquering Satan's powers; and (3) to apologetically show the fair-mindedness and openness of Roman officials.

72. Kapuściński, *Other*, 58 (emphasis original).

73. See also Luke 6:26; 2 Pet 2:1 (false prophets and false teachers disseminate destructive opinions); Rev 16:13; 19:20; 20:10.

words at Bar-Jesus' opposition to the "word of God." The narrator's positive evaluation of Paul as full of the Holy Spirit lends weight to Paul's subsequent evaluation of Bar-Jesus as full of deceit and villainy (cf. Luke 11:39). By prefacing Paul's judgment of Bar-Jesus with the narrator's description of Paul as full of the Spirit, Luke implies that Paul's words are God-inspired and thus superior. And Paul's evaluation of Bar-Jesus is truthful. Conversely, Bar-Jesus is identified as a disseminator of false prophecies or teachings and therefore as not inspired by God. Above, Peter and John's response to Simon implied that Simon's transgression was intransitive and reflexive, but Bar-Jesus' deceit affects someone beyond himself, i.e., the proconsul.

In response to Bar-Jesus' attempt to interfere with the dissemination of the "word of God," Paul renders him blind. Some readers will connect the blinding of Bar-Jesus by Paul with the narrator's evaluation of Bar-Jesus as a false prophet (13:11). The blinding of Bar-Jesus visibly inscribes his deception and prophetic impotency in his body. Luke foregrounds Bar-Jesus' status as a false prophet (*pseudoprophētēs*). Luke explicitly labels no other character in Acts as a false prophet, but the reader encounters several false witnesses (6:11; 7:58; 16:19–20; Luke 6:26).

Bar-Jesus' temporary blindness is reminiscent of Paul's Damascus Road experience during which he was temporarily blinded. Similar to Bar-Jesus, Paul's blindness compelled him to find someone to guide him by the hand (*cheiragogō*; 9:8). Blindness in both cases symbolizes liminality, transition, and reversal of vocational status. Paul remained blind for three days until Ananias anointed him with the Holy Spirit for his new appointment as apostle to the Gentiles (9:9–19). Bar-Jesus' physical blindness signifies the vocational liminality he experiences as a result of being publicly discredited before Sergius. That Bar-Jesus' blindness is temporary has no redeeming value. The omniscient narrator had already informed Luke's readers about Bar-Jesus' mendacity, but now the proconsul knows as well. When Paul renders Bar-Jesus blind, Paul demonstrates that he wields the greater power. Bar-Jesus' physical blindness confirms Luke's evaluation of him as a deceptive and false prophet (cf. Luke 22:63–64, where Jesus is blindfolded and mockingly told to prophesy).

Although Simon is known as a practitioner of magic and Bar-Jesus is called a magus, only Bar-Jesus is expressly linked with the devil.

No other character in Acts is explicitly characterized as a son of the devil. Unlike the account of the Pythian slave girl from whom Paul exorcises a Pythian spirit (16:18), Paul casts no unclean spirit or demon from Bar-Jesus in spite of the fact that Paul discursively demonizes him. It is Bar-Jesus' deceptive practices that earn him the designation *son of the devil*, and not any practice of magic or his position as a magus.

The demonological nomenclature creates a clear distinction between Bar-Jesus and the apostles thereby solidifying Bar-Jesus' status as external other. Paul discursively marginalizes and subjugates Bar-Jesus because of his activities as a false prophet and because he stood against the apostles when they attempted to explicate the "word of God" for the proconsul. The blinding of Bar-Jesus resolves the narrative instability—another charismatic is othered; Bar-Jesus is rendered impotent and becomes an external other.

The proconsul expresses astonishment (*ekplēssonmenos*) at Paul's miraculous blinding of Bar-Jesus (13:12), and Sergius becomes a believer as a result of the event. Thus, Sergius becomes the first Greco-Roman political figure in Acts to show an interest in the apostles and the "word of God." Paul displaces but does not replace Bar-Jesus as the proconsul's personal counselor or prophetic sage.

Transitivity Analysis

An ergative-based transitivity analysis shows that Bar-Jesus is a participant-actor in four ergative material process clauses (he opposed them [Paul and Barnabas], 13:8a; he attempts to turn the proconsul from the faith, 13:8b; he perverts the straight ways of the Lord, 13:10c; and he seeks someone to lead him by the hand, 13:12). He is a participant in two relational process clauses (he is with the proconsul, 13:7a and he is full of all deceit, 13:10). In comparison with other narrative actors, Bar-Jesus is a participant-actor in processes that express the highest degree of transitive agency—four ergative material processes affecting people rather than things.

Only one of the five clauses in which the proconsul is a participant-actor is an ergative material process clause (he summoned Paul and Barnabas, 13:7b). Of the four other clauses where the proconsul is a participant-actor, one is a verbal process (he asked, 13:7c); three are mental processes (he saw what had happened, 13:12a; he believed,

13:12b; and he was astonished at the teaching of the Lord, 13:12c). Like the people of Samaria whom Simon amazed, the proconsul demonstrates a lower degree of transitive agency than Bar-Jesus.

As usual, the apostles are the least active (or most passive acting) in the episode. Paul *and* Barnabas act together in one ergative relational process (they passed through the island of Cyprus, 13:6a) and one ergative material process (they found a certain man, 13:6b). Paul is a participant in two ergative clauses and one non-ergative clause; these do not involve material processes, but they consist of one ergative relational process (Paul is filled with the Holy Spirit, 13:9a), one ergative mental process (he stared at Bar-Jesus), and one ergative verbal process (he said, 13:10a). This verbal process clause is projecting speech. The projected speech or secondary clauses embedded in or attached to the verbal clause consists of two performative speech acts ("the hand of the Lord is on you";[74] "you will be blind"). It is through the latter speech act that Paul engenders Bar-Jesus' blindness, as noted above. The two speech acts constitute a cause and effect relationship. The act of rendering Bar-Jesus blind should evaluatively be understood as the result of the Lord acting decisively on him. Semantically and theologically, readers will attribute the blinding of Bar-Jesus to the Lord. Nevertheless, in spite of the lack of agency that Paul demonstrates in the grammatical structure, many readers will understand Paul to be the more powerful character in the story.

Summary and Conclusion

Like Simon, Bar-Jesus occupied a position of influence in the proconsul's court before Paul's arrival in the region. Bar-Jesus is a magus, but no magical practices or performance of signs are associated with this title (at least Luke does not mention any). Paul directs his negative evaluations of Bar-Jesus at his status as a false prophet. Paul and Barnabas perform only one sign, namely the blinding of Bar-Jesus. Otherwise, the text emphasizes their teaching, which is what Bar-Jesus opposes.

Bar-Jesus is an "outsider" as Rick Strelan argues. Bar-Jesus posed a grave threat because of his proximity to the Jesus movement.[75] Similar

---

74. Cf. Luke 1:66, where the narrative says of John the Baptist that "the hand of the Lord was with him."

75. Strelan, "Who Was Bar Jesus," 66–67.

to the apostles, Bar-Jesus is a Jewish person associated with the prophetic tradition (13:1). These similarities contribute to his status as a proximate other. Bar-Jesus is not a foreigner or stranger to the Jewish community. Both true and false prophets existed within the same communities, making similar claims to status and function.[76] Before Paul and Barnabas' arrival, Bar-Jesus presented himself to the proconsul as a legitimate prophet and Sergius accepted him as a legitimate *magos* and prophet. Luke's characterization of Bar-Jesus demonstrates a rejection of this claim. The omniscient narrator alerts the reader that Bar-Jesus is a false or illegitimate prophet. And Paul and Barnabas discern Bar-Jesus' illegitimacy and deceit through his interference with their teaching.

Bar-Jesus should *not* be classified as a magician or practitioner of magic in the same sense as Simon. The Greek word *magos*, which designates Bar-Jesus, "does not primarily emphasise [*sic*] a distinction between magic and true religion."[77] While Luke highlights Simon's magical activities and his post-conversion attempt to buy the authority to bestow the Holy Spirit, it is Bar-Jesus' role as a false prophet (and as such, a son of the devil) that Luke foregrounds. Smith argues that "[D]evil Worship' is a term of estrangement applied to others and represents a reduction of their religiosity to the category of the false but not . . . to the category of the impotent."[78]

After Paul renders Bar-Jesus blind as a result of his deception and interference, Bar-Jesus is rendered impotent as a court seer, and thus he is displaced. Another charismatic is left powerless and subordinated to the apostles. Thus, like Simon, Bar-Jesus' fate is sealed as external other in relation to the apostles.

76. Ibid., 69.

77. Delling, "Magos," *TDNT* 538.

78. Smith, "Towards Interpreting Demonic Powers," 425.

The Pythian Slave Girl—Acts 16:16–22

Third Encounter between a Charismatic Other and Approved Intermediaries

ANOTHER BORDER CROSSING: THE CONVERGENCE OF PAUL AND THE PYTHIAN SLAVE GIRL

As in the Simon narrative above, the story about Paul and the Pythian slave girl constitutes a border-crossing event. Paul had crossed the border into Macedonia (or Europe) because a man in a vision invited Paul to come help *us* (16:9). The first border-crossing meeting occurs between Paul (and Silas) and Lydia, immediately preceding Paul's meeting with the Pythian slave girl. Jeffrey Staley calls both women "borderland characters."[79] The Pythian girl's story functions as a borderland and bridging narrative. Her story also bridges the household conversion stories of Lydia and the jailer. If the Macedonian *us* that Paul has been asked to help are the jailer and his household, then both women form a literary drawbridge; they are a means to an end. But it is not certain this is the case since Paul returns to Lydia's house after being released from jail (16:40).

The two women do not represent two socioeconomic extremes or two sides of the same coin. Lydia and the Pythian girl are proximate, and in some ways they differ, but not unequivocally so. As the head of her household and the *ekklēsia* in her house, Lydia is responsible for the economic well being of her *materfamilias*. As a female slave, the Pythian girl represents the least of the members of a *paterfamilias* (patriarchal household). Yet she possesses a gift or skill that significantly contributes to the economic success of the household, which was not an unusual phenomenon in ancient slave societies (e.g., Luke 19:11–27; cf. Matt 25:14–30; Mark 13:34).[80] Both Lydia and the Pythian girl yield to male authority: the slave girl obeys her masters (*kurioi*), and Lydia voluntarily acquiesces to Paul's leadership in spite of his status as a migrant

79. Jeffrey Staley ("Changing Woman," 122) offers a post-colonial reading of the Lydia and Pythian slave girl stories. He reads their narratives together as opposed to some scholars who cast the two women as two-sides of the same coin—a good woman and a bad girl.

80. See Smith, "Slavery"; Harrill, *Slaves*.

foreigner. "Lydia functions as a passive hearer and helper of Paul," yet the slave girl is "an active announcer of and an anoy-er of Paul."[81]

Paul and the Pythian slave girl are functionally or vocationally and spatially proximate. Paul enters a new territory where another charismatic was already functioning among the inhabitants. Both Paul and the Pythian girl converge because of the divine revelations they receive. Paul's revelatory vision brought him to Macedonia where he proclaims the word. It is the Pythian girl's gift of divine revelations and oracles that make her as an asset to her masters in Macedonia. Paul and the Pythian girl cross paths in front of Lydia's *proseuchē*. Ironically, as Paul visits Lydia's house, presumably, to preach the word, the Pythian slave divines a meta-oracle about the act and content of Paul and Silas' proclamation.

Paul's border crossing, as well as the Pythian slave girl's persistent chanting and traipsing behind him and Silas, creates a narrative conflict. Paul becomes disturbed by the Pythian girl's words and by her persistent shadowing of them. Luke employs the present active feminine participle to designate the symmetry between her talking and walking: while tagging along (*katakolouthousa*) after them, she speaks (*legousa*). Her actions and words are connected performatively and grammatically.

According to the *we* narrator, for many days "[the Pythian slave girl] was shouting [*ekrazen*], 'These persons are slaves of the Most High God [*douloi tou theou tou hypsistou*] who are proclaiming to you[82] a way of salvation'" (16:17–18).[83] The Greek verb *krazō* (to cry out) is significant here. The verb foregrounds the manner and character of the slave girl's utterance connecting it grammatically with forensic speech and other exorcism stories. But this is the only time Luke employs this Greek verb for female utterances (cf. Luke 8:2; 9:39; 18:39). In Luke-Acts, *krazō* often signifies truthful and passionate speech. The verb also occurs in the context of forensic speech and/or public declarations involving the giving of testimony. This verb describes how Paul presented his defense speech before the "chief priests and [Jewish] council" (23:6); it demonstrates how Stephen cried out when an angry mob stoned him (7:60); it signifies the clamorous cry of mobs (7:57; 19:32–34; 21:28, 36;

81. Spencer, "Out of Mind," 146–49.

82. Some ancient manuscripts read "to us."

83. Conzelmann (*Acts*, 131) argues that the "'many days' does not fit" with v. 16 where the narrative says Paul and Silas met the slave girl "one day."

Luke 23:18); it characterizes the vociferous shout of demons (Luke 4:41; cf. 4:33; 8:28); and it describes the potential shouting of animated stones (Luke 19:40).

The first part of the public testimony the Pythian girl gives is that Paul and Silas are "slaves of the Most High God" (*douloi tou theou tou hypsistou*). The Pythian slave girl's testimony resembles other statements made in Luke-Acts, the veracity of which is not challenged in those narratives. The grammatical syntax of the statement is identical to that found in the story of the Gerasene demoniac, where the unclean spirit identifies Jesus as "son of the Most High God" (*Iesou huie tou theou tou hypsistou*; Luke 8:28//Mark 5:7; cf. Matt 8:29). Nothing in the narrative signifies that Jesus found the demoniac's statement to be false. The title *Most High* is repeatedly used to refer to the divinity: in Luke's Gospel Jesus is referred to as the "son of the Most High" (*hios hypsistou*; 1:32; 7:48); the "power of the Most High" shall overshadow Mary (*dunamis hypsistou*; 1:31–35); John the Baptist will be called the "prophet of the Most High" (*prophētēs hypsistou*; 1:76); and those who love their enemies will be "children of the Most High" (*huioi hypsistou*; 6:35; cf. Matt 5:45). The Pythian girl's oracle does not deviate from the rhetorical use of the phrase "of the Most High" in Luke-Acts, where it is attached to the name of Jesus or other people whom God has given a special purpose or ministry to fulfill.

The second public assertion that the Pythian girl makes about Paul and Silas is that they preach "a way of salvation" (*hodon sōtērias*). Instructively, in the Bar-Jesus story, Paul accuses Bar-Jesus of perverting the "straight ways of the Lord" (*diastrephōn tas hodous [tou] kuriou tas eutheias*), indicating that the Lord's ways are many (13:10). The Lord's ways are not singular or monolithic. In Luke's Gospel, Zechariah's prophetic oracle concerning his son John contains linguistic parallels with the Pythian girl's mantic utterance: "And you, child, will be called *a prophet of the Most High*; for you will go before the Lord to *prepare his ways* [*hodous*], *to give knowledge of his salvation* [*sōtērias*] to the people in the forgiveness of their sins" (1:76–77 NRSV).[84] The phrases

84. Cf. Luke 3:4–6, where Luke quotes Isaiah 40:3–5: "'Prepare *the way of the Lord, make his paths straight*. Every valley shall be filled and every mountain and hill shall be made low...and all flesh shall see *the salvation of God*'" (NRSV). Conversely, it seems to be those who have a pejorative view of Jesus or his disciples that refer unequivocally to "the way of God" as a monolithic social phenomenon in order to trap Jesus as one who does not follow "the way" (Luke 20:21–26). In Acts, "the way" refers to the Jesus

"to prepare *his ways*" and "to give knowledge of *his salvation*" constitute an instance of parallelism; they are symmetrical. Jesus' salvation, or salvation through Jesus, is envisioned in a multifaceted way. The Pythian slave girl's discourse does not deviate from discourse uttered elsewhere in Luke-Acts or from language that the apostles might otherwise affirm or embrace. The other as another self is both "a mirror and, at the same time, a foil."[85]

The slave girl likely is neither a Jewish woman nor a Godfearer, but she is a Gentile and a devotee of Apollo. We might assume that the girl either had already demonstrated her gift of divining (*manteuomenē*) before her enslavement—the spirit of Apollo filled her and she delivered oracles—or she is an imposter, a conclusion that does not accord with the semantic content her present oracle. In any case, *prima facie*, the veracity of her oracle cannot be disputed.

It is the subsequent exorcism that convinces some readers that the Pythian slave girl's oracle is false. The exorcism becomes the hermeneutical lens for evaluating her oracle and the authenticity of her gift. The exorcism obscures for many readers the functional and ideational (ideas reflected in her oracle) proximity between the apostles and the Pythian slave girl. When constructing self-identity *vis-à-vis* the other, clear boundaries must be marked between them and us to overcome proximity and to avoid ambiguity.

The Pythian slave girl (*paidiskē*; cf. Luke 22:56; Matt 26:69; Mark 14:66, 69) is the only female in Acts with a prophetic gift whose oracle is recorded. It seems, however, that the only reason her words are recorded is because they originate not from the Holy Spirit, but from another spirit, as the exorcism would prove (cf. 21:9–14). Thus, Paul is justified when he dismisses her utterances as an annoying noise despite the veracity of her words. "The focus on the 'other' as unintelligible has led, necessarily to 'their' silence and 'our' speech."[86]

---

movement as a new sect within Judaism, which Paul first persecutes and later joins (9:2; 19:9, 23; 22:4–5; 24:14, 22; 28:22); it does not represent a single absolute path to salvation. But it signifies a burgeoning and embryonic like-minded group who believe that Jesus is the resurrected Messiah who will usher in the *basileia* of God (18:25–26). The Jerusalem Council in Acts 15 stands as one example of the sect's evolving soteriology.

85. Benbassa and Attias, *Jew and the Other*, x.

86. Smith, "Differential Equations," 241.

Like the Delphic Pythia, the Pythian slave girl is articulate and coherent.[87] Possessed by a divine spirit, the ancient Pythia prophesied, and like the poets, she was eloquent, knowledgeable, fluent, and logical. Historically, "the Pythia at Delphi produced utterances that are a genuine expression of a cultural system which believed in the codified behaviours and speech that it understood as indicating the presence of the divine."[88] Devotees of Apollo regarded Pythia as authentic and her oracles as god-inspired: "The voice is not that of a god, nor the utterance of it, nor the diction, nor the metre, but all these are the woman's; [the god] puts into her mind only the visions (*phantasias*), and creates a light in her soul (*psychē*) in regard to the future; for inspiration (*enthousiasmos*) is precisely this."[89]

When Paul expels the spirit from the slave girl, he addresses the spirit and not the girl. That the girl has no say in the matter is not atypical of exorcism stories. Ordinarily, the exorcist addresses the demon since it is understood that the demon has taken possession of the individual's body. Either the demon speaks, or the demon *and* the possessed

---

87. Abrahamsen ("Women at Philippi," 21) argues that although the connection to the Delphic oracle is clear in Acts, Isis, Sylvanus (male cult), and the Diana worship were most popular among the Philippian women in the last half of the first century and early second century CE.

88. Maurizio ("Anthropology and Spirit Possession," 69–86, 79) uses paradigms for spirit possession from modern comparative anthropological studies to illuminate our understanding of the Pythia's function at Delphi. He further examines the use of randomizing devices to provide objectivity and to create resistance. The uses of these devices show the diviner's productions are not his own but the result of the power of spirit possession and believable. These devices involve the use of speech or body language by the divine. They take three forms: (1) the diviner's words are obscured, (2) the diviner's words are virtually unintelligible or incomprehensible, and (3) the diviner uses supplementary language such as unusual posture, voice tone, clothing or gestures. This use of randomizing devices does not mean that everything the diviner says or does is unintelligible, because a lot of what she says is comprehensible and like mundane language. Using the character of Cassandra as depicted by Aeschylus in Agamemnon, Maurizio argues that "verbal gibberish at the beginning of the Pythia's utterance and poeticized speech, that is, versified and ambiguous language," were perhaps the randomizing devices used by the Pythia at Delphi to prove her words were those of the god (81–86).

89. Plutarch, "Oracles at Delphi," *Moralia* 5.397.7. The discussion centers on the changes that have taken place in the oracles, i.e., why the oracles are no longer in verse but in prose and why they contain metrical and verbal errors. The gods use different vessels; some are poets and some are not. Some are well educated and some are poor peasants. In classical times the oracles were primarily in verse, but at times in prose as well.

person speak in unison, wherein the two appear indistinguishable (Luke 4:33–36; 8:26–30, 38; 9:38–39; cf. 11:14). Thus, Paul shows no compassion for the girl, just contempt for her words and vexing presence. The apostles only directly address women in Acts who are depicted as deceitful (Sapphira) or are dead (Tabitha). Using the name of Jesus Christ, Paul orders the spirit to abandon the girl (16:18).

No other reason is given for the "exorcism" but that the girl greatly disturbed (*diaponeomai*) Paul. This same Greek verb, *diaponeomai* (greatly disturbed or annoyed), describes the temple administrator (*stratēgos*) and the Sadducees' psychological state because of Peter and John's persistence in proclaiming the resurrection of Jesus and of the dead (4:1–2). In neither case does the stress derive from what the speakers' believe to be false teachings. The apostles have been the object and subject of the same verb; they have annoyed others and others have annoyed them over matters of speech.

In the eyes of her masters and quite possibly Luke, the slave girl functions simply as a medium and a means to an end. Luke's only interest in the girl is as "a narrative prop to show the power of God at work in Paul"; after the exorcism the story transitions to focus on the income lost because of her silence.[90] Luke also demonstrates that Paul's ability to exorcize the spirit from the girl is superior to the power of the spirit that inspires the girl. The spirit that inspires the slave girl is subordinated to the power operative in Paul. She is othered, and she, like the other charismatics, is the external other.

Differently from the exorcism stories in the Gospels, the exorcism of the Pythian girl is not widely reported, and amazed crowds do not congregate (Luke 11:14//Matt 12:22–33; Luke 9:38–43//Matt 17:14–21//Mark 9:14–29; Luke 4:31–37//Mark 1:21–28). The exorcism of the slave girl has no immediate impact on the growth of the *ekklēsia* or on any one individual's conversion. Conversely, when the proconsul witnesses the blinding of Bar-Jesus by Paul, he believes (13:12). When the evil spirit assaults and overpowers the seven sons of Sceva, it is rumored to all the Ephesians (Greeks and Jews), striking them with fear, and "the name of the Lord Jesus is exalted"(19:17). But at no time does the Pythian slave girl's testimony count.

---

90. O'Day, "Acts," 311.

Transitivity Analysis

The grammar demonstrates that the Pythian slave girl is the character constructed with the highest degree of transitive agency in relation to the apostle Paul. In terms of transitivity analysis, she affects other persons as much as her masters do. She exhibits nearly the same level of verbal agency as her masters. The Pythian slave girl is a participant-actor in three ergative material process clauses (she met us, 16:16; she was earning great profits for her masters, 16:16; she followed Paul, 16:17). She is a participant-actor in one ergative relational clause (she possessed a Pythian spirit, 16:16), one non-ergative verbal clause (while she was divining [*manteuō*], 16:16) and two ergative verbal clauses (she cried out, 16:17; she did this [crying out] for many days, 16:18).

As usual, the apostle Paul (and his companions) demonstrates the least amount of transitive agency, and any agency is expressed in verbal processes or speech acts. They exhibit the most passivity in the grammatical structure. Paul is *not* a participant-actor in any ergative material process clauses. Paul (Silas, and the *we* narrator) is a participant-actor in six clauses: two ergative relational process clauses (we were going to the *proseuchē*, 16:16; he turned to the spirit, 16:18), three ergative verbal process clauses (these are proclaiming a way of salvation, 16:17; he said, "I adjure you," 16:18; they proclaim customs, 16:21), and one non-ergative mental process clause (Paul was greatly disturbed, 16:18). Paul performs one speech act, embedded in a projecting clause ([he said] "I adjure you to come out of her," 16:18), which accomplishes the expulsion of the evil spirit.

The Pythian slave girl's masters are participant-actors in three ergative material process clauses (they seized Paul and Silas, 16:19; they dragged them into the agora, 16:19; they brought them before the magistrate, 19:20) and in one ergative mental process clause (they saw her, 16:19). The Pythian slave girl shows more transitive agency than the apostle Paul when she interacts with him. But when she disappears from the narrative and only her masters remain to interact with the apostle Paul (and Silas), the slave masters demonstrate a higher degree of transitive agency. Again, an analysis of the grammatical structure shows that the apostles are the most passive acting characters, but they are the most powerful on the level of the story.

Summary and Conclusion

Paul's encounter with the Pythian girl and resulting imprisonment serves as a segue from one household conversion story to another. The girl's masters identify Paul and Silas as Jews and accuse them of disturbing the city and teaching customs that are not lawful for Romans to practice (16:20–21). Paul and Silas are thrown into jail, and when, in answer to prayer, a violent earthquake shakes loose the prison doors presenting them with the opportunity to escape, they stay to convert the jailer and his household. Sandwiched between two household conversion narratives is the story of an encounter with the Pythian slave girl. She is most proximate to Paul in terms of her giftedness or functionality. The exorcism draws a clear line of distinction between her and Paul and renders her as categorically the external other. She is now an impotent external other like the other charismatics. In the minds of some readers, it is the naming of the spirit in her as "unclean" and the exorcism that convinces of the danger she posed to Paul and his ministry. It is Paul's evaluative words combined with the successful exorcism that discursively and theologically seal her fate as subordinated, triply marginalized other: she is female, slave, and vocationless.

Seven Sons of Sceva, the High Priest—Acts 19:13–20

Paul Builds a Reputation in Ephesus (Asia) for Performing Extraordinary Miracles

According to the immediate literary context, Paul spent over two years in Ephesus (and/or Asia) before the episode about the seven sons of the Jewish high priest name Sceva occurred.[91] Of the four charismatic others, the seven sons are the ones who have no direct narrative encounter with Paul. For three months Paul preached about the *basileia* of God in the synagogue. But because of rejection, Paul left the synagogue and began preaching the "word of the Lord" to a broader Jewish and Greek audience in the public lecture hall of Tyrannus (19:8–10).

---

91. Sceva is not mentioned among Josephus' listing of the Jewish high priests in *Ant.* 20.20. The number seven may be symbolic; in the Hebrew Bible, Job had seven sons and three daughters (Job 1:2), Jesse (King David's father) had seven sons (1 Sam 16:10), and the priest of Midian had seven daughters (Exod 2:16). While we know the names of the fathers, not all the sons or daughters are named.

Paul also performed miracles (*dunameis*); unclean spirits were cast out; and sick people who touched Paul's skin with their clothing were healed (19:11–12; cf. Luke 6:19; 22:51). When the people are healed by touching Paul's skin with their clothing, a cause-effect relationship is inferred as well as a "sympathetic bond." Historically, some might have labeled such healings with the use of "props" as magic.[92] The summary of Paul's activities in Asia ends with the clause *ta te pneumata ta ponēra ekporeuesthai* ("and the evil spirits went out," 19:12). This theme is continued and expanded in our text.

The narrative instability arises as a result of Paul's widespread success and the resulting reputation he gained in the region. The Jewish exorcists and Paul become spatially and temporally proximate with Paul's arrival and with his residing in the area for some time. In narrative time, Paul does not resolve to leave Ephesus until after the events surrounding the seven sons (19:21).

A Mimetic Attempt: Encounter between Seven Charismatic Others and an Unclean Spirit

After Paul's very public preaching, healings, and exorcisms in Asia Minor, the seven sons emerge as imitators of Paul (19:13–14).[93] I propose that

92. Hull (*Hellenistic Magic*, 54) argues that a miracle is partially or entirely magic if one or more of the following apply: (a) the only cause of the miracle is the will of the miracle worker; (b) an explicit cause-effect relationship is grounded on a notion of "sympathetic bonds . . . or something similar"; and (c) the miracle is understood to be caused by certain rituals, formal or informal, that themselves are considered efficacious—human effort through ritual brings about the miracle.

93. The textual tradition of 19:14 presents some difficulty because of the differences between the majority text and the much longer Western textual tradition. The primary Western witnesses to Acts 19:14 are P[38], D (Codex Bezae), and sy[hmg] (the margin of the Harclean Syriac). Depending on whether one interprets *en ois kai* (which is inserted in the Western text as the beginning of v.14) as "'among whom' the [seven] sons of a certain [Jewish] [chief] priest Sceva desired to do the same thing," as "'at this junction' seven sons of a certain priest Sceva desired to do the same thing," or "in this connection also," the seven sons are either a subgroup of the Jewish exorcists or they are a late and separate arrival to the incident involving the exorcists. The Jewish exorcists imitate Paul; the seven sons of Sceva attempt to mimic the exorcists. Metzger, *Textual Commentary*, 417. Strange ("Sons of Sceva") reconstructs "the earliest form of the Western text," which he proposes is the original and the majority is a "development from it by someone other than the author." Strange prefers a reading that presupposes Sceva to be a Gentile rather than a Jewish high priest. See also Mastin, "Scaeva"; idem, "Note on Acts 19, 14"; Delebecque, "La misadventure des fils."

the itinerant Jewish exorcists who were expelling unclean spirits (*ta pneumata ta ponēra*; v. 13) are *not* synonymous with the seven sons identified in v. 14. With the abrupt narrative shift to the seven sons, the grammatical number of the object of the exorcisms switches from plural to singular so that only one evil spirit confronts the seven sons (19:14–16). The seven sons are immediately identified as trying to imitate the itinerant Jewish exorcists. The itinerant Jewish exorcists had used Jesus' name to cast out evil spirits because Paul had preached Jesus' name. Since Paul preached to "all the residents of Asia," we can presume that the itinerant exorcists had also heard him. The plural form, *evil spirits*, as the object of the exorcisms also supports a conclusion that the itinerant exorcists had been successfully casting out evil spirits. Admittedly, the plural noun could also point to several failed attempts to use Jesus' name, but their failure would hardly motivate the seven sons to imitate them. The labeling of the group as itinerant Jewish exorcists suggests that they were already performing exorcisms in the region; what is new is their appropriation of Jesus' name.[94] This is true of the seven sons as well. Both groups of exorcists are functionally proximate to Paul.

The mimetic attempts of the seven sons may invoke the following questions: What happens when charismatic others who are functionally proximate to Paul attempt to appropriate the name of Jesus to expel unclean spirits? Will the name of Jesus work for others like it does for the apostles? What impact, if any, will the actions of the seven sons of Sceva have on the spread of the gospel?

By providing the father's name and position as high priest, Luke gives some readers the impression that the father is known and respected in the community. Also, by supplying the father's name and position and failing to provide names for the sons, Luke may want to give readers the impression that the sons have been relying on their father's reputation or name. And the exploitation of Jesus' name constitutes a continuation of a pattern of behavior.[95] The seven sons' anonymity is further foregrounded when the evil spirit fails to recognize them but does recognize the names of Paul and Jesus.

94. Gager (*Curse Tablets*, 108, 171) asserts that, historically, such an appropriation of a name was not extraordinary, for the use of names to cast spells and curses is well attested in the ancient world.

95. Conzelmann (*Acts*, 164) considers the high priest Sceva as "purely legendary."

The exorcism that the seven sons attempt to perform constitutes a double mimesis, or so the narrative sequence implies. The seven attempt to do what Paul had done, but this attempt is based on not having known Jesus but through the example of the itinerant Jewish exorcists. The itinerant Jewish exorcists were themselves imitating Paul; they had, it seems, no first hand knowledge of or encounter with Jesus (19:1–12). This double mimesis means that the seven sons are doubly removed from the Jesus reality. But in the end what matters is that the evil spirit has no knowledge of the seven sons.

Mimesis Gone Awry: The Name of Jesus Works for Some but Not for Others

The nature of the conflict between the seven sons and the evil spirit is ostensibly epistemic. The evil spirit that the seven sons attempt to exorcize brazenly confronts them. The evil spirit has no knowledge of the seven sons: "I know Jesus and I know Paul, but who are you?" (19:15b; cf. Luke 4:41; Mark 1:34). The demon associates authority with a knowing of persons and not merely a use of names; the demon refuses to obey the seven sons because he does not recognize them, in spite of their attempt to use Jesus' name. Differently, the Jerusalem leaders asked Peter and John by what power and name they healed the lame man (4:7). Peter and John respond to the Jerusalem rulers that there is no other name but Jesus by which anyone can be saved (4:12).

The anonymity of the seven sons renders them impotent as compared to Paul, whose name the evil spirit knows. No collaboration or collusion occurs between the seven sons and the evil spirit.[96] In fact, the two are at odds. The name that works for Paul in Acts does not work for proximate others.

If we presuppose continuity between Luke's Gospel and Acts, the seven sons' attempt at an exorcism in Jesus' name would not ordinarily be a problem, regardless of whether they knew Jesus or not. In Luke's Gospel, when the disciples want to stop someone who is not a disciple of Jesus from casting out demons in Jesus' name, the Lukan Jesus responds, "Do not stop him for whoever is not against you is

96. Cf. Matt 10:24. Contra Garrett (*Demise of the Devil*, 98, 99) who argues that "both the demon and the exorcists are working for Satan's side"; the only supporter of the seven sons was Satan, who was defeated.

for you" (9:50 NRSV; cf. Mark 9:38–41 NRSV, "whoever is not against us is for us"). Luke's revision from the first-person-plural object pronoun to the second-person-plural object pronoun anticipates a time when Jesus would no longer be with the disciples and they perform their own exorcisms. Either Acts represents a departure from Jesus' imperative at Luke 9:50 or something different is happening in Acts. I propose that Luke's attempt to construct a self-identity for the apostles in Acts takes precedence over Jesus' imperative at Luke 9:50. It is important that Luke draw boundaries between the proximate others and the apostles. The seven sons are functionally, spatially, ethnically, and religiously proximate to Paul.

Because of the epistemic dissonance between the evil spirit and the seven sons (the spirit knows both Jesus and Paul, but the sons know neither of them), the evil spirit rejects their mimetic attempt to expel it from the man's body. Thus, the man possessed of the evil spirit leaps on, subdues, and overpowers the seven sons.[97] The wounded seven sons sprint from the house having been stripped naked (19:16).[98] The stripping of clothing from their bodies represents the vulnerability and weakness of the seven sons. Conversely, the bringing of clothing into direct contact with Paul's body results in the healing of diseased and weakened bodies, as well as the expulsion of evil spirits (19:11–12). When the evil spirit prevails, the sevens sons are displaced.

Any reputation that the seven sons lacked before the botched exorcism attempt, they gained after their failed attempt to expel one evil spirit: "This [event] became known [gnōston] to all the Jews and Greeks dwelling in Ephesus, and fear enveloped everyone. And the name of the Lord Jesus was exalted" (19:17–19a). The seven sons' widespread infamy (to all the Ephesians) contrasts with Paul's ubiquitous fame (to all the Jewish and Greek inhabitants of Asians, 19:10). The story is not concerned with the man possessed with the evil spirit, only with the destruction of the seven sons. The seven sons are defeated; the evil spirit teaches the seven a painful lesson; and the name of Jesus is praised by all, but only to be used by a few approved intermediaries.

97. Conzelmann (*Acts*, 164) argues that the number seven "serves to heighten the effect: Seven against one"; seven men overpowered by one evil spirit.

98. This verse is difficult with the "both" (*amphoteroun*), which implies there were only two sons in the house. However, Metzger (*Textual Commentary*, 417) notes that *amphoteroi* can mean "all."

The people's subsequent exaltation of Jesus' name following the seven's defeat functions evaluatively. And some readers will understand the people's exaltation as proof of God's disapproval of the seven, notwithstanding that it is an *evil* spirit that has prevailed over the sons of a Jewish high priest. The same Greek verb, *ischuō* (prevailed), describes how the Lord's word triumphed (19:20) and how the evil spirit overpowered the seven sons (19:16).

The seven sons as persons who are ethnically, functionally, religiously, geographically proximate to the apostles are effectively othered. They are proximate others; they become external others.[99] The seven sons' failed attempt to exorcize the evil spirit in the name of Jesus results in the evil spirit rendering them impotent and subordinate to Paul. Ironically, the seven sons' defeat constitutes a win for the name of Jesus (19:17b). In Acts, proximate others cannot effectively use Jesus' name; this privilege is reserved for certain approved intermediaries, and the seven sons do not qualify.

Book Burning Ceremony: The Contagious Impact of the Creation of the Other

A larger group of Ephesians and their activities are associated with the defeat and othering of the seven sons, as manifested by the book burning ceremony. After the evil spirit's victory over the seven sons, some believers make confessions and disclosures about activities that remain enigmatic to the reader. These "disclosures" are followed by a book burning ceremony. Those who burn their books are said to have been practicing strange inefficacious things (*perierga*). Scholars interpret the Greek noun *perierga* as magic practices, presupposing that the seven sons are magicians; therefore, many scholars predetermine that *perierga* means magical practices.[100]

But Luke foregrounds the seven sons' *inability* to perform an exorcism in Jesus' name.[101] Luke's decision not to identify the seven sons as practitioners of magic warrants a more contextual interpretation for

99. Fitzmyer (*Acts*, 646) refers to the seven sons as outsiders with respect to "the Jesus that Paul preaches."

100. Conzelmann, *Acts*, 164.

101. Cf. Mark 9:17–18//Matt 17:14–17, where Jesus' disciples are unable to exorcise an unclean spirit.

perierga than a simple determination of magic practices. The immediate literary context favors an interpretation of *perierga* as ineffectual and/or strange practices and/or philosophies. The only other New Testament occurrence of this Greek noun is at 1 Tim 5:13, where young widows are described as "busybodies" (*periergoi*).

After the involuntary cessation of the seven sons' exorcism career, the people build a bonfire for the philosophical and how-to books related to their esoteric and ineffectual practices (cf. Augustine, *civ.* 10.16.321). The strange practices (*perierga*) based on diverse philosophies contained in the books and the failed actions of the seven sons fall into the same category of ineffectual things. Since *perierga* carries the sense of needless talk, efficacious or strange activities, it should not be strictly equated with magic or magical practices.[102] According to Plutarch, *periergos* would be considered normative behavior among some women, but odd behavior when practiced by others. He asserts that Olympia's strange behavior was typical of women in a certain region who were addicted to Orphic rites and the orgies of Dionysius; that they imitated the Edonian and Thracian women from which derives the term *threskeuein*, which refers to "extravagant and superstitious (*periergos*) ceremonies."[103] Here, as in Acts, imitating other persons' behaviors is known as *periergos*. Similar to the use of *perierga* in 1 Tim 5:13, the *Acts of Andrew* mentions magi and others as "meddlesome" (*periergoi*). Those meddlesome others are linked to the *inability* to drive out demons[104] (in the same way that the seven sons could not drive out one evil spirit). The *Acts of Andrew* may reflect influence from Acts or it may reflect a shared sociocultural knowledge. In the *Acts of Peter*, Albinus seeks permission from Agrippa to find and execute Peter as a meddler (*periergos*) because Peter persuaded their wives to refuse to fulfill their conjugal duties. The term can also be translated as "sorcerer."[105] In Chariton's novel (ca. mid-first century CE), *periergos* refers to naturally inquisitive or curious people or crowds; there the same word describes love as a naturally inquisitive thing.[106] Comparing the Acts context with the word's usage

---

102. Josephus, *Ant.* 15.11.1. Here it means idle and curious practices.

103. Plutarch, *Alexander*, 2.8.2.

104. *Act Andr.* 5.2; 42.18.

105. *Act Pet.*, *Martyrdom of Peter*, 34.17.

106. *Chaer.* 1.12.6; 3.9.4; 8.6.5.

in extra-narrative sources, a translation of *perierga* as "magic practices" in our pericope is misleading and is not unequivocally warranted.

In antiquity, individuals and groups publicly burned philosophical, prophetic, religious and/or popular books that were considered to be associated with strange or competing ideas and/or influential opponents. The forced burning of books was often politically or polemically motivated. Livy reminisces about how the Roman forefathers prohibited foreign or strange cults and required that prophetic books associated with them be burned.[107] Suetonius writes that upon assuming the office of *pontifex maximus* Augustus gathered Greek and Latin books in general circulation and burned them; he retained the sibylline books.[108] Lucian says that Alexander seized the philosophical books containing the beliefs of Epicurus and burned them in the middle of the marketplace as if burning the man himself. But Lucian asserts the books had brought peace, freedom, truth, and intelligence to many people.[109] King Jehoiakim burned the scroll containing the words of the Lord that Baruch, Jeremiah's scribe, penned (Jer 36:20–27). When King Antiochus commanded his subjects to adopt his religion and abandon their own customs, many people in Judah burned the books of the Law (1 Macc 1:56). Thus, book burning may also symbolize the switching of loyalties.

As in Acts, conflagration ceremonies were politically motivated and concerned the destruction of books associated with rival groups, prophecies, philosophies, or religious beliefs. Unlike the above examples, the Ephesians in Acts are not forced by anyone to burn their books. But they are compelled by an overwhelming and contagious fear resulting from the defeat of the seven sons, which the narrator discursively identifies as a victory for the name of Jesus (19:17b). In any case, the book burning ceremonies symbolize a transfer of the people's allegiance to the name of Jesus (19:18).

Transitivity Analysis

An ergative-based transitivity analysis demonstrates how Luke has foregrounded the man possessed with the evil spirit, and/or the evil spirit,

107. Livy, *History of Rome*, 39:16.

108. Suetonius, *Aug.* 31:1.

109. Lucian, *Alex.* 47.

as the most active character in the narrative. As in the other three narratives, the least active or most passive character is the apostle. Although Paul is not an actor in the immediate story, he is not absent from the grammar. Paul is a participant-actor in only one non-ergative verbal process clause (Paul preached, 19:13). Even the crowds exhibit more agency. The "considerable number of people" is a participant-actor in two ergative material process clauses, but their influence is primarily limited to things (they assemble their books; they burned them) and one non-ergative material process clause (they practice strange arts). The people's practice of strange things affects nobody beyond themselves. The human being (*anthropos*) possessed by the evil spirit exhibits the highest degree of transitive agency. He is a participant-actor in four ergative-based material process clauses (he leaped on [*ephallomai*] them, 19:16a; he subdued [*katakurieuō*] them, 19:16b; he overpowered [*ischuō*] them, 19:16c; and he wounded [*traumatizō*] them, 19:16d). The evil spirit is the participant-actor in one verbal process clause (he answered them, 19:15).

Transitivity analysis shows that the evil spirit surpasses the seven sons in terms of agency. This low degree of agency on the part of the seven sons represents a departure from how charismatic others are portrayed in the other three narratives; they usually demonstrate the highest degree of agency. The seven sons are participants-actors in only one ergative material process clause (they were doing this, 19:14b) and in only one non-ergative material process clause (they fled out of the house, 19:16).

Summary and Conclusion

In summary, the seven sons of Sceva attempt to imitate a group of Jewish exorcists who were using the name of Jesus which Paul preached. And at some point the apostle Paul enters and occupies the same geographical space as the Jewish exorcists and particularly the seven sons. In fact, it is not until after the seven blotch their attempt to exorcize an evil spirit that Paul leaves Ephesus. While Paul is still in the vicinity, one belligerent evil spirit destroys the influence and reputation of the seven sons. The seven are not magicians, but they are persons who attempt to imitate Paul's use of Jesus' name to perform exorcisms. Nor are the seven depicted as servants of the devil. Since they cannot imitate Paul's use of Jesus' name, the evil spirit prevails. But the seven sons' failure represents a win for the *ekklēsia*.

Significantly, this incident shares some commonalities with the story of the appointment of the seven Hellenists in Acts 6. In that passage the seven Hellenists are not allowed to engage in the same ministry as the apostles and are subordinated to the apostles, yet they are anointed and appointed to a table ministry. Similar to the seven sons, the seven Hellenists are constructed as other, but the seven Hellenists, as believers and coworkers in the ministry, are internal others. The seven sons constitute the marginalized and suppressed external other.

Conclusion

Using a theory of othering, I have shown how Luke constructs certain charismatic figures in the book of Acts as external others in relation to the apostles. The literary and discursive construction of Simon, Bar-Jesus, the Pythian slave girl, and the seven sons of Sceva as charismatic external others clearly identifies the apostles as the approved intermediaries and witnesses of God. This self-identity is constructed over against charismatic figures that are at least spatially and functionally or vocationally proximate to the apostles. The charismatic others are more like the apostles than unlike them. This proximity must be overcome to distinguish the apostles and their abilities as superior to the others.

I have further shown that reductionist efforts to identify all of the charismatic figures as magicians and associated with the devil are not substantiated by a close reading of the text. The Bar-Jesus episode serves as the centrifugal point from which Garrett argues that the devil, false prophecy, magic, and idolatry are integrally linked in Luke-Acts.[110] In other words, the connection made between the devil and false prophecy in the Bar-Jesus story is imposed on an interpretation of the other so-called magician narratives. Heintz correctly notes the tenuousness of Garrett's assertion that Luke categorically connects magic with the devil. Heintz argues that Garrett has systematically applied a "grid of demonological interpretation to the biblical texts."[111] He further notes that

---

110. Garrett, *Demise of the Devil*.

111. Heintz (*Simon*, 16) also argues that Garrett's use of *Jubilees* and other sources is problematic since in these texts the Exodus history is systematically reinterpreted so as to demonize all the obstacles to Moses' passage. Thus, Pharaoh's magicians are

Garrett has mingled "two distinct types of accusations: the accusations of magic and that of demonic collusion. The fusion of the two do not appear in a strict sense before the second century C.E. beginning with Justin" (*deux types of distincts d'accusations: l'accusation de magie et celle de collusion démoniaque. La fusion des deux n'apparaît pas stricto sensu avant le milieu du second siècle, en commençant par Justin*).[112] Simon is the only charismatic that is specifically identified as practicing magic, but it is not the practice of magic by others that causes conflict between the apostles and the charismatic others. Luke identifies Bar-Jesus as a magus, but he performs no magical acts; it is his false prophecies that get him in trouble. Bar-Jesus is also the only charismatic that Luke discursively associates with the devil, and this connection relates to his false prophecies.

Luke displaces the charismatics not because they are magicians, but because they are proximate others who perform or attempt to perform miraculous and powerful acts like the apostles, including prophetic utterance. They are proximate others who often simultaneously occupy the same space as the apostles and who seek to influence the same individuals or groups of people. The other is most dangerous when most like us.

---

only one of the instruments that the devil uses to oppose the plan of divine salvation. Heintz asserts that Garrett imposes an interpretation onto those texts as well as onto the *Martyrdom of Isaiah*. As for Garrett's use of the *Shepherd of Hermas*, she takes a risk in basing her argument on a later text when she wishes to show the shift to a demonization of magic in the Acts of the Apostles. Garrett's story begins with literary-critical reading of Luke-Acts and then she attempts to support her reading of Luke-Acts with extra-narrative sources. However, it is evident, as Heintz notes, that the extra-narrative sources provide a framework for her reading of Luke's narratives. Heintz refutes Garrett's argument point by point to first establish that Luke does not present Simonian magic as a satanic and demonic enterprise (22). Heintz proceeds to situate Simon within the much more widespread and stereotypical historical framework of ancient invective (28).

112. Ibid., 17. Heintz argues that even the writings of the apostolic fathers, which are dated between Acts and Justin, present no direct link between the devil and magic. Sorcery is only a sin among other sins.

2

The Construction of the Jews as the External Other

OTHERING SOMETIMES CREATES A SYNTHETIC AND DECEPTIVE BOUNDARY between the moral conduct of one group and another. Such constructions of difference are too often internalized and accepted as natural. This phenomenon of othering based on evaluating one group's behavior as inferior, or even demonic, to another group occurs often between proximate others inside the same collective. Many ethnic or cultural groups identify an other within their collective who is marginalized and rendered as categorically other. This happens when one segment of the group desires to distance or disassociate itself from another segment that it disdains and does not want to be identified with. Such otherness is sometimes manifested in contemporary society as classism. Some Whites identify other whites of lower socioeconomic status as "white trash," considering them ethically, morally, and culturally depraved. Some blacks identify other blacks as "niggers" because they are perceived as ignorant, morally diminished, and misrepresentative of the race.[1] Of course, in each case the reverse also occurs.

This same social and cultural phenomenon of intra-group othering gets inscribed onto texts, both secular and religious. When this othering is etched in texts we regard as sacred, we tend to overlook and/or discursively reinscribe it in our teaching, preaching, writing, and other public discourse and interactions. We uncritically appropriate and impose the inscribed image of the other on ourselves and on others. For many Christians, the Pharisees constitute categorically the eternal nega-

---

1. The two labels "nigger" and "white trash," of course, have historically, and continue to be, used pejoratively by some whites as a label for blacks and by some blacks to label whites.

tively ostentatious other against whom we measure piety. The Jewish people are the legalistic other who serve as a perennial reminder of how not to reject Jesus.

In this chapter I analyze Luke's othering of *the Jews* (*hoi Ioudaioi*) in Acts.[2] *The Jews* in Acts are also proximate others in relation to the approved intermediaries of the gospel. Luke ultimately discursively constructs *the Jews* as the external other. He accomplishes this in several ways. *The Jews* are consistently characterized as the stereotypical and synthetic other.[3] The gospel increases and is successful in spite of consistent and homogeneous opposition from *the Jews*. While *the Jews* actively oppose the Gentile mission, the approved intermediaries are portrayed as relatively passive objects of aggression. Thematic and/or stereotypical characterization of *the Jews* functions organically in the narrative; it contributes to the meaning of the text as a whole.

Luke's depiction of *the Jews* as highly active and negative eclipses positive representations of other Jewish people in Acts. *The Jews* are depicted as "the most violent opponents of the Christian community."[4] Because Luke repetitively depicts *the Jews* as hostile and fiercely opposed to Paul's gospel, some readers will compartmentalize the missionary successes among the Jewish people throughout Acts. As a result, Jewish people that are depicted as receptive to the apostles' message can be read as exceptional or are ignored altogether. And the negatively portrayed Jews become representative of all Jewish people in the minds of many readers;[5] all Jewish people become the dangerous external other.

2. From this point forward, when the term *the Jews* refers to the presence of the Greek plural with the definite article of *ho Ioudios* (*hoi Ioudaioi*) in Acts, it is italicized.

3. Luke does not expressly demonize *the Jews* in Acts as happens in the Johannine literature (John 8:44; 1 John 3:10). Pagels (*Origin of Satan*, 105) demonstrates how the Gospel of John, similar to the other Gospels, links the mythological character of Satan with particular human opposition when it implicates Judas Iscariot, the Jewish authorities, and then the Jews collectively. Some of the many works on the Jews in John's Gospel include: Reinhartz, "Building Skyscrapers"; idem, "'Jews' and Jews"; Pippin, "'For Fear of the Jews'"; Smith, "Judaism and the Gospel of John"; Culpepper, "Gospel of John and the Jews"; Cook, "Gospel of John and the Jews"; Townsend, "Gospel of John and the Jews"; Brown, *Community of the Beloved Disciple*.

4. Barbi ("[*Hoi*] *Ioudaioi* in Acts," 141) argues that *the Jews* are a model by which Luke shows "the ongoing rupture among Jews in relation to the gospel."

5. Tyson, "Problem of Jewish Rejection"; Sanders, "Jewish People in Luke-Acts"; idem, *Jews in Luke-Acts*, 303. See also Juel, *Luke-Acts*; Wilson, *Gentiles*; Haenchen, *Acts*, 729; Cook, "Mission to the Jews"; Tyson, *Images of Judaism*, 188. Also, Gilbert, "Disappearance of the Gentiles"; Sandmel, *Anti-Semitism*.

But throughout Acts, we notice a continual dialogue between the Jewish people and the Gentile mission. This dialogue is poignantly apparent in the context that gives rise to Paul's three declarations about turning to the Gentiles (13:46; 18:6; 28:28). I argue that these three declarations function as one element in the dialectic of discursive turning toward the Gentiles and an ontological remaining with *the Jews* and the Jewish people. It constitutes a dialectic between the language of abandonment and the practice of remaining in dialogue with the synagogue and the Jewish people.[6]

In spite of the language of abandonment (of *the Jews*) or turning toward the Gentiles, Jews *and* Gentiles continually join the Jesus movement in Acts. Daniel Marguerat argues that although the two images of Jewish persons (believing and unbelieving) stand in tension with one another, we do not have to choose a rejectionist reading over a more positive one. We can overcome the impasse if we assume one *and* the other, for they signal that "in Luke's work it is not reduced to one simple equation" (*dans l'oeuvre de Luc ne se reduit pas a une equation simple*).[7] The tension created by *le visage du judaisme* ("the face of Judaism") in Acts is peculiar to the text itself. Rather than reduce the tension, Marguerat interprets it theologically. He argues, like Jacob Jervell, that Luke wants to demonstrate historical continuity *and* discontinuity with Israel. If Luke, Marguerat asks, simply wished to establish the *ekklēsia* in place of Israel and to present a pro-Christian and anti-Jewish God, why would he go to lengths to compose such a complex narrative?[8] It is the continuity that forms the basis of proximity between *the Jews* and the apostles (and the mission). It is the discursive construction of discontinuity or disjuncture between *the Jews* and the mission that contributes to the othering of *the Jews* as the external other.

---

6. Regarding the continued relevance of the gospel for the Jewish people, see Jervell, *Luke and the People of God.* Also, Brawley, *Luke-Acts and the Jews;* Tannehill, "Rejection by Jews"; Tannehill, "Israel in Luke-Acts"; Trocmé, "Jews as Seen." Also, Fusco, "Luke-Acts."

7 Marguerat, "Juifs et chrétiens selon Luc-Actes," 156.

8. Ibid., 155–57.

The Problematic Proximate Other:
The Jews in Narrative Instabilities

The expression *the Jews* (*hoi Ioudaioi*) occurs seventy-nine times in Acts,[9] and these occurrences are mostly negative.[10] *The Jews* first appears at 9:22 as the apostles' opponents.[11] Prior to this, any reference to Jewish people is signified grammatically by the noun without the definite article or anarthrously. After 9:22, Luke's use of the expression *the Jews* and the progression of the narrative constitute interdependent phenomena. Narrative progression refers to how authors narrate their stories so as to engender, maintain, develop, and resolve readers' attention. The narrative as a dynamic event moves in its relating of the story; it progresses diachronically in its reception. An author can achieve this movement using narrative instabilities.[12]

Narrative instabilities involving *the Jews* are situations where Luke portrays Paul as doing or saying something that produces a negative reaction from *the Jews*. Luke's repetition of narrative instabilities between *the Jews* and the apostle Paul (and his companions) creates and maintains suspense. It makes for a dynamic story, particularly since *the Jews* often chase Paul out of their cities and from city to city.

Although instabilities between *the Jews* and the apostle Paul begin in Acts 9 and continue throughout the narrative from Jerusalem and towards Rome,[13] we encounter similar instabilities in the first half of Acts, prior to chapter 9. Luke has arranged the material so as to show correspondences between the activities of the *ekklēsia* in Jerusalem in chapters 1–7 and Paul's mission in the diaspora in the second half of Acts.[14] In the first seven chapters, the Jewish people that believe in the gospel are contrasted with the unbelieving religious leaders in Jerusalem. The Jewish believers are loyal observers of the Jewish customs and laws, par-

9. As to the Gospel of John, Culpepper ("Gospel of John and the Jews") counts seventy, and Pippin ("'Fear of the Jews'") counts seventy-one references to the Jews.

10. Rese, "Jews in Luke-Acts."

11. Tyson, *Images of Judaism*, 119.

12. Phelan, *Reading People*, 8.

13. Historically, some used the term *Jew* both as a self-designation and to distinguish the ethnic and religious communities of Jews outside of Judea. Cohen, *Beginnings of Jewishness*.

14. Talbert, *Literary Patterns*, 29, 98–99. Talbert divides Acts between chs. 12 and 13.

ticipate in the unity of the believing community, and share in the common fellowship. On the other hand, the Jewish leaders initiate conflict and oppose the apostles and the believers[15] (4:1–4; 5:17; 6:12).

The Jews as a collective are not a necessary phenomenon in the first half of Acts. They emerge only when the Gentile mission begins. However, the narrative conflict that arises between some synagogue Jews and Stephen (one of the seven Hellenists, 6:1–7) foreshadows the narrative instabilities concerning *the Jews* whom Luke later depicts as Paul's opponents:

> Some men from the so-called synagogue of the Libertines—
> Cyrenians, Alexandrians, and some from Cilicia and Asia—rose
> up [*anthistēmi*] and disputed with Stephen. But they could not
> stand up against [*anthistēmi*] the wisdom and spirit with which
> he spoke. So they secretly enlisted men to say that they heard
> him speak blasphemous words against Moses and God. They
> incited [*sunkineō*] the people [*laos*], the elders, and the scribes.
> And they seized [Stephen] and carried him to the Sanhedrin.
> (6:9–12)

The behavior of these synagogue members prefigures the behavior of *the Jews* who become Paul's opponents:[16] they dispute, incite others, seize Stephen, and are ultimately implicated in Stephen's death. Nevertheless, Luke adeptly refrains from referring to this group as *the Jews*. He reserves this definite plural noun, *the Jews*, for the opponents of the Gentile mission. Stephen's opponents are identified as an ethnically mixed and geographically diverse group recruited by the synagogue members, the elders and the scribes. Stephen's opponents incite the people (*laos*),[17] whereas Paul's opposition arouses the crowds (*ochloi*). Otherwise, their behavior is identical to that of *the Jews* who subsequently emerge. Both Stephen and Paul's opponents come from various geographical areas, but Luke lumps Stephen's opponents together in one

15. Thompson, "Believers and Religious Leaders." Also, Tyson, *Images of Judaism*, 109–11.

16. Matson (*Household Conversion*, 101) places the culpability on the synagogue, rather than on *the Jews*. I do not consider the synagogues and *the Jews* as equivalent, even though *the Jews* are associated with the synagogues.

17. Jervell (*Theology of the Acts*, 23) asserts that *laos* occurs 142 times in the NT, and Luke alone uses it 84 times (60 percent of all occurrences). The "unqualified" use of the term refers to Israel as a name, but sometimes it is a synonym for the Greek word *ochlos* indicating a crowd of Jews.

episode. This is because of Stephen's anticipated and forthcoming death. Stephen's opponents kill him at the end of the episode where we meet the apostle Paul for the first time.

The Jews oppose and instigate violence against Paul (and others) primarily when Paul visits cities that have not been previously evangelized by approved intermediaries (i.e., Damascus, Psidian Antioch, Iconium, Lystra, Thessaloniki, Berea, Corinth). The places where no one, not even *the Jews*, oppose Paul are cities where other missionaries have preceded him. For example, when persecution erupted after Stephen was martyred, the Jerusalem *ekklēsia* dispersed (all except the apostles).[18] Members of the *ekklēsia* fled to Syrian Antioch, Phoenicia, and Cyprus, preaching only to Jewish persons (11:19–20). Some Cypriots and Cyrenians were among the scattered members of the *ekklēsia*, and they preached to the *Hellenistas* in Syrian Antioch (cf. 6:1; 9:29).[19] The reception of the message in cities where the "scattered ones" migrated to was positive (11:20–21). Paul visits Syrian Antioch, Phoenicia, and Cyprus after "the scattered ones" had already preached there, and he receives a positive Jewish response, but no opposition from *the Jews*. Syrian Antioch also served as the base from which the Antiochene *ekklēsia* commissioned Paul and Barnabas (13:2–3).

Paul preaches in the synagogue of *the Jews* in Salamis (Cyprus) and no trouble erupts. The lack of trouble in Salamis may again be attributed to the groundwork already laid by the scattered ones. Paul does not preach publicly in Paphos (Cyprus) (13:6–7), but he has a private audience with the proconsul. Paul passes through Perga on his way from Cyprus to Psidian Antioch (13:13), but Luke records no preaching there. Paul preaches in the city of Derbe, making disciples, but any activity in the Jewish synagogue is not mentioned, and therefore Luke reports no opposition by *the Jews* there (14:21). As for Phrygia,

18. These scattered women and men were likely the pioneers of the Gentile mission. Käsemann, "Paul and Nascent Catholicism."

19. Here, I understand *Hellenistas* to mean Gentiles that were either Godfearers or proselytes (cf. 6:5). According to Metzger (*Textual Commentary*, 342) *Hellenistas* refers to "'Greek-speaking, persons,' meaning thereby the mixed population of Antioch in contrast to the *Ioudaioi* of ver. 19." Moule ("Once More, Who Were the Hellenists?"), Hellenists were Jews and Jewish Christians who spoke only Greek. Also, Wilson, *Gentiles and the Gentile Mission*. Juel (*Luke-Acts*, 69) says they were probably both Greek-speaking and Aramaic-speaking Jews. Tyson ("Acts 6:1–7") argues that the Hellenists were Gentiles. Also, Cadbury, "Hellenists."

the narrator says that the Holy Spirit prevented Paul from preaching in Asia[20] (16:6). At the beginning of his ministry Paul does not witness in Caesarea Maritima. He only passes through Caesarea Maritima on his way to Tarsus (9:30), possibly because the Antiochene *ekklēsia* had not yet officially commissioned him. But Luke places Peter in Caesarea Maritima ahead of Paul so that it is Peter who converts, arguably, the first Gentile—Cornelius and his household (10–11). To repeat, *the Jews* oppose Paul primarily in cities where Paul is the first to preach the gospel, i.e., in towns where no other approved intermediaries have already preached. This way Luke constructs an identity for Paul (and other apostles) exclusively over against certain proximate others.

As we shall see, the narrative instabilities occur between *the Jews* and Paul because of his apparent success among the Gentiles to whom salvation is extended without circumcision. These instabilities remain unresolved in the narrative. At the end of Acts, these collective unresolved instabilities result in tension between the narrator and some readers. The author creates tensions throughout Acts with discursive evaluations or ethical judgments. Ethical tensions encourage readers to accept certain evaluations, form judgments, and establish expectations.[21] For example, Gamaliel predicts that the Jesus movement would fizzle out as did those of Judas and Theudas (5:36–38). If the Jesus movement does not decline, its opponents are to be understood as ultimately opposing God. This prediction serves to positively evaluate the *ekklēsia* and the apostles as the approved intermediaries of the gospel; in spite of opposition, they are successful. As the narrative unfolds, it is *the Jews* who actively and unsuccessfully oppose the Gentile mission and may be construed as fighting against God.

It is historically unlikely that *the Jews* as Paul's opponents emerged mainly in places where Paul was the first to preach and that each time *the Jews* acted in very similar ways (or even identically). Luke's negative portrayal of *the Jews* consists of some synthetic dimensions. According to Phelan, synthetic attributes are always present in characterization.[22] Some aspects of characterization will inevitably constitute fabrications since authors cannot replicate exactly the situations or individuals to

---

20. Conzelmann, *Acts*, 126. In Luke's day part of the territory of Phrygia lay in the province of Asia and part in Galatia.

21. Phelan, *Reading People*, 8.

22. Ibid., 14, 91.

which they refer. Characterizations are not absolute images of the reality that they signify. This does not mean that there is a total absence of historicity in such literary constructions of character. But it is unlikely that *the Jews* existed as a monolithic stereotypical collective oppositional group in the exact manner that Luke constructed them in Acts.

The Construction of Difference and Sameness: The Stereotypical Other

Luke constructs *the Jews* so as to give readers the impression that they are an authentically ubiquitous group that acts harmoniously, homogeneously, and violently to oppose the Gentile mission. Luke depicts *the Jews* as different from those who accept the gospel (Jewish and Gentile believers), and this difference is always the same *everywhere*. Lawrence Wills has noted the "stylized" way that Luke negatively portrays *the Jews*, and he attributes this depiction to an apologetic "imperial sociology" motif. This motif asserts that the masses are naturally inclined toward rioting and insurrection. Because of the constant fear of revolt, the Roman ruling classes must keep the crowds under control. Wills further argues that *the Jews* in Acts are seditious while the "Christians" are orderly. *The Jews* are involved in riot scenes in Acts that "reflect common Roman assumptions about the nature of the masses and insurrection, which appear especially in Roman historical writing."[23] According to Wills, a theory of society is at work in Acts where "the good order of the empire is taken as an ideal, and the lower classes are perceived as potentially seditious." But he also acknowledges that all opposition does not stem from *the Jews*, and that the crowds whom *the Jews* incite are not necessarily from the lower classes.[24]

In support of his argument, Wills cites an excerpt from Tacitus (*Annals* 1.16), which Erich Auerbach treats as an example of antique historiography. Auerbach notes the biased nature of this piece of historiography, and he argues that it demonstrates no interest in the contemporary sociohistorical forces that motivated the revolt. Tacitus does not discuss the grievances in detail. He does not discuss whether the soldiers are justified, or how the Roman soldiers' situation had evolved

23. Wills, "Depiction of the Jews," 634–35, 647.
24. Ibid., 635, 644.

since the period of the Republic. Tacitus presents the soldiers' grievances as those of the ringleader Percennius. Auerbach further asserts
that Tacitus is more interested in presenting his own perspective, which
is that "the whole thing is merely a matter of mob effrontery and lack
of discipline."[25] So in Acts, Luke presents a one-dimensional view of
the Jews as "ringleaders" of baseless and violent opposition against the
ekklēsia.

Unlike Tacitus and Luke, some ancient writers betray some sympa-
thy for opposition parties rather than simply casting them as the fren-
zied mob. Diodorus of Sicily reports that Thrasybulus (one of four sons
of a certain Deinomenes) succeeded two of his brothers (Gelon and
Hieron) as ruler in Sicily and over the Syracusans. Thrasybulus acted
more avariciously and violently than any of his sibling predecessors.
In fact, many subjects had wished to revolt (*aphistasthai boulomenoi*)
under Hieron, but, remembering Gelon's good reputation (*doxan*),
they restrain themselves (*parakateschon tas idias hormas*). According
to Diodorus, Thrasybulus' many crimes included unjust killings, exile
based on false charges, and seizure of property to enrich the royal treasury. Eventually, Thrasybulus' actions compelled the victims to revolt
(*tous adikoumenous apostenai*) in order to destroy the tyranny.[26]

Significantly, Luke does not accuse *the Jews* of sedition or *stasis*
(revolt) in Acts. In Acts, *stasis* signifies disputes between individuals
and civil revolts, as in other ancient literature.[27] In fact, *stasis* occurs
four times in Acts, but never to refer to *the Jews* as the instigators: (a)
in Asia, the town clerk admonishes the popular assembly (*ekklēsia*) that
they are in danger of being charged with *stasis* (19:40); (b) when some
people from Judea arrive at Syrian Antioch teaching the brothers they
must be circumcised to be saved, a significant *stasis* breaks out between
Paul (and Barnabas) and the Judeans (15:1–2); (c) the rhetor Tertullus

25. Auerbach, *Mimesis*, esp. 33–40. The ancients did not "see forces [socio-histori-
cal] [but] . . . vices and virtues, successes and mistakes" (38). For a more recent work on
mimesis, see GeBauer and Wulf, *Mimesis*.

26. Diodorus Siculus, *Bibliotheca Historia* 11.67.1–7. Diodorus also reports a case
in which a man's daughter is unjustly sold into slavery (ibid., 12.25.3–12). Rather than
allow his daughter to suffer the fate of a slave, the man kills her. He then instigates
the army to revolt against the Roman government on account of his daughter. Again,
Diodorus seems sympathetic to the revolutionaries.

27. Plutarch (*Sulla* 6.1.1) reports a stasis that occurred between the Roman general
Sulla (first century BCE) and Marius.

accuses *Paul* of being a pest and of stirring up a *stasis* among all *the Jews* throughout the known world (24:5); and (d) in Jerusalem, Paul causes a *stasis* to erupt between the Pharisees and the Sadducees over the issue of the resurrection of the dead (23:7). The military tribune feared a great *stasis* would result from this dispute (23:10).[28]

Modern historians, according to Martin Goodman, have expressed an interconnection between Judaism as a unique religion and exceptional Jewish rebelliousness under the Roman Empire. Contrary to modern scholarly opinion, which has been "concocted from systematically biased evidence," the Jewish people were not historically any more committed to starting revolts than any other conquered peoples in the Roman provinces in the first century CE. Historical sources report the immediate cause of revolts to be the levying of taxes or extortion of taxation. Different subjugated groups invoked religious ideas to stoke the fires of dissent after a revolt commenced.[29]

Nevertheless, Wills correctly argues that the potential for the arousal of crowds is central to Acts.[30] Even though *the Jews* easily arouse the Gentile crowds to collude with them against Paul, he continually succeeds in converting both diaspora Jews and large numbers of Godfearing Gentiles. Since the conflict between *the Jews* and Paul concerns whether or not the Gentiles/Godfearers should be allowed to participate with the Jewish people in God's salvation without submission to circumcision (Acts 15; cf. Gal 2), it is logical that Luke should construct *the Jews* as the primary opponents. Circumcision is central to Jewish covenant identity as the people of God. Literary characterization is to some degree always an artificial construct in both fictional and nonfictional works. I hope to bring the synthetic, mimetic, and thematic characterization of *the Jews* into greater relief with transitivity analysis. Such an analysis is useful since Luke obfuscates the synthetic aspects of his story. One way he accomplishes this obfuscation is by preempting any suspicion about the complete authenticity and truthfulness of the reality constructed in Acts. He has claimed to write an accurate chronology superior to previously written accounts (Luke 1:1–4; cf. Acts

28. At other times, Roman officials are nonchalant about *the Jews'* accusations against Paul, since they do not concern Roman law (e.g., Gallio, 18:12–17).

29. Goodman, "Opponents of Rome," 222, 228–30, 237–38. See also Goodman, *Ruling Class of Judaea.*

30. Wills, "Depiction of the Jews."

26:26). As the single canonical text that functions as a witness to the beginnings of a Holy Spirit-empowered and guided *ekklēsia*, Acts does not invite critical reflection on characterization.

Transitivity Analysis and the Foregrounding of the Jews

Transitivity patterns help reveal foregrounding in Acts. Foregrounding is motivated prominence. This means that foregrounding strategically contributes to "the meaning of the text as a whole." In foregrounding, transitivity patterns as syntax are a part of the story.[31] A transitivity or linguistic analysis can bring into relief how starkly Luke contrasts *the Jews* with other participants in Acts.[32] Luke differentiates *the Jews* from others, particularly the apostles, and he maintains this project of differentiation throughout Acts. A transitivity analysis of the grammatical clauses elucidates how Luke subtly portrays the apostles as participant-objects in grammatical clauses. Conversely, a transitivity analysis demonstrates how Luke systematically portrays *the Jews* as participant-actors or -subjects in material process clauses in which they are doing something to someone or something else. Paul and his traveling companions, in contrast, are rarely participant-actors in material processes. The low degree of transitivity and causal agency displayed by the apostles renders prominent the high degree of transitivity and agency of *the Jews*. And the high degree of transitivity displayed by *the Jews* highlights the apostles' low degree of casual agency. Paradoxically, Paul is primarily a passive participant-object in grammatical clauses, but his mission activities among the Gentiles succeeds in spite of the violent opposition of *the Jews*.

I have examined seventeen episodes in which *the Jews* are participants. In the majority of these episodes, *the Jews* are participant-actors. However, Paul and his companions (Barnabas, Silas, and Timothy) are primarily the participant-objects in these same episodes. The episodes are: (1) Damascus, 9:19b–25; (2) Psidian Antioch, 13:14–52; (3) Iconium, 14:1–7; (4) Lystra, 14:8–20a; (5) Thessaloniki, 17:1–10a; (6) Berea, 17:10b–15; (7) Corinth, 18:1–11; (8) before the Proconsul Gallio

31. Halliday, "Studies in Linguistics," 98, 120.

32. Sanders (*Jews in Luke-Acts*, 38) argues that the inconsistencies in Luke's portrait of *the Jews* show that he depicts them in "subtle shades," rather than in "vividly contrasting colours."

of Achaia [Corinth] 18:12–17; (9) Ephesus, 18:19–23; (10) Asia/Ephesus, 19:28–41; (11) Hellas, 20:1–3; (12) arrest in Jerusalem after performing purification rites in the Temple, 21:27–36; (13) between Jerusalem and Caesarea, 23:12–35; (14) Caesarea, 24:1–27; (15) Jerusalem, 25:1–5; (16) Caesarea, 25:6–12; and (17) Rome, 28:17–31.

Most often *the Jews* are participant-actors in material processes (acting on someone or something outside of themselves). Luke employs a variety of synonymous verbs and grammatical constructions to express those processes.[33] The most frequently occurring material processes in which *the Jews* are participant-actors are the following: (a) twelve times *the Jews* incite/arouse crowds or form a mob;[34] (b) twelve times *the Jews* mistreat, seize, cast out, drag, attack, beat, or stone (the apostles or other individuals);[35] (c) five times *the Jews* make a plot, conspire or attempt to kill Paul;[36] (d) four times *the Jews* accuse Paul, inform someone about him, or bring him before the tribunal; (e) once *the Jews* mock (*chleuazō*) Paul; they embitter (*kakoō*) the Gentiles against Paul; and they make an oath (*anathematizō*) to harm Paul. In addition, on two occasions *the Jews* oppose (*antilegō, antitassō*) either what Paul preaches or Paul himself. Significantly, these two occasions occur in the context of Paul's first and second declarations about turning to the Gentiles (13:45; 18:6), as noted below. These two verbs (*antilegō, antitassō*) provoke the dialectic of discursive *abandonment* or turning toward the Gentiles and the ontological *remaining* or returning to the synagogues to dialogue with the Jewish people, as more fully addressed below.

Immediately one notices that most often Luke constructed *the Jews* to behave violently. *The Jews* instigate, act violently, and plot more often than they simply oppose or dispute the apostles' message. However, when Luke characterizes *the Jews* as simply opposing the apostles, some readers view, consciously or unconsciously, the less violent character-

---

33. Cadbury, "Four Features of Lukan Style," 92. The combination of similarity and variation is numerous in Luke-Acts. The story of Ananias and Sapphira is a perfect example (5:1–11).

34. The equivalent Greeks verbs are: *saleuō, parotrunō, epegeirō, sygcheō, thorubeō, tarassō, peithō, ochlopoieō, proslambanō.*

35. The equivalent Greek verbs are: *hubrizō, epiballō, ephistēmi, epilambanomai, katephistēmi, ekballō, syrō, synepitithēmi, tuptō, lithoboleō.*

36. The equivalent Greek verbs are: *ginomai, epiboulē, systrophē poieō, enedra, parapēreō, analuō, symbouleuō.*

izations as part of an overall pattern as inscribed in the text. Some readers aware of the more violent characterizations of Jewish persons (as angry murderous mob types, both in Acts and in the Gospels) see single disparate snapshots as part of a behavioral pattern ascribed to *the Jews*.

What might Luke's use of different but semantically similar Greek verbs to describe the most violent behaviors of *the Jews* accomplish? It is not enough to say that Luke has a penchant for variety. Luke's pattern of lexical variation constitutes a foregrounding norm in this case. Foregrounding that is based on a pattern of deviation is referred to as "congruence of foregrounding."[37] The fact that the semantically similar Greek verbs are not cognates reinforces the text's message that *the Jews* are many groups, from many distinct places, but they behave in similar or identical ways. Although *the Jews* come from different areas throughout the diaspora, they act predictably and in harmony (*homothymadon*).[38] They are all opponents of the Gentile mission as Paul represents it. This polymorphic linguistic imagery emphasizes the distinct localism and the sameness of *the Jews*. This linguistic pattern gives the impression, as the Jewish leaders in Rome state, that distinct groups of Jews everywhere have opposed the mission (28:22).

In metanarratives (and in speeches) Luke reinforces this negative construction of *the Jews* (22:6–21; 26:2–23; 28:17b–20). For example, Claudias writes a letter to Felix, which is intertextually inserted into the story. In that letter Claudias informs Felix about events that happened earlier in Acts: *the Jews* seized Paul, were about to kill him, accused Paul concerning matters of their Law, and plotted against him (23:27–30; cf. 21:27–36; 23:12). This metanarrative restates and reinscribes previous narrative constructions of *the Jews*. And when Luke recontextualizes the negative and violent literary construction of *the Jews* by placing it in an official letter, he credibly establishes and reifies that pejorative characterization. Luke thus maintains continuity between the narratives and the metanarratives portraying *the Jews* as highly active and aggressive opponents of Paul on both literary levels.

37. Halliday, "Studies in Linguistics," 98, 120.

38. In other ancient literature the Greek adverb *homothymadon* refers to an intentional united group effort in response to potential or actual perceived deprivation, threats of violence, or abuse and suffering inflicted on a group by external forces. For example, see Josephus, *Ant.* 15.277, 19.357; idem, *Ag. Ap.*, 1.242; Philo, *Mos.* 1.72; Philo, *Flacc.* 121, 122; Cyprian, *Test.*, "Covenant of Nephtali," 6.10; *Ps.-Clem.*, *Epitome Prior* §172, *Epitome Altera* §180.

Most often Paul and his companions are the passive recipients (participant-object or goal) in clauses where *the Jews* and others act on them. In contrast to *the Jews*, Paul and his traveling companions are primarily participant-actors in verbal, rather than material, processes (e.g., he/they confound, persuade, prove, encourage, respond, preach, say, speak boldly and semantically equivalent verbal actions). Paul is secondarily a participant-actor in relational clauses (e.g., he enters, departs, returns, turns, and stands in the midst of them).

The few times that Paul (and his traveling companions) is a participant-actor in material processes, they seldom affect other human beings: Paul shakes the dust off his feet or clothes (13:51; 18:6), shakes a viper off of his arm (28:5), gathers dry sticks for a fire (28:3), and breaks bread (20:11). In two clauses Paul affects only himself (reflexive actions): in 21:40 he motions with his hand, and in 24:10 he nods [his head] at Felix.

In a few clauses Paul is a participant-actor affecting other people: he heals Publius's father (28:8); he bends over and falls on the dead body of Eutychus, wrapping his arms around him, and Eutychus is resurrected (20:10); and he and Barnabas appoint elders in the *ekklēsia* (14:23). When Paul is a participant-actor in a material process that affects other human beings, some readers presuppose, as the story implies, that it is not Paul who ultimately brings about the outcome; God acts through Paul. And this mediation primarily occurs through prayer or the laying on of hands (28:8). In Martin-Asensio's analysis of ergative-based foregrounding in Acts 6–7, 21–22, and 27, he concludes that Luke's selection of processes and participant roles (Stephen, Paul, and God, et al.) is central to a foregrounding scheme that shows an "extraordinary concern to underline the overriding power of divine purpose . . . upon the stage of human affairs."[39] God causes everything in the *ekklēsia*. And even in Luke's Gospel, Christ is remarkably passive in comparison with other New Testament writings.[40] In Acts, the narrator informs the readers early on that all the mighty deeds and witnessing activities associated with the apostles are the work God, God's Holy Spirit, or the angel of the Lord (1:8; 2:4, 33; 12:7–11). So any agency attributed to the apostles in the grammatical structure, which is comparatively very little, is circumscribed at the level of the story.

39. Martin-Asensio, *Transitivity-Based Foregrounding*, 20.
40. Jervell, *Theology of the Acts*, 20. "God's Will and Acts Are Irresistible" (21).

On the story level, some readers will recognize that the low degree of agency Luke attributes to the apostles is part of his theological agenda, which is to demonstrate how the apostles are God's agents. In Acts, God's agency employs little human effort. Paul and the apostles do not act in their own volition, because God's Spirit works through, guides, and even prohibits them (1:8; 8:29, 39; 15:28; 16:6). Bovon argues that in Luke-Acts one observes collaboration between God and human agents (i.e., the apostles). God acts through and with humans to reveal God's self and God's gospel. This mediation signifies a cultural and social reality. All revelation, posits Bovon, passes through human language, and this language remains human in spite of the divine revelation that it communicates.[41]

A synchronic (collective and thematic) analysis of the character dimensions that Luke attributes to *the Jews* shows that, in addition to readily resorting to physical violence and plotting to commit murder, *the Jews* incite crowds against Paul (and his traveling companions). These dimensions that Luke attributes to *the Jews* do not grow progressively worse as the narrative moves in time and in its telling.[42] A diachronic (through story time) analysis shows that *the Jews* do not become increasingly more violent. More in line with Luke's theological program, they are consistently violent and persistently opposed to the Gentile mission as represented by Paul. At the very outset of Paul's preaching activity in Damascus, albeit before the Antiochene *ekklēsia* officially commissions him, *the Jews* conspire to kill Paul (9:23). (At 2 Cor 11:32–33, it was the ethnarch of King Aretas of Damascus who conspired to kill Paul.) And again toward the end of the narrative in Jerusalem, *the Jews* plot to kill Paul (23:12f). *The Jews'* plotting and conspiring frames or forms an *inclusio* around Paul's ministry in Acts.

At times, Luke illustrates *the Jews'* behavior more vividly, but contrary to Marguerat, *the Jews* do not evolve. *The Jews* consistently act the same way, and this consistency gives the impression that they are a predictable and unified group with respect to their response to the Gentile mission as Paul preached it. Thus, Luke characterizes *the Jews* as closed-ended characters that are not "subject to further speculations and enrichments, visions and revisions," as opposed to open-ended characters. Closed characters are the same as flat characters, which are

41. Bovon, "L'importance des médiations," 38–39.

42. Contra Tyson, *Images of Judaism*, 100. Also Wills, "Depiction of the Jews."

highly predictable.[43] The predictability is established by the repetition of the same character dimensions attributed to the various localized groups of *the Jews*. Phelan would agree in principle with Chatman that when readers encounter characters acting in the narrative plot, they sort through the paradigm of traits (attributes for Phelan) previously ascribed to those characters, and they then attempt to account for certain actions of those characters.[44] These stereotyped dimensions linger in some readers' minds and create for them a social reality beyond the narrative.

The Jews *as the Synthetic Other: The Mimetic and the Thematic Function of Characterization*

Authors develop the mimetic aspect of character by providing background information and an inside view of the character: by revealing a character's beliefs, assumptions, desires, likes, dislikes, intelligence, and education, etc.[45] Mimetic function results from the way mimetic traits (dimensions) are employed together to produce the "illusion of a plausible person and, for works depicting actions, in making particular traits relevant to later actions, including of course the developing of new traits."[46] The first time that *the Jews* oppose Paul, Luke describes them as jealous (13:45; cf. 5:17; 17:5). Also, Herod describes *the Jews* as pleased when he murders James (12:2–3). These mimetic traits are relevant as the motivation for future opposition by *the Jews*. In terms of beliefs, *the Jews*, like the people from Judea (15:1), hold to an interpretation of the Law and the Prophets that requires Gentiles to submit to circumcision to participate in God's salvation.

---

43. Chatman, *Story and Discourse*, 119, 132.

44. Chatman (ibid., 125–29) understands traits as adjectives and adjectives as personal quality. Phelan (*Reading People*) argues the trait is not the basic unit of character. The fundamental unit of character is the attribute—attributes participate in all three spheres of meaning (thematic, mimetic, and synthetic) simultaneously (Phelan, 11).

45. Writers refuse to fully develop the mimetic function when they avoid providing the reader with an inside view of the character (Phelan, *Reading People*, 84–91).

46. Ibid., 9, 11.

THE FUNCTION OF MIMETIC TRAITS

The second and most vivid portrayal of *the Jews* is in Psidian Antioch. Luke ascribes to them the mimetic dimension of jealousy:

> When the Jews [*hoi Ioudaioi*] saw the crowds, they were filled with jealousy [*eplēsthēsan zēlou*]. They opposed [*antelegon*] that which was spoken by Paul and they blasphemed him. . . . [Paul and Barnabas] carried the word throughout the entire region, and *the Jews* [*hoi Ioudaioi*] aroused [*parōtrunan*] the God-fearing, well-bred women and the leaders of the city. And they stirred up [*epegeiran*] a persecution against Paul and Barnabas and cast them out of their borders. (13:45, 49–50)

Luke provides an inside view of *the Jews* as jealous. In fact, they are "filled with jealousy." Luke attributes the mimetic trait of jealousy to *the Jews* in Thessaloniki as well (17:5). The absolute adjective "filled" gives the impression that *the Jews* are completely overcome by their jealousy and therefore out of control as their subsequent actions prove.

In Acts, Satan fills people's hearts so that they lie to the Holy Spirit (5:3). It is not a huge leap for some readers to connect Luke's mimetic portrayal of *the Jews* as jealous with Satan,[47] even though Luke does not directly connect the two. In Stephen's speech, he describes the patriarchs as filled with jealousy when they sold their brother Joseph into Egyptian slavery (7:9). The Hebrew Bible attests that jealousy motivates people to do terrible things (Prov 6:34; cf. 1 Cor 10:22; 2 Cor 11:2). However, as in the case of Joseph, actions motivated by jealousy do not hinder God's plans (Gen 37–42). This negative mimetic dimension will stick with some readers, especially since it is juxtaposed in the same episode with the description of the disciples as "filled with joy" (13:52). Also, the notion that the apostles are filled with the Holy Spirit (2:4; 4:8, 31; 9:17; 13:9; cf. Luke 1:41, 67) is pervasive in Acts.

When Luke mimetically describes *the Jews* as jealous he gives the illusion that plausible people are acting. Some readers may view this description of *the Jews* as a trivializing of their reaction to the Gentile mission. Other readers will conclude that *the Jews* have no legitimate grounds for opposing the mission because their actions are motivated by selfish emotion.

---

47. Arator, the sixth-century CE orator and subdeacon in Rome (*Acts of the Apostles*, 43) referred to the Jews as "savage men."

Thematic dimensions are individual or collective attributes that function as vehicles for expressing ideas representative of a class or group. "The distinction between the mimetic and thematic components of character is a distinction between characters as individuals and characters as representative entities."[48] The collective attributes of *the Jews* that function thematically are the following: they instigate crowds, act violently, oppose the apostles, and conspire to kill them. Collectively, these attributes express the manner in which *the Jews* oppose the Gentile mission. Regardless of where Paul and his traveling companions encounter *the Jews*, the majority of the time Luke schematizes these encounters. Whether *the Jews* are in Damascus (9:22–23), Psidian Antioch and Iconium (13:45f; 14:19), Thessaloniki (17:13), Asia (21:27), or Jerusalem (25:7), Luke constructs them as stereotyped opponents of the Gentile mission.

The Jews were likely relatively few in number. Luke's use of the definite plural noun, *the Jews*, does not necessarily signify a large group or the majority of the Jewish people. Josephus mentions fifty Jewish ambassadors from the Jewish nation that were sent to Rome. He refers to these ambassadors as "the Jews."[49] Here the collective term literally refers to a relatively small representation. Yet, in Josephus their role as ambassadors makes them representative of the general body of Jews. *The Jews* that oppose Paul are not ambassadors for the Jewish nation; they are not even the leaders.

Historically most Jewish synagogues did not hold large numbers of people, since many were converted from private homes into synagogues.[50] Therefore, the overall number of Jews and Godfearing Gentiles in the Jewish synagogues that Paul frequented was probably not a very large number.[51] Are Luke's readers to believe that an overwhelming number or the majority of Gentiles believed, or just some Godfearing Gentiles? In the majority of instances where *both the Jews* and Gentiles are converted, Luke employs adjectives like "many" (13:43, 48; 18:8), "great number" (14:1–7; 17:4), and "some" (17:4, 34; cf. 21:34; 28:24) to describe the quantitative success among both groups collectively. Most

48. Ibid., 12–13.

49. Josephus, *Ant.* 17.11.1–3.

50. Cohen, *From Maccabees to the Mishnah*, 114.

51. As an exception to the smaller synagogues, according to Josephus (*Life*, 277) a rather large *proseucha* or house of prayer was located in the Jewish city of Tiberias.

often *the Jews* appear less confident in their numbers than are some exegetes, since *the Jews* must enlist the help of the crowds when they oppose the apostles and the believers. The Jewish people as a whole are not hostile to the proclamation of the word, but it is *the Jews* as Luke has constructed them that oppose the mission.

Historically, one or two persons were sufficient to incite crowds for protest or revolt. In the example from Tacitus mentioned above, one common soldier named Percennius was "well qualified to stir up the passions of a crowd."[52] And of course, Gamaliel mentions Theudas and Judas (5:36–37). *The Jews* that oppose the Gentile mission could be as few as two and as many as over forty (23:13, 21). This is a small number compared to the thousands of Jewish persons and proselytes who Luke says became believers in the first five chapters of Acts. "Mythical" or not, the one explicit number (i.e., forty) that Luke provides for Jewish opponents relative to the Jewish converts (about 3,000 at 2:41; about 5,000 at 4:4; large crowd of priests at 6:7; myriads at 21:20) is minute. According to the Jerusalem brothers, there were many thousands among *the Jews* that were both believers and zealous for the Law (21:20).

Regardless of where Luke locates *the Jews* geographically, there is no shortage of individuals or groups that they can influence to collude with them against Paul and his comrades. *The Jews* successfully incite the Gentiles to oppose and treat the apostles violently. Luke refers to these accomplices as Gentiles (14:2), the crowds (14:19; 17:13; 21:27), some evil men from the marketplace (17:5), and Godfearing noble women and leaders of the city (Psidian Antioch) (13:50). *The Jews* generally rally the support of the Gentiles, except in Damascus and Greece. Some Gentiles oppose Paul and his companions without any nudging from *the Jews*. These include the Gentile masters of the Pythian slave girl (16:16–22) and the people of Asia (19:23–40). Significantly, the Pythian girl is constructed as a charismatic other over against Paul, as I have shown in chapter 1.

The frequent collocation of *the Jews* and the crowds is a part of Luke's literary construction. Most often the crowds are the indispensable medium through which *the Jews* attack the apostles. The presence of the crowds transforms the negative encounter between *the Jews* and the apostles from a semi-public gathering (i.e., the synagogue) into a public event. The *populus* in the late Roman Republic were public

52. Tacitus, *Annals* 1.16.

witnesses to all the functions of the *res publica*.[53] The crowds are witnesses to the interaction between *the Jews* and the apostles.

Although they are part of Luke's foregrounding of *the Jews'* opposition to the apostles, the crowds exhibit even less agency than do the apostles. *The Jews* generally act on the crowds. Most often, the crowds are divided either as a result of Paul's preaching or someone else's speech, such as Demetrius in Ephesus (19:24f.). While *the Jews* collude with pagan Gentiles, the Gentiles that accept the apostles' messages and become believes are Godfearing Gentiles. The construction of complicit crowds function as part of the othering of *the Jews*.

Complicity between crowds and jealous rivals is demonstrated in the Hellenistic novel. In Chariton's novel (first century BCE to middle of first century CE), an angry crowd of men and the instigator of that crowd, the tyrant Acragas, were rivals for the affection of the heroine Callirhoe. The rival suitors were jealous because Callirhoe married Chaereas instead of one of them. Here, jealousy as a mimetic trait functions in practically the same way as it does in Acts. Because of their common interest, Acragas incites them to plot against Chaereas.[54] The crowds and the instigators share a stake in the conspiracy.[55] In the late Roman Republic politicians incited the *populus* in order to gain massive support for their political intrigues by appealing to any vested interest the crowds may have had for supporting them.[56]

The frequent collocation of *the Jews* and the crowds may also obscure the extent of any real Jewish opposition. It is possible that, historically, the majority of the Jewish people paid little attention to the emerging new sect. Meeks notes that what the author narrates "may be distorted, or, at best, may not represent the whole movement."[57] However, Luke may want his readers to believe otherwise. If the amount of space

---

53. According to Millar (*Crowd in Rome*) during this period all the functions of the *res publica* are to be executed publicly and oral or written explanations addressed to the people often accompanied such functions. Understanding the elected office as *beneficium* conferred by the people was a fundamental element of the ideology of elected office at Rome.

54. Chariton, *Chaer.*

55. Tacitus, *Annals*, 1.16.

56. Millar, *Crowd in Rome*. Between 55 and 50 BCE, political corruption and abuse of power led to the need for politicians to incite the crowds/populus in the Forum for their support.

57. Meeks, "Breaking Away," 94.

Josephus gives to the "tribe of Christians" is any indication, it may have been the case that few Jewish persons opposed the Gentile mission because they believed the new sect would fizzle out or be of little significance.[58] We know Luke exaggerates. For example, in Damascus "all" the Jews were amazed and confounded, yet *the Jews* in Damascus also conspire to kill Paul (9:19b–24). Since Luke frequently uses the verb "amazed" to describe positive reactions (3:10, 11; 8:9, 11, 13; 12:16), *the Jews* that conspire against Paul are likely not the same as "all the Jews." This shows: (a) that Luke does not hesitate to use the categorical adjective "all" when he so desires, and (b) that when Luke uses absolutes, we cannot always interpret them literally. Aspects of Luke's characterization of the crowds are synthetic as well. As Gerd Lüdemann remarks about the Jews in Damascus at 9:22–25, "it was Luke who portrayed the Jews as instigators of the attack on Paul," for this was not historically the case.[59]

Authors can create three different relations between the mimetic and thematic functions of character: "subordination of one to the other, equality along parallel tracks of interest, and fusion."[60] Luke fuses the mimetic and thematic functions of *the Jews* by constructing them as a collective group of characters who are motivated by the same mimetic trait of jealousy.

The Dialectic of Turning Toward Gentiles and Remaining with the Jews

Paul's Three Declarations of Movement toward the Gentiles

As noted above, Marguerat asserts that a dialectical relationship exists between the *ekklēsia* and Israel characterized by continuity and discontinuity.[61] Similarly, I argue that Paul's three declarations about movement toward the Gentiles constitute dialogical sites of struggle between

---

58. Josephus (*Ant.*, 18.3.3) says Jesus attracted many Jews and Gentiles, but he says nothing of Jewish opposition to Jesus. As Koester (*History and Literature*, 14) notes this text "is not preserved in its original form, but it was thoroughly redacted by a Christian scribe."

59. Lüdemann, *Acts*, 134.

60. Ibid., 83.

61. Marguerat, "Juifs et chrétiens," 158.

the Jews and Paul.[62] This dialogicality results in a dialectic of turning toward (or abandoning) and remaining or maintaining dialogue with the synagogue. This struggle is precipitated by Paul's introduction of a different interpretation of the Law and the Prophets that allows for Gentile salvation without submission to covenantal circumcision. Sanders correctly states, "throughout Luke-Acts, the hostility of non-Christian Jews towards Christianity and of Jewish Christians toward Gentile Christianity is provoked by the inclusion of Gentiles."[63] More precisely, it is the truncated means of granting salvation to the Gentiles that provokes *the Jews*, namely, without covenantal circumcision and solely through "the grace of God."

An insistence on Gentile circumcision does not mean that the outpouring of the Holy Spirit on Gentiles is denied, but that Gentile converts must be obedient to God or God's law.[64] In Acts, Gentiles remain Gentiles. Gentiles are never considered to be Jews, unlike Josephus' account of the royal house of Adiabene, in which Azates would become thoroughly a Jew should he be circumcised.[65] Historically, before 100 CE Judaism did not require all outsiders to convert fully, but they were satisfied with "sympathetic support and appreciation."[66]

The Jerusalem Council officially decided the no-circumcision policy toward the Gentile brothers (ch. 15; cf. Gal 2) after Paul had begun his mission among the Gentiles, and after Paul's first declaration about turning to the Gentiles. When certain people from Judea arrive in Antioch, they are concerned that the Gentiles are offered salvation without the requirement of circumcision (15:1).[67] Historically, "only Jews

62. Sanders (*Jews in Luke-Acts*) argues that Luke's three declarations do not pertain to Jerusalemite Jews but to Antiochene Jews, Corinthian Jews, and Roman Jews, respectively. Tyson (*Images of Judaism*, 141–42) agrees with Sanders that the three declarations are localized, but, following Haenchen (*Acts*), *the Jews* are simultaneously "the Jews in general." According to Tyson, the three announcements "function as general summaries: *Jews have heard* but *rejected* the *message, which* is *accepted by Gentiles*" (emphasis original).

63. Sanders, *Jews in Luke-Acts*, 316.

64. Bauckham, "James, Peter," 118.

65. Josephus, *Ant.* 20.2.

66. Goodman, *Mission and Conversion*, 102–3.

67. Bauckham ("James, Peter," 116) argues that "those from the circumcision" are not a faction from the Jerusalem church, but simply "Jewish believers in Christ." "Luke first uses it at the precise point in his narrative at which there are, for the first time, Gentile believers in Christ (10:45), and then again, in 11:2, to highlight the difference

(circumcised if male), obedient to the Torah, could really be trusted to be morally pure."[68] An attempt to compel Gentile believers to submit to circumcision causes a dispute among Paul, Barnabas, and the Judeans. We can assume that the accusations against Paul are based on Paul's missionary activities heretofore in the narrative in Psidian Antioch, Iconium, Lystra, and Derbe. So prior to the Jerusalem Council's decree Paul had not required that Gentiles submit to circumcision. Thus, the Jerusalem Council functions in the narrative to legitimize Paul's previous activities among the Godfearing Gentiles.

The occasions for the three declarations, like other encounters between Paul and *the Jews* in Acts, constitute narrative instabilities. Instabilities can be local or global. The progress that local instabilities create is limited to one or two scenes, and they are quickly resolved. Global instabilities engender progress, but they are complicated later by other actions.[69] Paul's declarations do not so simply offer local resolution since he returns continually to the synagogues immediately follow-

---

between the Jerusalem believers, all Jews, and the newly converted Gentiles" (117). Cf. Rom 4:12; Col 4:11; Gal 2:12; Eusebius, *Eccl. Hist.* 4.5.3. Bauckham (91–142) also explores what it meant in the late Second Temple period to consider Gentiles "profane and impure" in order to understand disputes over Gentile converts in both Acts and Gal 2. Bauckham asserts that in the late Second Temple period Gentiles generally are considered morally impure and profane (not members of sacred people of Israel). Moral impurity included idolatry, sexual sins, and eating blood. "Our evidence suggests that the use of the language of moral impurity for Gentiles may have been more common in Palestinian Judaism than in the diaspora, though it is not absent from diaspora sources" (98). See also Klawans (*Impurity and Sin*) ,who notes that ancient sources distinguish between ritual impurity and moral impurity. Klawans argues that not all Jews in antiquity agreed on what constituted either one: "[T]he relationship between defilement and sin in ancient Judaism was the subject of sectarian debates"; NT figures such as Jesus, John, and Paul "may have agreed with some groups and not others," or decided on a path of their own (138). The apostle Paul was more concerned with moral impurity, which he often juxtaposed with moral sins such as adultery (Rom 1:21–5; 6:19; Gal 5:19–21) (151–53). Klawans also argues that we should not assume that "Jews considered Gentiles to be a source of ritual defilement. Moreover, . . . even if Jews considered Gentiles to be ritually defiling, it would not necessarily be unlawful for Jews to associate with Gentiles, for it was not considered sinful to contract ritual impurity" (151). John the Baptist, Jesus, and Paul tended to prioritize the need for moral purity, and for them baptism (formerly more often associated with ritual impurity) was a means of obtaining moral purity (154).

68. Bauckham, "James, Peter," 102.
69. Phelan, *Reading People*, 51.

ing the first two declarations, and this complicates the narrative.[70] The three declarations of turning to the Gentiles are inscribed in the text as verbal events. But these inscribed verbal events do not directly correspond with Paul's subsequent actions also inscribed in the text world of Acts. Luke has constructed a dialectical relationship between inscribed verbal events and the referential reality inscribed in the text. While the verbal events discursively point to a turning away from *the Jews* and toward the Gentiles, the inscribed referential reality demonstrates that Paul never stops confronting, dialoging, or preaching to *the Jews* and/ or in the synagogues.

Each declaration employs a different verb tense. The first declaration is in the present tense (13:46), the second is in the future tense (18:6), and the third is in the past tense (28:28). This switch to past tense in Paul's final declaration recapitulates and reaffirms, in brief, the *ekklēsia's* hermeneutical position regarding the mission to the Gentiles. The tense Luke employs in each declaration, as we shall we, is appropriate to each context.

These three discursive sites of struggle constitute dialogue between Paul and *the Jews*, but they are also dialogical on the literary level in two ways. First, dialogicality is marked by convergence of two texts. Dialogicality relies on "meeting or encounter, on coexistence and interaction. . . . The encounter between discourses is an encounter between word and alien word."[71] A word is formed in "dialogical interaction"

70. Sanders ("Jewish People," 71) argues that the Lukan Paul *always* visits the synagogue first and *the Jews always* oppose him, except in Athens (emphasis original). Tyson (*Images of Judaism*, 134) notes that Luke's narrative never shows a positive response to the gospel from an entirely Jewish group. Nevertheless, as Wills ("Depiction of the Jews," 639–44) proposes in his schema, the initial success of the Gentile mission is always followed by opposition. *The Jews* most often initiate this opposition, which is followed by movement and the realization of new successes. When the Gentiles oppose the mission, "the narrative is more neutral in terms of resultant missionary success. Where there is no Jewish opposition, there is no dramatic expansion of the mission." The pattern that Wills observes in Acts consists of three dramatic movements that are cyclically repeated. The movements are "positive missionary activity, opposition and constriction, and release and expansion," which serve as an organizing framework. Vanhoye ("Juifs selon les Actes," 75) notes that although the scheme is easily recognized with variation, it is never repeated identically so as to render the story monotone.

71. Patterson, "Mikhail Bakhtin," 132. Acts has been shown to have some novelistic characteristics. See Pervo, *Profit with Delight*; Wills, *Jewish Novel*. Also, Bonz (*Past as Legacy*) argues that Luke-Acts is epic (the antecedent of the Hellenistic novel) similar to Virgil's *Aeneid*.

with an "alien word."[72] Luke creates intertextuality (a dialogical relationship between two texts) when he recontextualizes scriptural quotations by inserting them into the contexts of the first and final declarations. This is also the case when Luke inserts logia (sayings of Jesus) into the immediate context of the first two declarations. The logia in question are as follows:

> And he commanded them, "Take nothing in the way except a staff. Do not take bread, a leather bag, or any money in [your] belt. But put on sandals, and do not clothe yourself with two tunics." He said to them, . . . "Whatever place neither receives nor hears you, while *departing* from there, shake the dust from under your feet for a witness against them. . . . Whatever city you *enter*, if it does not receive you, go out to the gates of [the city] and say, We are wiping off the dust from your city that has accumulated on our feet. But know this, The Basileia of God is near. I say to you, It will be more bearable for Sodom in that day than for that city." (Luke 9:3–5; 10:10–12//Mark 6:8–11//Matt 10:9–15)

A portion of these logia is inserted into the first two declarations, and they echo the instructions that Jesus communicated to the Twelve and the Seventy/Seventy-two when he commissioned them in the Gospels.

In the context of the first two declarations, *the Jews* are described as opposing the apostles. Paul retorts that he is turning to the Gentiles. In the first declaration (13:46), the Greek verb used to describe this opposition is *antilegō* (to oppose). In the second declaration (18:6), Luke uses the semantically equivalent verb *antitassō*. In the third declaration (28:17–31), Luke uses *antilegō* again, but not to describe the actions of the Jewish leaders in Rome. There *antilegō* occurs in a metanarrative in which Paul recounts to the Jewish leaders at Rome that *the Jews* in Jerusalem opposed his release and how he was compelled to appeal to Caesar (28:19). *Antilegō* occurs for the *last* time at 28:22 when the Jewish leaders in Rome claim that their knowledge of the sect is limited to the fact that it is opposed everywhere.[73] Thus, Luke reserves these semantically equivalent Greek verbs for the context of these three dec-

72. Bakhtin, "Discourse in the Novel," 279.

73. The only other occurrences of these Greek words in Luke-Acts are in the Gospel (2:34; 20:27; cf. John 19:12; Rom 10:21; Titus 1:9; 2:9).

larations to linguistically designate the discursive encounter between Paul and *the Jews*.

FIRST DECLARATION: SEE, WE *ARE TURNING* TOWARD THE GENTILES (13:46)

The characterization of *the Jews* in the context of Paul's first declaration of turning to the Gentiles is paradigmatic. It serves as the model on which subsequent declarations are based. This first declaration incorporates more instances of intertextuality (or dialogicality) than the other two declarations: (a) the recontextualization of a Jewish Scripture and (b) the recontextualization of a Jesus logion.

In the immediate literary context Paul and Barnabas arrive in Psidian Antioch on the Sabbath and join the synagogue gathering. After the Scripture reading, the synagogue leader invites Paul to encourage the people (*laos*). Paul offers an interpretation of the prior reading of the Law and the Prophets. He employs the rhetoric of proximity to address the audience: "Israelites and those who fear God" and "brothers and children of Abraham and Godfearers." Both Jews and Gentiles/Godfearers attend the gathering. In Paul's midrash he states that John the Baptist proclaimed a baptism of repentance for all the people of Israel.

The Jews and Paul are proximate on several levels: their Jewish ethnicity; their claim to the same spiritual ancestors; their understanding of the Scriptures as sacred; their temporal and spatial observance of the sacred Sabbath at a specified time and place; and their acknowledgement that the Scriptures allow for the inclusion of Gentiles. A group or individual that is considered to be radically other is simply other and of little consequence. However, the proximate other is problematic and rarely considered an object of indifference.

Paul continues to invoke language of proximity, but he also foregrounds difference. The Jerusalem residents and their leaders acted in ignorance of salvation when they killed Jesus, but God raised Jesus (13:27–30). God extends forgiveness to *all* through Paul's proclamation. The end of Paul's midrash echoes the Paul of Romans: "you were not able to be justified by the Law of Moses but in Jesus *everyone* who believes is justified" (cf. Rom 8). Jesus accomplished *for everyone* what the Law of Moses failed to do (13:39). While *the Jews* hold to an understanding of the Law of Moses (i.e., circumcision) as the standard to which the Gentiles must conform if they are to share in God's salvation, Paul presents his hermeneutic as the definitive *word* for the inclusion of the Gentiles. As Rosemary Radford Ruether argues, each represents two exegetical traditions of the same texts,[74] i.e., the Law of Moses and the Prophets. *The Jews* believe that in order for the Gentiles to be saved, they must be circumcised as demanded by these texts.

The production of such a hierarchical relationship that subordinates one discourse to another by judgments and evaluations is politically motivated. When groups or individuals are proximate to one another and one group needs to distinguish itself claiming for itself or for its group certain rights (i.e., the right to claim one's interpretation as *the* definitive word of God) "otherness" is constructed.

The literary context implies that the *Israelites and the Godfearers* receive Paul's midrash positively, or at least with curiosity, since they invite Paul to speak again on the next Sabbath (13:42). When Paul and his companions leave the synagogue site, the term *Israelites* is no longer used to refer to the Jewish audience (13:16b; cf. 13:43). When Paul and Barnabas left the synagogue many of *the Jews and Godfearing* proselytes followed them, and they were persuaded to remain in the grace of God (13:43). Thus, the linguistic transition from *Israelites* (and the Godfearers, 13:16b) to *many Jews* (and the Godfearing proselytes) marks a transition in the narrative from semi-public space (the synagogue gathering) to pubic space, and from proximity to hostile differentiated space. While Luke continues to refer to the Gentiles as *Godfearers* (adding the designation *proselytes*), the Jewish people from the synagogue gathering become *many Jews*. This linguistic transition, together with the admonishment to the *many Jews and Godfearing proselytes* to remain in the *grace of God*, by which they obtain salvation, anticipates the conflict that follows. For Paul, the grace of God replaces the requirement of circumcision for the Gentiles believers (cf. 15:11).

74. Ruether, *Faith and Fratricide*, 64. Schüssler Fiorenza (*In Memory of Her*) understands Luke's story of the Sabbath synagogue healing of the woman bent over double (Luke 13:10–17) as a controversy dialogue in which Luke has transformed the healing story into a debate about healing on the Sabbath. The woman's story, Schüssler Fiorenza argues, has become a site of struggle "between Christian and Jewish men over the religious authority to interpret the 'law of the Father,'" and this emphasis opens the door for an anti-Jewish reading (208–9).

On the following Sabbath, the entire city (Lukan hyperbole) gathers (*synagō*) (13:44).[75] When *the Jews* see the crowd, they are filled with jealousy. Marguerat argues that the Jewish reaction here is more than simple jealousy because of the success of the "Christian" missionaries. It is the diffusion of the word to the Gentile crowd that seems intolerable to the Antiochene Jews.[76]

However, just the diffusion of the gospel alone is not responsible for the reaction. *The Jews* oppose Paul's *word* as definitive, i.e., his interpretation of the Law and the Prophets that allows for the inclusion of the Gentiles by the grace of God and without circumcision. Jewish identity is at stake, but the story is about the early *ekklēsia* and its construction of self-identity as a burgeoning sect within Judaism. *The Jews'* "jealousy" is motivated by the fact that the large Gentile crowd accepts Paul's word as truth and as God's word. Luke constructed the scene so that only *the Jews*, and not the Godfearing proselytes, are "jealous" of the crowds who become believers. The crowd (*ochlos*) is distinct from the people (*laos*) that gathered on the previous Sabbath day.

In this public gathering of the crowds, Paul reacts to the opposition of *the Jews* in two ways. First, he emphasizes the election priority of the Jewish people to hear the gospel. According to Jervell, Israel's priority has nothing to do with strategy, but it has to do *mit göttliche Notwendigkeit* ("with divine necessity").[77] Paul invokes Israel's priority before he declares that he is turning toward the Gentiles. Second, Paul claims that his own words are *the* word of God. Finally, Paul retorts, "Since (*epeide*) you are rejecting it and do not consider yourselves worthy of life, we are turning toward the Gentiles" (13:46; cf. 7:27–39; Rom 11:1, 2). He is turning toward the Gentiles because *the Jews* are rejecting salvation for the Gentiles by grace alone (cf. 3:26; 9:15–20). This dialogical encounter marks *the Jews'* first negative diasporic reaction to Paul's preaching to

75. Kee, "Defining the First-Century CE Synagogue," 493. With the exception of Luke 7:5, the synagogue in the New Testament and in pre-70 CE Jewish writings signified "a gathering rather than a distinctive type of religious structure." See also Levine, *Ancient Synagogues Revealed*; White, *Building God's House*.

76. Marguerat, "Juifs et chrétiens," 160. According to Vanhoye ("Juifs selon les Actes," 76) the connection between *the Jews'* jealousy and Paul's success among the non-Jews is significant. That which is at stake for *the Jews* with the success of the Gentile mission, according to Vanhoye, is their Jewish identity and their privileged place as a chosen people.

77. Jervell, *Apostelgeschichte*, 336.

the Gentiles. These words have the force of negatively evaluating *the Jews* as those who reject *the* word of God and who do not value their own life or the lives of others. Paul discursively places blame on *the Jews* differentiating them from those who do not reject God's word.

Luke recontextualizes and edits the Septuagint citation from Deutero-Isaiah (Isa 49:6 LXX). When Luke inserts the Deutero-Isaiah citation in the dialogical encounter between *the Jews* and Paul, he re-contextualizes it. Luke prefaces this citation with, "For thus, the Lord has commanded us" (13:47). "The Lord" here can only be God, and not Jesus, because *Lukas hat keine Vorstellung davon, dass Jesus in der Schrift redet. . . . die Schrift befiehlt die Heidenmission* ("Luke does not present Jesus as speaking in the text. . . . The text [Isa] commands the Gentile mission.")[78] The word *us* primarily refers to Paul and his companions. This language is typical of othering where the distinction is made between *us* and *them*. Of course, *us* and *them* as object pronouns are synonymous with *we* and *they* as subject pronouns. The self-constructed *we* serves to construct the other, and this *we* often constitutes distortion and idealism.[79]

Luke does not introduce the quotation in his usual manner with phrases such as "as it is written" or "that which was spoken by the prophets" (7:42; 13:40; 15:15, etc.). "The Lord" replaces "the Prophets" in Paul's midrashic interpretation, and Paul and his companions apply the Scripture to themselves as *us*.[80] When Luke recontextualizes the citation, he also deletes the Septuagint wording: "for a covenant [*diatheken*] of a people [*genous*]." Interestingly, the "covenant" language is absent from 49:6 in the Masoretic Text, but it is included at verse 42:6 in Deutero-Isaiah's first Servant Song. Luke writes instead: "I have placed you as a light to the nations; you are to be for salvation to the end of the earth" (13:47). Paul discursively excludes *the Jews* from collective Israel (as the *people*) as bearers of the light to the nations. The generic second person plural, *you*, replaces the *people*. The Lukan Paul does not consider the phrase "the covenant of the people" (symbolized by circumcision) relevant to Gentile salvation. Ruether asserts that "Christianity did not ask Judaism merely to extend itself in continuity with its past, but to

78. Ibid., 364.

79. Wills, *Insiders and Outsiders,* 13.

80. Soards, *Speeches in Acts,* 88.

abrogate itself by substituting one covenantal principle from the past for another provided by Jesus."[81]

A third instance of intertextuality occurs at 13:51, "When they shook [ektinaxamenoi] the dust [koniorton] off their feet, they went to Iconium." This verse echoes Jesus' commissioning instructions to the Twelve and the Seventy/Seventy-two (Luke 9:3–5; 10:4–12//Mark 6:7–13//Matt 10:9–15). Matthew and Luke's version is based on Mark, which they slightly revise and insert wording from Q (the hypothetical sayings source used by both Matthew and Luke). While Mark's version allows the Twelve to take sandals with them, Q does not. The most significant change is that Q attaches eschatological significance to the symbolic act. Q asserts that Sodom and Gomorrah will fair better on judgment day than the city that rejects the sent ones (Luke 10:12; Matt 10:15). Unlike Jesus' instruction to the Twelve in Luke's Gospel, Luke de-eschatologizes Paul's symbolic act in Acts. Thus, in Acts the judgment against *the Jews* is effective here and now and not at some eschatological future. The rite of shaking dust from the feet is not a curse; it throws back onto *the Jews* the responsibility for the rejection and absolves Paul of all accountability.[82] Nevertheless, despite that Paul discursively condemns the Jews' opposition and declares that he is turning toward the Gentiles, Paul returns to the synagogue in the immediately following literary context (14:1–7). There at Iconium, the same dialogical drama unfolds. Thus, the first instance of the dialectic of turning (or abandoning) and returning is inscribed in Acts.

SECOND DECLARATION: FROM NOW ON I *SHALL* GO TOWARD THE GENTILES (18:6)

While the first declaration contains two instances of dialogicality or intertextuality, this second declaration contains only one, namely, the recontextualization of a logion similar to the first declaration. The Septuagint scripture is absent. In the immediate literary context Paul encounters fellow tentmakers Priscilla and Aquila in Corinth, and he stays to work with them (18:1–3). As usual, every Sabbath Paul attends the synagogue gathering where he persuades both Jews and Greeks (18:4). Here Luke does not call the Gentiles attending the synagogue

---

81. Ruether, *Faith and Fratricide*, 80.

82. Marguerat, "Juifs et chrétiens," 161.

services Godfearers as he does in Psidian Antioch, but he calls them Greeks. Next, Luke foregrounds *the Jews* as Paul's sole interlocutors. He informs his readers that when Silas and Timothy[83] arrived in Corinth, Paul was busy witnessing to *the Jews* that Jesus is the Christ.

Luke foregrounds *the Jews* in hostile dialogue and based on the pattern repeatedly inscribed in the text as his opponents (18:6). In response to the opposition, Paul shakes off his garments (*ektivaxamenos ta himatia*), as opposed to the dust from his feet in the previous declaration, as a symbolic gesture. Paul then interprets this embodied symbolism: "Your blood is on your head. I am clean. From now on I *shall* go to the nations" (18:6). Again, Paul's shaking his clothes is de-eschatologized as in the previous declaration. The consequence of *the Jews'* opposition is immediate and pertains to the present. Paul's negative evaluation of *the Jews* contributes to a construction of them as external other in relation to the apostles and the Gentile mission.

Different from the incident in Psidian Antioch, *the Jews'* opposition at Corinth seems directly related to Paul's preaching about Jesus. Luke does not reiterate *the Jews'* jealousy over the crowds of Gentile converts. But the repetition is not necessary. Many readers will indiscriminately apply this attribute to all *the Jews* in Acts, since Luke characterizes *the Jews* as a homogeneous group with a unified purpose. The narrative gives some readers the impression that all *the Jews* behave similarly and for the same reasons.

Looking more closely at this episode, we notice that *the Jews* offer no opposition until Silas and Timothy arrive. *The Jews* oppose all three coworkers. *The Jews* had ample opportunity to oppose the preached word before Silas and Timothy arrived, but Luke reserves their opposition until Timothy and Silas arrive. Why does Luke show *the Jews* opposing Silas and Timothy, as well as Paul? All three represent *another word*, namely, that Gentiles can be saved without being circumcised, as Paul preaches and as the Jerusalem Council affirmed (15:22). Silas is one of the brothers that the Jerusalem *ekklēsia* appointed to accompany Paul and Barnabas to disseminate the Jerusalem Council's decision regarding the inclusion of the Gentiles. As for Timothy, Paul picks him up in Lystra, and he joins Paul and Silas in transmitting the Council's decree throughout the cities (16:1–5). All three coworkers are connected with

---

83. Cohen ("Was Timothy Jewish?") argues that Luke thought of Timothy as a Gentile; Paul and the Jews would have considered him a Gentile as well.

disseminating another word that says Gentiles can be saved without submitting to circumcision. By placing all three disseminators of this other word in the same space with the opponents, Luke does not want his audience to miss this point.

Just in case the reader missed the precise reasons for the opposition surrounding Paul and his coworkers, Luke provides a more explicit explanation (18:12–17). While Gallio is proconsul in Achaia, *the Jews* with one accord (*homothymadon*) rise up against Paul and drag him before the proconsul. Luke's use of the term *homothymadon* gives the impression that we are dealing with a substantial group of people acting in unison. *The Jews* accuse Paul of persuading people to worship God contrary to their Law. *The Jews* consider Paul's preaching alien to their understanding of the Law. Gallio rules that Paul has not committed any wrong or evil act over which he should exercise jurisdiction (18:14–16). Since *the Jews* are unsuccessful with their attempt to persuade Gallio to formally charge Paul, they seize and beat Sosthenes, the leader of the synagogue (18:17).

Returning to the initial encounter, after *the Jews* oppose Paul (and his coworkers), Luke inserts what ostensibly amounts to a directional or temporal shift. This time his declaration is in the future tense: "From now on I *shall* go to the nations." But Paul has already been preaching to the Gentiles in the Jewish synagogues and just recently on the Areopagus in Athens. Recall that in the previous declaration, Paul says "*we are* turning to the Gentiles." In this second declaration the tense has changed from present to future. And the subject pronoun changes from the first-person plural, *we*, to the first-person singular, *I*, even though Silas and Timothy have joined Paul. An explanation for these shifts in grammatical tense and number may be found in the immediate literary context.

Immediately after this second declaration, Paul enters the home of the Godfearer Titus Justus, whose house is attached to the synagogue. This may account for the first-person-singular subject. Thus, Paul's declaration does not point to some distant future, but to a more immediate future. Paul entered a more hospitable home similar to what Jesus had instructed his disciples to do. But the disciples were to leave the city that rejected them. Yet, Titus Justus's home is not any ordinary home in the scheme of Acts. This second declaration is accompanied by a boundary crossing similar to what Peter did when he entered Cornelius's home, a Godfearer. Paul explicitly enters a Gentile's home for the first time in Acts, unless we also presume that he entered Lydia's home. In Acts, Luke informs his audience twice how it is unlawful for a Jew or a circumcised person to have intimate contact with Gentiles, and both occur in the Cornelius narrative (10:28; 11:3).[84] I propose that the story of Paul's entrance into Titus Justus' house parallels the story of Peter and Cornelius. Although Lydia, the leader of the house of prayer in Philippi, urged Paul to stay at her home, Luke does not expressly state that Paul accepted her offer. Instead he continued to visit her house of prayer (*proseuchē*, or synagogue gathering) (16:13–16), which is not necessarily the same venue as her home. But even if we concede that Lydia hosted Paul in her home, Luke has situated Paul's visit to Justus' home immediately following this second declaration for a reason. Paul's boundary crossing does not mean he will cease preaching to his fellow Jews. This second declaration, like the first, is a part of the dialectic of Paul's turning toward the Gentiles and remaining in proximity with and maintaining a priority for the Jewish people. This remaining is evidenced by the household conversion that takes place after Paul leaves Titus' home. Crispus the leader of the synagogue and his whole house become believers, as well as many of the Corinthians (18:8).

THIRD DECLARATION: THIS SALVATION OF GOD *WAS* SENT TO THE GENTILES (28:17–31)

This last declaration differs from the first two in several respects. Paul is no longer included in the grammatical subject (*I* or *we*), but the subject is the abstract phrase "this salvation of God." Dupont argues that the phrase "this salvation of God was sent to the Gentiles" is synonymous with the phrase "all flesh shall see the salvation of God" at Luke 3:6. This

---

84. Bauckham, "James, Peter," 112–13. While daily associations between the Jews and Gentiles were virtually impossible to avoid, "Luke takes pains to represent the Jerusalem church as exemplary in their religious observance and on that account respected in Jerusalem." In spite of Cornelius' stellar reputation among the Jewish nation, he is not exempt from the prohibition of intimate relations between Jews and Gentiles. This may indicate there was "no general recognition of a category of righteous Gentiles occupying a third position, neither law-observant Jews nor morally impure Gentiles" (114). But Peter's dream teaches him that Gentiles who accept Christ are neither morally impure nor profane. Bauckham ("James, Peter," 115) further argues that the dividing lines of pure Israel and impure Gentiles and sacred Israel and profane peoples were abolished during the "Gentile Pentecost" at Cornelius' house.

history that Luke recounts in Acts "is to be determined as that of the manifestation of God's salvation in favor of all flesh." (*se définit comme celle de la manifestation du salut de Dieu en faveur de toute chair*).[85] The universal *all flesh* ensures that God's salvation will include the Gentiles, but also does not exclude the Jewish people. *The Jews* are ultimately constructed as the external other in Acts.

Another way that this declaration differs from the previous two is that Paul exhibits a higher degree of agency than the other characters in this episode. Paul summons the Jewish leaders, and they come. The characters and the circumstances are different from those in the previous two declarations. Paul tells the Jewish leaders in Rome that *the Jews* opposed him, and that he is in Rome because he appealed to Caesar. Proximity is linguistically foregrounded in the dialogue.

Paul preemptively declares that he has done nothing contrary to Moses. "The story seems intent on demonstrating Paul's Jewish 'orthodoxy.'"[86] The Jewish leaders inform Paul that they received no evil reports about Paul from Judea. Both Paul and the Jewish leaders at Rome continue to refer to each other as "brothers" (28:17, 21). From the beginning to this final chapter, the apostles do not express an attitude of rupture with their Jewish compatriots.[87] But Paul's declarations constitute one element of the dialectic of turning toward another while remaining with the Jewish people.

The Jewish leaders know that Paul belongs to a sect, that the beliefs of the sect are generally not believed within Judaism, and the sect is opposed *everywhere*. This is another Lukan hyperbole, which reinforces the idea that the apostles took the gospel everywhere in spite of ubiquitous opposition from *the Jews*. The Jewish leaders' reference to the *ekklēsia* as a sect shows that they considered it harmless and not

---

85. Dupont ("Salut des gentils," 137) argues that Luke uses the expression *this salvation of God*, which does not derive from Isa 6, to bring the end of Acts into harmony with the beginning of the Gospel. In Luke 3:1–6, according to Dupont, Luke situates "gospel history in comparison to universal history" (*l'histoire evangelique par rapport á l'histoire universelle*) when he adds the Isa 40:3–5 quotation, which also gives the narrative a theological perspective.

86. Juel, *Luke-Acts*, 84. Paul's defense speeches, as well, focus on issues of "orthodoxy" (77).

87. Vanhoye, "Juifs selon les Actes," 71.

a threat. They considered it a phenomenon not unlike the sects of the Pharisees, Sadducees, Essenes, or the followers of Judas the Galilean.[88]

When the Jewish leaders at Rome return with a larger constituency to hear Paul after their initial meeting with him, their response to Paul's message is mixed; some are persuaded and some remain unconvinced (28:23–24). The unconvinced group does not act violently against Paul as in the other two dialogical encounters. And Luke reports no mixed audience of Greeks and Jews. As they leave, Paul interjects one more word (*rhēma* in Greek):

> Correctly, the Holy Spirit spoke through Isaiah the prophet to your ancestors, saying: "Go to this people and say, 'surely you will hear and not understand and certainly you will see and not perceive; For this people's heart is hardened. They hear with their ears with difficulty and they closed their eyes, lest they might see with their eyes and hear with their ears and understand with their heart and turn, and I would heal them.'" (28:26–27//Isa 6:9 LXX)

We have here two quotes and not a single quote. According to Bovon, we have a quote within a quote, which Luke conveys as "one unique word." Bovon further states, "Paul's last speech, a mixture of the quotation and his own speech, is observed by Luke as [Rhema]. [Rhema] is not here simply a Word. . . . It is the biblical [Rhema] that stands here and not a logos. Luke has reserved [rhema] as inspired speech from God for the Hebrew tradition, for the Word of God, and for humankind." (*Die letzte Rede des Paulus, eine Mischung von Zitat und eigener Rede, wird, von Lukas als [rhema] betrachtet. [Rhema hen] is hier nicht einfach ein Wort. . . . Es ist das biblische [rhema], das da steht, und nicht [logos]. Lukas behalt sich [rhema] für die hebräische Tradition, für das Wort Gottes und für die menschliche, von Gott inspirierte Rede vor*).[89] Thus, Paul claims his interpretation of the immediate situation and of the Gentile mission as God inspired. In contrast with the disunity of the Jewish people, Paul unites his voice with the Holy Spirit and Isaiah.[90]

Paul's claim to divine inspiration extends to this third declaration. Yet as context shows, Paul continues to preach to whomever comes to

88. Josephus, *Ant.* 18.1.2–6. We may not be able to totally rely on the information Josephus provides.

89. Bovon, "Schön hat der heilige Geist," 230.

90. Gaventa, *Acts*, 367.

hear him. Dialectically, the gospel is directed toward the Gentiles even while it remains as a dialogical reality for the Jewish people. Note in the Isaiah quotation that the verb in the sentence, "I will heal them," is future tense, and the verb in the last sentence of Paul's declaration, "they will listen," is also in the future tense. At a future time, Paul envisions that those Jewish people who now refuse to believe will respond more favorably to his inspired interpretation of the Law and the Prophets. This presupposes a continued dialogue. Luke does not identify the future messengers of "the salvation of God." Nevertheless, this future acceptance by the Jewish people stands in tandem with the future of the Gentiles. In Luke's eyes there is room and hope for both the Gentiles and the Jewish people in general.[91]

After the previous two declarations, Paul continues to preach to both Jews and Gentiles. In this last declaration, the text says that Paul preached unhindered to *all* that would approach him.[92] In Acts, Luke never expressly excludes the Jews from God's salvation.[93] Although *all* have access to Paul, he says that he is in chains.[94] Paul is unhindered in the sense that anyone can visit him and he can speak freely without fear of retaliation. The dialogue continues. Yet, closure is achieved in that

91. Fitzmyer (*Acts*, 790–91) argues that this verse "is not a judgment, but a description of the hardening of the hearts of Jews of old." Luke is comparing the obduracy of those in Israel who refuse to accept the gospel with the obstinacy of their ancestors; Fusco ("Luke-Acts") argues that the hermeneutical key lies in the theologoumenon of blindness and hardening (28:7–31) that must be viewed in light of the Hebrew Bible usage where the possibility of redemption or healing always exists. This final section shows that there is a future in which Israel will be restored; Bovon ("Schön hat der heilige Geist," 230) asserts that the phrase "I will heal them" is a positive expression of a last hope (*letzte Hoffnung*) for Israel.

92. Gaventa (*Acts*, 369) posits that since "Luke allows 'all' to remain ambiguous, perhaps interpreters must do the same." Some Western witnesses insert at 28:30 that he expressly preached to both Jews and Greeks (614.2147 *pc* (gig p) vg^mss syh**).

93. In the Hebrew Bible, God is willing to save a remnant in Israel. In the wider context of Isaiah 6:9, God promised Israel that a remnant would return from exile (Isa 10:20–23; cf. Rom 9:27). God did not require that every individual in Israel be saved (Isa 37:31–32). In Deutero-Isaiah, God's salvation is for the remnant in Israel (46:3, 13). The remnant will serve as God's servant for a light to the nations (Deut-Isa 49:3, 6; cf. Isa 26; Zech 8:6, 13).

94. Mealand ("Close of Acts") argues that the three Greek terms *akolutos*, *dietia*, and *misthoma* are technical terms derived from a civil law context. Luke recontextualizes them to support his theological aims (28:30–31). Historically, Luke probably leased property, which would allow him to come and go freely. Such leases are mentioned in the papyri as lasting for a term of two years.

Paul's desire (and God's promise to Paul) to see Rome is fulfilled (19:21; 23:11). *Closure* is the manner in which a narrative indicates its end, but "completeness refers to the degree of resolution accompanying the closure. Closure need not be tied to the resolution of instabilities and tensions but completeness always is."[95] The picture is far from *complete*. Acts closes on an unresolved dialectical tension.[96] The dialectic of turning toward the Gentiles and remaining with or maintaining a dialogue with *the Jews* and/or the Jewish people continues. The dialectical dance continues as seeking and leaving, leaving and seeking. As is the case between the Jews and their proximate others in the Hebrew Bible: "[At] every step of the way, the Jew and the other are bound up with each other and separated from each other, seek each other and abandon each other. But either never forgets the other."[97]

Conclusion

The Jews as Luke constructed them are stereotypical and in some respects synthetic. Sandmel aptly asks whether the Jews in Acts are actual people or the author's puppets. Can we accept Acts as a true account of events with respect to *the Jews*?[98] My answer is not without critical reflection and an acknowledgment that all characterization is synthetic and mimetic. Mimesis in narrative provides a representation of a social reality and/or social practice, but it does not and cannot imitate perfectly the empirical world.[99] Nor is it always the author's desire to imitate fully the empirical world that the text represents, but sometimes the author wants to construct a world that is fluidly descriptive and prescriptive. Wills has argued that the picture we have in Acts is "ideal" and not "real."[100] *The Jews* are the ideal negatively romanticized opponents of

95. Phelan, *Reading People*, 18.

96. Marguerat, "Juifs et chrétiens," 175. Wills ("Third Maccabees") argues that ancient histories more often remained relatively open at the end of the account, whereas the novels were more often relatively closed when the story was completed. The term "relatively" refers to the fact that works can have opened or closed endings with respect to some variables but not all variables (7).

97. Benbassa and Attias, *Jew and the Other*, 4. See also Machinist, "Outsiders and Insiders."

98. Sandmel, *Anti-Semitism*, 100.

99. GeBauer and Wulf, *Mimesis*, 15, 23.

100. Wills, "Depiction of the Jews," 653.

the *ekklēsia* and its gospel message. Luke characterizes *the Jews* with homogenous mimetic and thematic attributes as the primary opponents of the apostles. The fact that *the Jews* emerge in many different venues and yet act in very similar ways gives some readers the impression that *the Jews* are an organized and harmonious group. Thus, Luke's narrative discursively creates the illusion that *the Jews* in Acts are the Jewish people in general. The only power in Acts that is able to transcend the hostility of *the Jews* is the power of God, which, according to the narrative, is on the side of the *ekklēsia* and not on the side of *the Jews*.

Such a literary construction of *the Jews* as the external other risks denigrating Jewish people in general since many readers will not differentiate *the Jews* as constructed in Acts from historical or contemporary Israel or Jewish people. All audiences are not aware of the synthetic component of character or they do not expect synthetic character construction in what many believe to be "historical" narratives that are understood as the unadulterated "word of God." Such a discursive construction can promote anti-Jewish understandings of all Jewish people as potentially volatile and homogenous, and as enemies of the *ekklēsia*.

When Luke constructs *the Jews* in dialogical relationship with the apostles, who are the representatives of the *ekklēsia* and the "winners" whose interpretive words are *the* word of God, Luke effectively desacralizes the words of *the Jews* regarding God's salvation in Acts. This desacralization subjugates *the Jews'* interpretation of the Law and the Prophets to that of Paul's and/or the *ekklēsia's*. This subjugation creates a hierarchical relationship between *the Jews* and the *ekklēsia*. In this way Luke discursively constructs *the Jews* as the external other. A project of othering is a linguistic one because it takes place on the level of discourse.[101]

While the discourse of *the Jews* is virtually muted and embodied in their volatility, Luke foregrounds and evaluates Paul's discourse concerning the Gentile mission by (a) Paul's appeal to Scripture, (b) his repeated declarations in direct speech of turning to the Gentiles, and (c) the valuation of his speech as the "word of God." It is difficult for contemporary Christian readers to critically engage character construction in a sacred text, especially when such constructions are discursively framed in theological language.

---

101. Smith, "What a Difference," 45–46.

3

The Construction of Women as Internal Other
and Peter

WOMEN IN ACTS ARE PROXIMATE OTHERS OVER AGAINST WHOM THE self-identity of males as approved intermediaries are constructed. Emmanuel Levinas has argued that woman constitutes the absolute other; she is "essentially other." For him, otherness is about alterity and not sameness.[1] Simone de Beauvoir refutes Levinas' claim and argues that "man defines woman not in herself but as relative to him." The male is absolute, and she is the other. Woman can never be the subject, but she is always men's object.[2] Beauvoir further argues that woman as man's other embodies passivity, diversity, matter, and disorder as opposed to males, who represent activity, unity, form, and order.[3]

While in Acts *the Jews* and the charismatic others constitute the external other, women are constructed as the internal other and associated with passivity and disorder. Like the external others, internal others function as a foil for the construction of self-identity for approved intermediaries.[4] The literary and discursive construction of women functions to form a self-identity for the apostles. I have divided women in Acts into two groups: those who emerge in narrative instabilities with Peter, or with Paul. In this chapter, I examine women in relation to Peter within the framework of a theory of otherness. I argue that named women are juxtaposed with Peter when he is the spokesperson for the Twelve. These named women enhance Luke's portrait of Peter and/or redeem him from negative traits associated with him in Luke's Gospel.

---

1. Levinas, *Time and the Other*, 86.
2. Beauvoir, *Second Sex*, xvi, 70–71.
3. Ibid., 80.
4. Boyarin, "Other Within," 434. They "share in common the making of ourselves."

When Luke introduces a group or class of women, as opposed to individual named women, Peter is not the spokesperson for the group, but the Twelve speak and act in unison. This is the case with the Hellenists widows.

Luke attempts to redeem Peter from character or leadership deficiencies attributed him in the Gospel by juxtaposing him with women who engender disorder or who are problematic to community order. The pairing of these women with Peter privileges him and diminishes women as credible witnesses, or as witnesses at all. This diminishing or silencing of women who are situated within the community renders them the internal other.[5] The internal other constitutes a greater threat than the external other. The internal other serves as a perennial reminder of the constructed nature of the community and its leaders' self-identity; therefore the internal other must be kept in order to maintain an objectivistic ideal of an "authentic" self-identity.[6] For example, if a community constructs its identity upon the belief of the superiority of male preaching, and females emerges within the community with superior preaching skills, the authenticity of the community's identity is called into question. Those females must either be deemed as exceptional, demonized, silenced, or the community must rethink and reconstruct its self-identity.

Women as the internal other are never agents of the resolution of instabilities or the facilitators of order. This is strategic on Luke's part. Males who are approved intermediaries engender resolution of conflict or disorder and facilitate or embody order. Women, as well as some men (e.g., Sapphira's husband Ananias), embody disorder and function as a foil for the developing image of an orderly *ekklēsia*. Luke acknowledges women's presence, but women's speech or lack thereof and women's activity or inactivity foregrounds men's presence, speech, and authority, particularly Peter's authority. Foregrounding and evaluation constitute "two sides of the same coin. . . . [E]verything that is foregrounded is

---

5. Wills (*Other in Acts*, 205) argues that the "Jews and charismatic opponents are equal but external to the male apostles, while women within the movement are unequal but internal."

6. Benbassa and Attias, *Jew and the Other*, 73. The Samaritans or the "imaginary Gentile or idolater against whom Judaism constructs itself" are the internal others who pose the greatest threat because they serve as a "reminder that authentic Judaism does not exist any more than the wholly other that it invests in order to invent itself."

expressly evaluated, but not everything that is evaluated is textually foregrounded."[7]

Brief Review of Some Relevant Studies of Women in Acts

Although Luke-Acts contains a relatively significant female presence, scholars have noted that Luke depicts women as either passive, silent, or absent from the text.[8] Thus, Elisabeth Schüssler Fiorenza argues that exegetes must view Luke's texts with a hermeneutic of suspicion and/ or with a consciousness of the patriarchal and/or androcentric biases and "kyriarchal" (from the Greek *kurios* and signifying all forms of oppression or lordship) oppression inherent in the work. A hermeneutic of suspicion requires deconstructing the text and reconstructing an imagined historical reality.[9] Jervell argues that one could imagine Acts *without* the women since they are incidental to Luke's story. One could erase women from Acts, Jervell asserts, without changing its nature.[10] This assertion presumes that we can know with certainly the nature or the entirety of Luke's theological and literary intention or that Luke inadvertently included the women in his narrative. But we could no more erase the women from Acts than we could erase *the Jews* and the charismatic others without altering Luke's literary project.

Turid Seim is one of few scholars that have employed narrative ("redactional-compositional") criticism to study Luke's characterization of women. Seim analyzes gender in Luke-Acts within the framework of the patriarchal household. The household is an important interpretive context because of its burgeoning significance as the locus for the gathering of the early church community. The growing centrality of the household as the gathering place of the *ekklēsia*, however, does not alter women's place within the patriarchal structure of the house, which ac-

---

7. Fleischman, *Tense and Narrativity*, 183–84.

8. For example, Martin, "Acts," 777; Koperski, "Luke 10:38–42." Bauckham (*Gospel Women*) provides a historical study of individual women in the Gospels (i.e., Anna, Elizabeth, and Mary in Luke, et al.). He includes a chapter on women and the resurrection in which he questions the absence of women in the kerygmatic summaries in Acts and 1 Cor in light of the fact that women appear as witnesses to the resurrected Christ and/or the empty tomb in the Gospels. See also Levine, *Feminist Companion to Luke*.

9. Schüssler Fiorenza, *In Memory of Her*. Any reconstruction of women in Acts must be supplemented with material from authentic Pauline literature.

10. Jervell, *Unknown Paul*, esp. 152.

counts for the tension between Luke and Acts.[11] "Certain conditions are drawn up to define the context in which [women] may speak . . . when women appear with the power of the word, the text closes frameworks around them socially and locally."[12]

An investigation of narrative situations involving women in Acts should include character analyses of women and others with whom they interact. These character analyses should also include both synchronic and diachronic analyses. By synchronic I refer to women's characterization in Acts thematically or compositely without respect to time. What character traits contribute thematically to the overall characterization of women? By diachronic I mean characterization in the context of narrative progression through story time. Do the character traits that Luke ascribes to women change or remain the same as the story progresses? With the help of transitivity analysis, I address the following questions: How are women characterized individually and collectively? How do the characters interact with each other? How are the women differentiated as the internal other in relation to Peter and other male characters?

Scott Spencer has studied composite characterizations of slave girls and widows in Luke-Acts using a literary and social framework. With regard to slave girls, Spencer's literary framework considers narration, context, characterization, and the relationship between character motivation and plot.[13] In his article on widows in Luke-Acts, Spencer

11. Seim, *Double Message*.

12. Ibid., 118–19. Women are not commissioned to preach, nor are they public preachers or witnesses in Luke-Acts. As the community moves into the private space of the house, which was typically women's domain, Luke's depiction of women is also more consistently linked to "the house." Women had already had a place in the private space of the house. "When the private and the public converged, as the outer world found a place in the house, this . . .was not without ambivalence with regard to its implications for equality, because women, protected by the private sphere, were given new scope for their abilities within the community; on the other hand, the association with the order of the household could contribute to an intensification of the demands for subordination in the community, and thus provide a useful path to the reinforced patriarchal development of the household of God" (125).

13. Spencer, "Out of Mind." Motivated by Peter's citation of the Joel prophecy, Spencer examines slave girls or maidservants in the context of the right to speak or prophesy. Luke's version of the Joel prophecy contains a double emphasis on female and male prophesying as a major sign. After the appearance of Anna the prophetess in Luke, women's speech decreases. Martha is rebuked for speaking and the women who witness the empty tomb are not believed. By placing the Joel prophecy at the beginning

examines six episodes featuring widows in terms of plot sequence. He asserts that Luke-Acts reveals a stereotypical character profile of widows as "destitute, dependent women vulnerable to exploitation by corrupt authorities.... Thus, [subject] to deprivation of essential economic, practical, social, and emotional support."[14]

Similar to Spencer, Shelly Matthews[15] focuses on a particular class of women. She investigates the rhetorical function of high-standing and/or noble women in the missionary propaganda in Acts (esp. ch. 16), Josephus's *Antiquities of the Jews,* and in the mystery religions. Matthews concludes that Luke constructed his narrative so that noble women in Acts serve to support his apologetic aims. As part of Luke's narrative strategy, the presentation of noble and/or high-standing women allows Luke to deflect the presence of women of lower status among the early Jewish Christians and to refute the notion that popular religions in which women were the majority involved immorality and sexual promiscuity.[16]

Ivoni Richter Reimer has offered the first expansive investigation of women in Acts.[17] Reimer employs a sociohistorical, feminist liberation/ theological reconstruction. Although Reimer's commentary explores all the named and unnamed women in Acts, she reconstructs women's history with respect to business and community. She analyzes stories of women within the narrative sequence, but not schematically or thematically,[18] as Matthews and Spencer have done with noble women and slave girls and widows, respectively. Reimer is more interested in the history behind the text than the message of the text.[19] She is quite gener-

---

of Acts, Luke leads the reader to anticipate a return to the activity seen at the beginning of the Gospel. The reader, however, is frustrated when Peter's speech addresses males only. Spencer's social framework considered: (1) status and occupation, (2) race and religion—Jewish or Gentile, (3) Gender and locale—public or private discourse, (4) and deviance and denunciation. Spencer asserts that servant girl images in Luke-Acts reinforce hierarchical norms.

14. Spencer, "Neglected Widows," 732.

15. Matthews, *First Converts.*

16. Ibid., 67.

17. Reimer, *Women in the Acts.* See also Schottroff, *Let the Oppressed Go* and *Lydia's Impatient Sisters.*

18. Reimer (*Women in the Acts*) does classify named and unnamed women as well as women mentioned briefly, if at all.

19. For example, Reimer (*Women in the Acts*) examines the story of Ananias and Sapphira in Acts 5 in its context of Jewish women's rights under the marriage con-

ous in her historicizing of the Sapphira story by equating Sapphira's situation with later Rabbinic understandings of Jewish women's *ketuba* rights (a share of the husband's property that was to be transferred to the wife if the marriage dissolved).[20]

This chapter builds on Ann Graham Brock's comparative study of Mary Magdalene and the apostle Peter in canonical and non-canonical resurrection narratives.[21] Brock shows that Luke's Gospel exalts and privileges Peter as a disciple by omitting, altering, and supplementing Petrine traditions. In traditions where the author exalts Peter, Mary

---

tract (*ketuba*) and in the immediate context of "community of goods practiced by the Christians of Jerusalem." Reimer presumes the existence of a community of equals among the early Christians and asserts that Sapphira would have had nothing to fear if she had resisted her husband. Under the *ketuba*, Sapphira would have had to sign her rights over to her husband in order for Ananias to sell the property. By signing over the property, Sapphira broke her oath to the community, thereby submitting herself to patriarchal demands. Such demands "reduce women to immature beings and make them incapable of resistance to the injustice that is often planned within their houses" (15).

20. Although Kauffman's work, on whom Reimer (*Women in the Acts*) depends for information on *ketuba*, states that not every marriage contract included *ketuba*, Reimer seems to rely on the much later Talmudic claim that every wife had to have a *ketuba*. Such *ketuba* could only be relinquished with the wife's signature. Thus, Reimer first presumes that the couple also had to have a *ketuba*. Next she concludes that the land Ananias and Sapphira sold was security for Sapphira's *ketuba*, and that Sapphira's signature was required as a precondition for the sale. Reimer asserts that Sapphira gladly helped to execute the sale by affixing her signature. The historical possibility that the land sold was a part of a *ketuba* contract between the couple has been made a historical fact in Reimer's analysis. She states that "[i]n surrendering this part of her marital right, Sapphira had abandoned some future financial security, even though it may not have been especially significant" (6). Reimer seems to treat the information about community of goods in the summaries of Acts (2:42–47, 4:32–37) as historical. From these passages she concludes that when persons entered the community their property became communal property but remained their legal property to be sold by them as necessary for the use of the community. "Business dealings must still have been the legal responsibility of private individuals, but they were done for the sake of the community" (14).

21. Brock (*Mary Magdalene,* 17) examines canonical and non-canonical gospels (e.g., *Gos. Pet.* and *Gos. Mary*) to elucidate "how each gospel lays the ground work for apostolic authority in its resurrection narrative." Schüssler Fiorenza (*In Memory of Her,* 50) states that Luke's resurrection narrative should be situated in a discussion as to whether Peter or Mary Magdalene was the first resurrection witness. This competition between Peter and Mary Magdalene is also apparent in *Gos. Mary, Pistis Sophia,* and *Gos. Thom.* Seim (*Double Message*) notes that Luke's account of the women at the cross differs from Mark's account. Luke's account is more concise, and he does not mention the women's names or their function, 27. See also Bovon, "Mary Magdalene's Paschal Privilege."

Magdalene is diminished.[22] Luke's Gospel varies in two significant ways from the other Gospels: Luke asserts that "the risen Lord first appeared exclusively to Peter" (Luke 24:34; cf. 1 Cor 15:5–8); and Mary's interaction with the disciples after her encounter with the two messengers at the sepulcher does not take the form of a kerygmatic announcement as in John's Gospel (John 20:18).[23] Brock argues that "Luke's unique presentation of Peter as the recipient of an individual resurrection appearance is the keystone of the evangelist's overall program for enhancing the status of Peter as a leader of the early Church."[24] This programmatic enhancement of Peter's leadership extends to apocryphal texts that privilege Peter, such as the *Gospel of Peter* and the *Acts of Peter*.[25] Peter is also privileged as the spokesperson (*Wortführer*) for the apostles in the *Acts of Peter and the Twelve Apostles*, however, this non-canonical text contains no resurrection narrative *per se*, and it mentions no individual women.[26]

The Construction of Women as Internal Other and Redemption of Peter

In Acts, encounters between women and Peter always occur within the confines of intimate communal settings. This communal situatedness bolsters Peter's authority as a leader within the community. The community of believers serves as the venue for redeeming the deficiencies that Peter demonstrated as a significant figure in the Jesus movement in Luke's Gospel. In Acts, we witness a defining of women's place in the community over against the apostle Peter as representative of the Twelve.

Brock points to several minor additions in episodes where Luke exalts or privileges Peter as the leader of Jesus' disciples. For example, in the episode concerning the woman with the chronic hemorrhage who touched Jesus' garment, it is Peter who responds to Jesus' inquiry about who touched him (8:45). But in Mark, the disciples as a group

22. Brock, *Mary Magdalene*, 19.

23. Ibid., 19, 29, 33–34.

24. Ibid., 20.

25. Ibid., 65–71, 104–22.

26. Jesus is represented by several characters and undergoes transformation and ultimately recognition. See Smith, "'Understand Ye a Parable!'"

respond to Jesus' inquiry (5:31). This privileging of Peter by attributing to him additional dialogue is also evidenced elsewhere in Luke's Gospel (12:40–41; 22:8; cf. Matt 24:44; 26:17; Mark 14:13).[27] In his eagerness to push Peter to the forefront of the group, Luke (intentionally or unintentionally) also highlights a deficiency in Peter's character. Luke's portrait of Peter in this episode involving the woman with the hemorrhage demonstrates that Peter lacks spiritual discernment. This is different than in Acts, where Luke often attributes spiritual discernment and/or authority to Peter. Peter does not know what Jesus knows about the woman's touch which results in her healing (8:45b–46). But in Acts, Luke redeems Peter of this leadership deficiency in the story of Ananias and Sapphira.

Sapphira—Acts 5:1–11

The story of Ananias and Sapphira is significantly longer than other stories of named women in Acts and thus demands more hermeneutical attention than other episodes. This narrative situation centers on a breach of a community "rule" by the couple.[28] Ananias and Sapphira sold a piece of land, retained a part of the price for themselves, and lied about the net profits. Derrett argues that the point is the issue of "withholding what belongs to God" rather than lying.[29] But Luke foregrounds the fact that the couple lied to the Holy Spirit and portrays Sapphira as caught in the very act of lying. Luke adjudicates the couple separately so that they are individually and collectively discursively determined to have lied. The couples' withholding of property constitutes

27. Brock, *Mary Magdalene*, 22.

28. Derrett ("Ananias, Sapphira," 227) argues that the church had no "rule that property should be legally pooled." Members voluntarily brought together their assets to the apostles who acted as trustees.

29. Ibid., 218. Ascough, "Benefactions Gone Wrong." The list of women at Luke 8:1–13 is one example of how Luke and his community relied on patronage. Just as people were expected to emulate the practices of the benefactors, Luke's community was expected to imitate the actions of donors within the early church. By putting the story in the context of benefactions in the Greco-Roman world through an investigation of ancient inscriptions, Ascough conjectures that the couple's motivation for lying was to gain more earthly honors than they deserved. Benefactors received honors comparable to their donations. Ananias and Sapphira pretended to have turned over a greater donation than they actually gave in order to obtain greater honor. Thus, they were compelled to lie to the Holy Spirit.

the first deception, which they cover up with a second one. The couple's "dissing" of community order is methodically resolved as Peter negatively evaluates their actions in turn.

First, Peter deals only with Ananias' crime, which momentarily raises the question about how Peter will deal with Sapphira, as his wife. Will she suffer the same punishment as her husband or is her guilt and punishment mitigated because she merely consented to the sale? Readers who know well the Scriptures of Israel will anticipate that her punishment will not be mitigated. But the same readers may not anticipate the adjudication of her case apart from her husband's.

As other scholars have noted, the Ananias and Sapphira story recalls the Achan story in Joshua 7. Luke Timothy Johnson notes that, similar to the Achan story, property is deceitfully retained (*nosphizomai*), God's spokesperson confronts the guilty party, and the guilty party is cutoff from the community by death.[30] But as Marguerat notes, here both a male *and* a female are implicated in a crime against God and the community. Marguerat argues that the story is an echo of the story of the fall in Genesis 3 rather than a parallel to the Achan story.[31] Price views the story as a combination of simple parallelisms to the Achan story and of features that conform to the Naboth story of 1 Kings 21.[32] In the Achan story, members of the family are found guilty by association and suffer the same fate as does Achan. But in Sapphira's case, she is found guilty in her own right of tempting the Spirit. In all cases, the corollary sin of the protagonist is the deception or cover-up, forcing the community leader to call them on the carpet, so to speak.

Also, different from the Achan account in Joshua 7, where an entire family is wiped out because of Achan's sin, Luke portrays Sapphira as sealing her own fate. If Sapphira is simply complicit in the crime and if the primary crime is the retaining of proceeds from a sale of communal assets, why construct the narrative so that the husband and wife are adjudicated separately? In the Achan story, Joshua interrogates Achan who does not commit a second deception but quickly confesses

30. Johnson, *Acts*, 91–92.

31. Marguerat, "Mort d' Ananias et Saphira."

32. Price (*Widow Traditions*, 220, 223) argues that Luke added Ananias to offer a parallel with Ahab, and thus, Sapphira was transformed into the "new Jezebel in tandem" with Ananias. Luke uses the name *Ananias* for two imaginary characters, namely, the husband of Sapphira and Paul's sponsor (Acts 9:10; 22:12), both of which are fabrications (Paul denied that any human taught him the gospel; Gal 11:1, 11–12).

to the crime. Achan's family is not questioned separately, *but* the entire family and property are carried to the Valley of Achor where they are all consumed together at one time. Interestingly, a wife is not mentioned, only his sons and daughters (Josh 7:24–25). The separate adjudication of Ananias and Sapphira allows Luke to attribute damning speech to Sapphira.

SAPPHIRA AS PROXIMATE INTERNAL OTHER

Sapphira is the second named woman juxtaposed with Peter in Acts (cf. 1:14 where Mary the mother of Jesus is the first). The women Luke uses as a foil to enhance and privilege Peter as the leader of the Twelve are named. This naming is mimetic; the naming of the women adds to the realistic representation of persons and events. Luke may want to show that both the people and the situations represent real events and that the events are accurately represented (Luke 1:1–4).

Sapphira and Ananias are part of a larger believing community characterized by tremendous growth. Thousands of believers daily joined the new community (2:41, 47; 4:4; 4:32). But Sapphira's story constitutes the "first detailed characterization of a woman."[33] And she is the first woman attributed with direct speech. Sapphira is first described as being *with* (the Greek preposition *sun* plus the dative case) her husband. Luke uses the Greek construction *sun* plus the dative to describe the proximate relationship between male and female characters. He uses the same construction at 1:14 to show that Mary the mother of Jesus and certain other women gathered in the upper room *with* the eleven apostles. In both instances the men with whom the women are connected are mentioned first. Luke refrains from using the Greek phrase *anēr kai gynē*, translated "men and women," to describe the distinct genders of the new converts until after Sapphira's story.

The women in both episodes (1:14 and here) are engaged in identical or similar activities as their male counterparts. The women in the upper room are praying and waiting for the outpouring of the Holy Spirit just as are the male apostles. Both Ananias and Sapphira sell property and retain part of the profits, even though the grammar may tell a slightly different story, as noted below. Sapphira is complicit with

33. Martin, "Acts," 779.

her husband Ananias in his mendacity.[34] In both stories Peter emerges as the spokesperson for the community. In the upper room, Peter initiates the selection of Judas's replacement. Luke's pattern of juxtaposing named women (Mary the mother of Jesus, et al.) with Peter begins in that upstairs room. The women in the upper room are diminished when they are excluded from the decision-making process, as many scholars have already noted. Although women are members of the *ekklēsia*, approved intermediaries deprive them of the opportunity to actively help define or construct its identity.

Luke's juxtaposing of Sapphira and Ananias with other characters begins in the immediately preceding context (4:32–37) where Luke portrays Barnabas as a paragon of communal sharing of property. Barnabas' behavior mirrors the norm for communal sharing portrayed in the second of three major summaries in Acts (4:32–35; cf. 2:42–47; 5:12–16). Barnabas sells his property and places the proceeds at the apostles' feet. Ananias and Sapphira, on the other hand, deviate from the pattern, creating an instance of disorder in the community. Although Luke sometimes parallels male and female characters (e.g., Simeon and Anna), here a single male character, Barnabas, is juxtaposed with a married couple (similar, but not identical, to Prisca and Aquila with Apollos at 18:24–28). The parallelism negatively evaluates the couple in relation to Barnabas and contributes to Luke's construction of them as the internal other.[35] They threaten a pristine and idyllic self-identity of a

---

34. Reimer, *Women in Acts*, 55.

35. Price (*Widow Traditions*, 219, 220) argues that the original tradition was solely about Sapphira, and Luke later added Ananias. He surmises what happened to Sapphira's story: "When it was decided that a man must have been needed to mastermind the scheme, he [Ananias] was brought in to do it, and Sapphira was shunted aside.... [In the original story,] the sin of the widow Sapphira was to keep back some of her inheritance from the church because perhaps she rightly did not trust the stewardship of the male authorities who thought a widow complained too much if she was not satisfied with a thread-bare coat." Price's speculations are based on dating Luke later than 80–90 CE. He places Luke's text in the same period as 1 Tim where he finds evidence for the existence of an order of widows. Thus, for Price, Luke retrojects concerns from the widows' tradition back into the period of the church and recontextualizes them. It is possible, as Price asserts, that original paralleled texts consisted of episodes about Barnabas and Sapphira, since (1) Luke often uses male/female parallels, and (2) by inserting Ananias into Sapphira's story, Luke diminishes Sapphira's portrait as a totally independent woman who may have inherited or purchased the land and thus became the sole owner. But it is also possible that Sapphira was added to a story that mainly centered on Ananias to provide a narrative parallel to the episode involving

harmonious *ekklēsia* in which property owners care for the needs of indigents. The interjection of disorder or conflict that is quickly resolved functions as a mimetic foil.

The parallelism between Barnabas and the couple is strategic on Luke's part, as is the quick and successive resolution of the problem resulting in the restoration of a romanticized orderly community. A similar story appears in the Coptic Berlin papyrus 8502, which is a fragment of the *Acts of Peter*. A certain Ptolemaeus bequeathed some property to Peter's daughter because Ptolemaeus credited her with leading him to faith in God. Ptolemaeus entrusted the property to Peter as the girl's father. Peter says, "I executed it with care. I sold the land, and—*God alone knows*—neither I nor my daughter kept back any of the price of the land, but I gave all the money to the poor."[36] In this story Peter's behavior is the reverse of Ananias and Sapphira's. As a male, Peter has power over property in which a subordinate female has an ownership interest. The *Acts of Peter* differs from the Sapphira story in another respect: the author introduces no third party to judge whether or not Peter actually retained any of the profits. Instead Peter remarks, "Only God knows." In the Sapphira story, the reader is expected to accept the narrator and Peter at their word about the couple's community tort. God knows *and* Peter knows.

REDEEMING PETER: LYING TO PETER MEANS LYING TO GOD

As soon as Ananias places the supposed net revenue at the apostles' feet, Peter makes three evaluations about Ananias in the form of two questions and one assertion: (1) "Why has Satan filled your heart to lie against the Holy Spirit and to retain a part of the price of the property?" 5:3; (2) "Why did you place this act in your heart?" 5:4a; and (3) "You have not lied to humans but to God," 5:4b. Ananias lies to Peter about the profits of his real estate transaction. Ananias' lie to Peter constitutes lying to God. It is indisputable that Peter regards Ananias' greatest fault as lying against the Holy Spirit and to God. The act of retaining profits that should belong to the community results from the self-deception

---

Paul, Prisca, and Aquila. In any case, what is important for my purposes is the narrative in its current form.

36. Acts Pet., 139–141.

that they could fool God. The lie was conceived when Satan took up residence in Ananias' heart, and the deceptive actions followed.[37]

Similar to Peter's evaluation of Ananias' behavior, when Jesus predicted that Peter would deny him three times, Satan was accused of desiring to sift him (Luke 22:31–34). The same Peter who lied about knowing Jesus is now entrusted with discerning when others are lying to God. Peter's judgment and the concomitant punishment of Ananias and Sapphira stand in stark contrast to Peter's three denials in the Gospel of Luke (22:54–6//Mark 14:53–72//Matt 26:57–75). Peter's false statements to the high priest's servant girl and others are euphemistically referred to as "denials," as opposed to lies. In Luke's account of the prediction of Peter's denial of Jesus, Peter receives a special commissioning "by Jesus to strengthen the other disciples (Luke 22:31–32)."[38] Thus, Luke alone demonstrates Jesus' continual support of Peter before the denial even occurs "rather than a condemnation of Peter's behavior."[39]

The idea of a person being filled signifies a dispossession as well as a possession—a taking over of the heart. Peter's first question to Ananias about Satan filling (*plēroō*) his heart is the first negative use of this metaphor in Acts. And it is used to explain the first case of disorder within the community of believers. The state of being filled is a theme throughout Acts (and Luke's Gospel; see 1:35, 41, 67; 4:1). Luke often depicts people or places in Acts as either filled with the Holy Spirit, filled with envy, or by Satan.[40] In either case, filling is an internal phenomenon with external demonstrations. And when Satan or envy fills a person, the external manifestation is a negative or destructive one. Some readers might assume that Satan is the agent or cause in all the subsequent negative instances in Acts where a person or a group of people is filled with envy (5:17, 28; 13:45; 19:29) or even when someone is deceptive.

37. Derrett, ("Ananias, Sapphira," 228) argues that Peter is "courteous . . . to allege that Satan [rather than Sapphira] tempted Ananias to deceive or cheat the Holy Spirit."

38. Brock, *Mary Magdalene*, 39.

39. Ibid., 21.

40. Of the thirteen times that the verb occurs in Acts (2:2, 4; 3:10; 4:8, 31; 5:3, 17, 28; 9:17; 13:9, 45, 52; 19:29) seven times the object of the verb is a place or people who are filled with the Holy Spirit (2:2, 4; 4:8, 31; 9:17; 13:9; 13:52). Five of the remaining six occurrences are negative and one is positive (3:10; 5:3, 17, 28; 13:45; 19:29). All refer to people who are filled with fear or envy, or by Satan. The one positive occurrence is at 3:10, where after the healing of the lame man by Peter and John all the people were filled with fear and amazement because of the miraculous healing. Luke also uses the adjective to describe persons such as Stephen (6:5).

Yet, the narrative does not say that Satan filled Sapphira's heart. Of course, it could be that the reader is to assume that if "Satan" filled Ananias causing him to lie, then "Satan" is also the cause of Sapphira's deception. On the other hand, the question arises as to whether Peter invoked "Satan" as a metaphor for Sapphira, especially given that Sapphira becomes a nameless female pronoun in her dialogue with Peter.[41] This solution may also account for why Luke attributes direct speech to Sapphira and none to Ananias.

Peter evaluates the couples' acts as crimes against the Holy Spirit and God. Although God is absent from this episode as a participant-actor, God's presence is implied throughout Peter's speech. "Luke portrays a radical connection between the apostles, especially Peter, and God.... God and the Holy Spirit are present in the community in her leaders.[42]" Like a true prophet, Peter cut "through their conspiracy" and he "read their hearts."[43] By framing Ananias and Sapphira's offenses in theological language, Luke gives the appearance of objectivity and fairness. This theological framing puts the onus of the couple's death on God and/or the Holy Spirit.

Luke's characterization of Peter in relation to Sapphira (and Ananias) allows Luke to redeem Peter from his reputation in the Gospel as deficient in spiritual discernment. In the episode about the woman with the chronic hemorrhage, mentioned above, and in the transfiguration scene (Luke 9:28–36//Mark 9:2–8; cf. Matt 17:1–8), Luke portrays Peter void of spiritual discernment. The story of Sapphira and Ananias also permits Luke to position Peter on the side of truth telling as opposed to denial or lying, which is what Peter is infamous for in the Gospels. Peter is the disciple who lied about his association with Jesus (Luke 22:54–62//Matt 26:57–75//Mark 14:53–72).

---

41. Derrett ("Ananias, Sapphira," 227–28) places the onus on Sapphira as an Eve figure who coaxes her husband to keep back that part of the purchase price that represents her *ketuba* (that portion of the husband's property that would go to the wife in the event of divorce).

42. "O'Toole, "'You Did Not Lie.'"

43. Johnson, *Acts*, 92.

The Strategic Use of Proper Names Diminishes Sapphira

The narrative demonstrates a privileging of Peter over against Sapphira in the strategic occurrence of proper names. The proper name *Ananias* occurs three times in the narrative, and the proper name *Peter* appears once in the same narrative. The three mentions of Ananias's name by Peter when he questions Ananias gives the impression that Peter may have had a more personal relationship and is more sympathetic with him. However, the proper name *Sapphira* occurs only once at the beginning of the narrative about Ananias when the narrator introduces her as his wife. When the narrative switches to the dialogue between Peter and Sapphira, the proper name *Sapphira* is never used. Three times the text references Sapphira with the Greek feminine pronoun *autēn* (*her*), and once with the Greek feminine definite article translated as *she*. Thus, when Peter interrogates Sapphira, she is not called by her name. In contrast, in the same dialogue, the proper name *Peter* occurs twice. This is twice the number of times that Peter's proper name occurs when he questions Ananias. This pattern effectively diminishes Sapphira as a person while foregrounding her complicity as a female. Conversely, the pattern foregrounds Peter as the unsympathetic, authoritative leader. Without her husband, she is reduced to a feminine pronoun. Her gender embodies her identity. She is reduced to her gender and her complicity, but her punishment will equal that of her husband's.

Deadly Dialogue: She Must Speak and Speak a Lie

Luke provides no response for Ananias to Peter's direct questioning and accusations, but Sapphira's response to Peter's question provides an opportunity for Peter to refute her words, to render them false, and to explicitly foretell of her impending fate. Different from Ananias, Sapphira's lie is reified as direct speech like black ink against white paper. Sapphira indicts herself with her speech. Peter asks Sapphira about the purchase price of the property: "Peter said, 'Tell me, whether you [two] gave up the property for this amount?' And she said, 'Yes, for that amount'" (5:8). When Peter questions Sapphira, her husband has been dead for several hours, but Peter gives her the impression that her husband is still alive by asking what the two of them got for the sale of the property. Peter does not inform her before he interrogates her that her husband is dead;

she has not a clue. Unlike Peter, she has no spiritual discernment. This silence keeps Sapphira ignorant with regard to her husband's death, and infers that the goal is not to give her a chance to repent, but to obtain direct evidence to prove her guilt.

Peter's second question to Sapphira is both rhetorical and adjudicatory. Why was she complicit with her husband in testing the Lord's Spirit? As Jervell asserts, "Peter's question here constitutes more of a pronouncement of judgment than an actual question. An answer does not follow, and it was not demanded" (*Die Frage des Petrus ist hier [5:9] eher Urteilsverkündigung als eigentliche Frage. Eine Antwort erfolgt nicht, und sie wird auch nicht verlangt*).[44] Her words confirmed her guilt; there is nothing more she can say.

REDEEMING PETER AGAIN: AUTHORITY AND RESTORATION OF ORDER

While Ananias's death is more spontaneous, Peter prophesies Sapphira's impending fate. Once her fate is sealed when she lies to Peter, Peter announces that what has happened to her husband is now going to happen to her. Peter's speech act facilitates her death. He speaks for God to condemn her deception and his words embody God's judgment. The one who once lied acts as judge over those who lie—not unlike Moses who killed an Egyptian and became the deliverer and mediator of the Decalogue containing a prohibition against murder (Exod 2:12).

Like her husband, Sapphira collapses at Peter's feet. The same men who buried her husband immediately appear to collect her body for interment (5:10). Why is it that the woman and not the male is portrayed as falling dead at Peter's feet? Sapphira's falling at Peter's feet may symbolize the full restoration of community order as was modeled by Barnabas when he sold his property and laid it at the apostles' feet. Thus, Peter is credited with the restoration of order.

In Acts, Peter operates as God's spokesperson empowered by God's Spirit to speak or bear witness. The subsequent death of the couple is to be considered as proof that Peter does in fact have authority to speak for God and that he speaks truthfully. According to Gail O'Day, the purpose of this story is "to warn the Christian community of the dangers

---

44. Jervell, *Apostelgeschichte*, 198.

of deceiving the Holy Spirit and lying to God."[45] Clarice Martin asserts that the narrative is "designed to demonstrate to both the church and wider society an appropriate respect and reverence for the spirit-filled community."[46] But, more pragmatically, the story warns of bringing disorder to the community by failing to imitate authoritative models of order (e.g., Barnabas). The story also cautions about underestimating the power of God's Spirit at work in God's spokesperson who has the discernment to recognize when an act of disorder has occurred and the authority to restore order. While named women as the proximate but differentiated internal other are placed at the center of disorder, it is Peter as God's spokesperson who restores order.

Sapphira's False Speech Impacts the *Ekklēsia*

The effect of this restoration of order spreads throughout the community. While the death of Ananias results in the fear of all who heard about it, Sapphira causes fear to fall on the entire *ekklēsia*. The impact of her fear is more narrowly defined as affecting the *ekklēsia*. This is the first time we encounter this Greek noun, *ekklēsia* (usually translated "church"), in Acts. Not until after the Ananias and Sapphira episode do we find the Greek phrase *anēr kai gynē*, as noted above, which is translated as *male and female* in Acts. O'Day is correct that this is probably no coincidence.[47] The phrase occurs four times (5:14; 8:3, 12; 9:2). It occurs after 9:2 in a similar but different construction. For example at 13:50, it is "devout women and the leaders [grammatical masculine] of the city." The last instance of *anēr kai gynē* appears at 9:2 where Paul has bound, persecuted, and dragged "men and women" belonging to the Way into Jerusalem. The phrase first emerges in the context of the deaths of a man and a woman, and it last appears in the context of the murder of both men and women.

I propose that Luke uses *anēr kai gynē* after the Ananias and Sapphira story to show that the incident surrounding Sapphira did not prevent women from joining the church and participating, albeit in a limited way. And more significantly, to demonstrate, negatively, the basis on which women could expect to remain members of the

45. O'Day, "Acts," 309.

46. Martin, "Acts," 779–80.

47. O'Day, "Acts," 309.

ekklēsia. They must act according to the rules of the community and be limited in speech. After Paul's conversion we no longer see the exact phrase *male and female*, except in speeches where Paul recounts his persecution of the church. Schüssler Fiorenza argues that this phrase is often a way to include women syntactically while limiting their significance, relevance, and voice. She further notes that in Acts, women are important in relation to men. The usage of grammatically masculine or generic language under which *woman* is subsumed is not evidence of inclusivity or equality.[48] The phrase *male and female* may function apologetically to show that women continued to join the church, even after the Sapphira incident, and they willingly submitted to its rules and authority. Women's speech will be limited, and when they do speak they will be judged by their words. Significantly, no other named woman in relation to the apostle Peter will speak for herself until we get to Rhoda!

TRANSITIVITY ANALYSIS

From the beginning, Ananias is in the foreground of the story as an active participant. Similar to Barnabas, Ananias is a participant-actor in ergative clauses affecting property and money and indirectly affecting people. A transitivity analysis shows both Barnabas and Ananias as agents in ergative clauses involving material processes. Ananias is a participant-actor in one clause involving a mental perception process (he hears Peter's words). Ananias is a participant in two non-ergative relational clauses (or one, actually an asyndeton) (*he falls and he dies*).

In contrast to both Barnabas and Ananias, a transitivity analysis does not show Sapphira engaged in any material processes affecting things or property. The action verbs in 5:1–2 (*epōlēsen*, he sold; *enosphisato*, he kept back; *enengas*, he carried; and *ethēken*, he set) are all third-person singular, and the subject of those verbs is Ananias. All clauses in which Sapphira is the participant-actor are verbal (she says), negated mental perception (not knowing), and relational (she enters, falls, dies) clauses. Her actions are primarily reflexive. Thus, it is difficult to consider Sapphira as an independent moral agent, at least grammati-

---

48. Schüssler Fiorenza, *But She Said*, 26. "An inclusive translation is not necessarily identical with a feminist translation."

cally, contrary to what Martin has asserted.[49] She is passive and verbally limited.

Similar to Sapphira, Peter is not an agent in any ergative clauses of material processes. He does not explicitly do anything in terms of transitivity that affects any bodies. Peter is a participant-actor in ergative clauses involving verbal processes (saying something). Peter's transitive agency equals Sapphira's, but it is less than Ananias's. But Peter's agency continues to be expressed as speech acts embedded in verbal process clauses.

Summary and Conclusion

The story may serve as a model of the miraculous signs and wonders mentioned in the third major summary (5:12–15), and it serves as a counter example for Barnabas.[50] As a counter example, it functions to differentiate Ananias and Sapphira from Barnabas. They are proximate others to Barnabas and Peter. Ananias is judged to have lied to God and the Holy Spirit; Sapphira is judged to have tested God's Spirit. But Peter interrogates Ananias and Sapphira separately. The separate adjudicatory procedures for husband and wife forces Sapphira to speak for herself. And she does speak, and her speech becomes the basis of her ultimate condemnation. She embodies her lie; she speaks her lie. Sapphira's story privileges Peter, redeeming him from his negative reputation in the Gospel and enhancing his leadership image. In contrast to Peter, Sapphira is constructed as one who is ignorant of her husband's fate, devoid of truth, and unable to escape fatal divine judgment through Peter as the authoritative arbitrator of truth and order. Sapphira functions as a foil; she is Peter's internal other against whom Peter is redeemed from his previous negative image in the Gospels. She is at the center of community disorder, but she has no part in its resolution or the restoration of order. It is her lifeless body that symbolizes the ultimate restoration of community order.

49. Martin, "Acts," 779.
50. Marguerat, "Mort d' Ananias et Saphira," 212, 214.

Hellenist Widows—Acts 6:1–7

The Ananias and Sapphira episode foregrounds Sapphira's complicity and speech so as to highlight Peter's ability to discern when community members are lying to God and consequently bring order to the assembly. Both the Ananias and Sapphira story and the episode about the Hellenist widows concern disorder and the restoration of order within the community.[51] In the episode involving the Hellenist widows, disorder occurs when the widows are neglected in the daily service. In this episode, the women are anonymous, and Peter is not the spokesperson. Luke provides no individual proper names for the women. Reimer correctly observes that "women are explicitly named [i.e., mentioned] precisely when and where such conflicts appear in Luke's narrative."[52]

In Acts, the conflict occurs after a dramatic increase in the number of disciples. The neglect of the Hellenist widows is the object of and the cause of the complaining of the Hellenists against the Hebrews (6:1). The text does not state that the widows are grumbling as some exegetes assert.[53] Nevertheless, the disciples and apostles take action as a result of the conflict, but it is questionable whether the group addresses the actual neglect of the widows in the daily service (kathēmerinos diakonia).

This is the first mention of widows in Acts (although for the space of three hours Sapphira was a widow, 5:7). This is also the first we hear of the existence of these two distinct cultural groups. The Hebrews were probably Jews whose mother tongue was Aramaic, and the Hellenists were Greek speaking Jews, as noted above[54] (cf. 9:29; 11:20). The text

51. Other widows mentioned in Luke-Acts include Anna (Luke 2:36), the widows of Zarephath (Luke 4:26; cf. 1 Kgs 17:8–24), the widow of Nain (Luke 7:11–17), the persistent widow (Luke 18:1–8), the widow who put all she had into the temple treasury (Luke 21:3–4), and possibly Dorcas (9:32–43).

52. Reimer, Women in Acts, 237.

53. Spencer (Portrait of Philip, 209) asserts that "the widows' grumbling is treated sympathetically, and the final result of satisfying their need is community growth (6:7)." Price (Widow Traditions, 211) argues that the "grumbling of, or on behalf of, the widows" should be categorized with similar external problems, such as heresy (8:9–12), simony (8:18–19), persecution (5:17–18, 21b–33), and competition from Jewish magic (19:13–14). Price further asserts that the resolution of these problems is more of "a fending off of another dart from Satan" than it is the church working out its "own kinks."

54. Fitzmyer (Acts, 347) argues that the best solution is to understand the Hellenists as Jews who spoke only Greek and the Hebrews as Jews who spoke both Aramaic and Greek. Similarly, Jervell (Apostelgeschichte, 216) says the Hebrews spoke Aramaic and

implies that the Hellenists hold the Hebrews responsible for the neglect of the widows in the daily ministry. Or maybe what we see is an appeal to the Hebrews as the majority of the Jerusalem *ekklēsia*.

The Division of Labor: Daily Service, Table Ministry, and the Word

In response to the complaint of the Hellenists, the Twelve summon the entire community of disciples. This is the first occurrence of the term *the disciples* in Acts (6:2).[55] Prior to this the believers are called *brothers* [*and sisters*] (1:15).[56] The Twelve explain to the disciples that God would be displeased with them if they should abandon the "word of God" to serve tables (*diakonein trapezais*, 6:2). This response implies that it may have been suggested that the Twelve take over or supervise the daily ministry and that for them to do so would constitute abandonment of the "word of God."[57] Or the statement is introduced into the narrative in order to justify the subsequent selection of the Seven Hellenists. Or the Twelve may have panicked and are blowing the situation out of proportion. The daily ministry could have constituted a significant ministry and was not simply confined to serving meals.

Significantly, the "word of God" is not initially referred to as a ministry until the decision is made that they will select seven to provide a *table* ministry as opposed to *daily* ministry (6:2). After which it is stated that the Twelve would devote themselves to "the *ministry* of the word" (*hē diakonia tou logou*, 6:4). The ministry under question is first described as a *daily* ministry, but when juxtaposed with the ministry of the word, it is called "the *table* ministry" (6:4; cf. 1:25). I propose that

---

the Hellenists spoke Greek. "Many Hellenistic Jews who were born abroad lived in Jerusalem and had their own synagogues in the city, Acts 6.9, cf. 9:29. Both groups [Hellenists and Hebrews] are Jews since the first Gentile of the community first appears in chs. 10–11. . . . *Hellenist* can also mean Gentile" ("[In Jerusalem] wohnten viele hellenistische Juden, im Ausland geboren, die in der Stadt ihre eigenen Synagogen hatten, Apg 6,9, vgl. 9:29. Beide Gruppen bestehen aus Juden, denn der erste Heide in der Gemeinde erscheint erst Apg 10–11. . . .'[Hellēnistēs] könnte an sich auch Heide bedeuten.")

55. Conzelmann, *Acts*, 44.

56. Witnesses to the Western text such as D E 1739ˢ substitute *disciples* for *brothers*.

57. Spencer ("Neglected Widows," 729) argues that the "apostles co-opt the widows' ordeal; they suppose that their right to proclaim the word is as much in jeopardy as the widows' right to receive food."

the two words *daily* and *table* refer to the same phenomenon, but they signal a structural change. I further propose that this structural change constitutes the formal creation of a new division of labor within the community, which is why the "multitude of disciples" are involved in the selection process. The mention of the increase in the number of disciples at 6:1 anticipates and signals the need to adjust ministry to the needs of a growing community.

The Twelve make it clear that their primary role is to devote themselves (*proskartereō*) to prayer and to preaching the the "word of God." That the Twelve have the authority within the community to determine which ministry they will and will not perform presupposes at least an informal hierarchical relationship between the Twelve and proximate others who are potential or known leaders in the wider community. While the Twelve reject table ministry (*diakonein trapezais*), they are still involved in ministry (*diakonia*).[58] Luke does not explicitly state that the Seven should serve tables and do nothing else.[59] Spencer argues that "menial" forms of *diakonia* (feeding widows) are subordinated to the more "spiritual" ministries of preaching, teaching, and prayer. But the basis for the Twelve's rejection, that the table ministry would cause them to abandon the "word of God," does not signify that the table ministry is menial or trivial.[60] Although Stephen does perform signs and wonders, and he speaks (*laleō*), he does not preach the word. And Philip does not preach the word of God until he is forced to leave Jerusalem as a result of the persecution surrounding Stephen's death. If the table ministry was centered in Jerusalem and was a ministry to the entire Jerusalem community, this might explain why the Twelve imply that it would be time consuming and why Philip does not preach the word until he is forced to flee to Samaria (8: 4,12, 14). This does not mean that the table ministry would *never* have permitted the Seven to preach the word of God. But it is possible that the table ministry could have been a more geographically confined and/or localized ministry. Concerning the fusion of feeding and preaching ministry, the Lukan Jesus combined

---

58. Seim, *Double Message*, 110.

59. Price, *Widows Traditions*, 211.

60. Fitzmyer (*Acts*, 344) says that "[u]nity and peace have to be preserved, but not by having the Twelve spend time on such trivia; the Twelve are depicted manifesting a proper sense of priority."

the ministries of compassion with ministries of teaching and preaching (Luke 9:1–6, 10–17; 12:37–42; 17:7–10; 22:14–27).[61]

Scholars do not agree on the meaning of *diakonia*. According to Tyson, the rift between the Hellenists and the Hebrews concerned the exclusion of some widows from a daily common meal.[62] Reimer contends that table service extends beyond the daily apportioning of food for the indigent or common meals. The table service pertains to daily distribution and participation in the daily cultic activities of the community, similar to what we see at Matt 25:35–40.[63] Schüssler Fiorenza asserts that Paul refers to the *table of the Lord* as a eucharistic table (1 Cor 10:21) and that historically it consisted of purchase, distribution, preparation, service, and cleanup, as well as the proclamation of the word.[64] It is quite probable that *diakonia* in the text includes proclamation of the word since (a) as noted above, the Seven (Philip) subsequently engage in preaching and performance of miracles (6:8–10; 8:7; 11:19); and (b) Luke makes a direct connection between the election of the Seven and the increase of the word.

Luke's limiting of the table service to the seven males may also be an attempt to circumscribe a ministry that the Hebrew widows had already been performing. Luke discursively likens and subordinates the newly consecrated table ministry to the ministry of the word, but he does not do so gratuitously. This subordination has more to do with the construction and naming of approved intermediaries, over against non-approved intermediaries or internal others, and with making a distinction between the ministry of the Twelve and other named approved intermediaries.

---

61. Spencer, "Neglected Widows," 729–30. Similarly, Seim (*Double Message*, 108) argues that Luke's "interest is to set a priority, so that one service is subordinated to another."

62. Tyson ("Acts 6:1–7," 154–55) argues that if the phrase *diakonein trapezais* refers to the duties of the seven and means serving meals, "it is difficult to avoid the conclusion that the daily *diakonia* of Acts 6:1 was an actual meal. The implication is that it is a meal like that described in Acts 2:42, 46, a common meal."

63. Reimer, *Women in Acts*, 236–37.

64. Schüssler Fiorenza, *In Memory of Her*, 165; idem, *But She Said*, 64. Contra Reinhartz ("Narrative to History"), who argues that *diakonia* did not include proclamation of the word; the term refers broadly to the service of servants.

FROM SERVICE TO SILENCE: THE TRANSFER OF *DIAKONIA* TO SEVEN MEN?

What is the Hellenist widows' relationship to this daily ministry? Does the overlooking of the Hellenist widows mean that ministers of the daily service were neglecting them? And does it mean that the ministers who neglected the Hellenist widows were widows themselves?[65] In other words, was it the Hebrew widows who were initially performing the daily service? In other words, were the Hebrew widows serving the other widows as may be implied in the case of Tabitha and her good works (that she was a widow like her constituency)? I propose that the Hebrew widows were performing the daily diakonia for all widows but their service to the Hellenist widows was less than thorough. Yet the widows are not the ones complaining; the Hellenists as a group are complaining in their behalf. Luke solves the problem of this disorder and grumbling by turning the Hebrew widows' ministry into a ministry role (i.e., table ministry) exclusively for approved intermediaries and populating it with Hellenist men. The table ministry (*diakonein trapezais*) semantically and administratively replaces the universal daily (*kathēmerinē*) ministry (*diakonia*) the Hebrew widows were engaged in. This way the approved intermediaries continue to be male, as was required when the Eleven replaced Judas (1:25), and the women continue as the proximate internal other.

If the disorder rested solely on the matter of missing a meal, the situation could have been remedied without ordaining men. Although the Hellenist widows are being neglected, we do not know the exact nature or extent of the neglect.[66] In the Gospels, when persons were hungry, Jesus fed them; when Jesus wanted to organize his disciples for a ministry, he commissioned them. And this is what the disciples do here. They convene a meeting, set the selection criteria, select candidates, and consecrate seven men. Some scholars argue that the problem does not fit the solution,[67] but it depends on how one perceives the problem.

---

65. Schüssler Fiorenza (*In Memory of Her*, 166) asserts that either "they were not assigned their turn in the table service or that they were not properly served."

66. Tyson ("Acts 6:1–7," 158) argues that widowhood in Luke-Acts is primarily associated with grief, piety, and poverty, so to exclude the widows from a common meal would have been "an act of extreme cruelty and impiety." The situation required an urgent solution. See also Bassler, "Widows' Tale," 30–35.

67. Johnson, *Acts*, 111; Conzelmann, *Acts*, 44.

Although the neglected Hellenist widows find themselves at the center of the controversy, they are rendered silent. Seim attributes the silencing of women in Acts to Luke's "special concept of apostleship and acceptance of the public sphere as a man's world."[68] The women have no input into the decision-making process. Luke renders women ineligible for election among the seven, and thus, "leadership is defined as the business of men."[69] Together with the Hellenists and Hebrews, the widows disappear into the crowd of disciples.

The brothers or disciples are told to examine seven men (*anēr*)[70] among them who have been witnesses, and who are full of the Spirit and of wisdom (6:3). These qualifications are not what one would anticipate for persons who will only "sling hash."[71] Of course, the gender restriction alone enables the group to exclude the widows and other women from eligibility. And Luke strategically describes no individual women in Acts as full of the Spirit; Tabitha is only full of good works. In Acts boundaries are being drawn between approved intermediaries and internal others, particularly women, who silently perform good works.

THE CONSECRATION OF THE SEVEN AND THE INCREASE OF THE WORD

After the seven are consecrated, the *word of God* increases, as well as the number of disciples, including the addition of a large number of priests (6:7). Luke makes a direct link between the increase of the *word of God* and the addition of the seven to the *diakonia*. This may confirm that the newly instituted *diakonia* included the proclamation of the word. Thus, strategically, putting men in charge of ministry and silencing women proves good for the growth of the community. The explicit mention of

68. Seim, *Double Message*, 162.

69. Ibid., 112.

70. D'Angelo, ("ANHP Question," 51) argues that Luke's use of ANHP together with the silencing of women is because of a Roman apologetic. Luke tries to show that the Christian messengers and their messages comply with the Roman civil ideals of what it means to be proper "ambassadors suitable for the public and civic forum" (52). These civic ideals include "gender correctness." This means women's silence serves only to bolster males' reputations as ideal ambassadors (66–67).

71. Price, *Widow Traditions*, 212. Spencer (*Portrait of Philip*, 191) asserts these qualifications "may suggest recognition on Luke's part that this company already constituted an acknowledged leadership body distinct from, though not necessarily in competition with, the Twelve."

the priests seems to imply that they did not relinquish their official positions or the prestige and authority associated with those offices when they joined the community of believers. This brief instability involving discord or disorder is dealt with by a division of labor resulting in a hierarchical and yet harmonious organizing structure that positively affected the spread of the word and the subsequent increase of the Jerusalem community.[72] This romanticized image of the community is contingent upon the internal other remaining in her place. She is the most significant threat to this constructed self-identity.

Transitivity Analysis

Transitivity analysis shows that the Twelve demonstrate the highest degree of transitive agency in this episode where ministerial agency is an issue within the community. This is a departure from the lack of transitive agency expressed by individual apostles (i.e., Peter and Paul) in relation to external others. The disciples elect the Seven, and they place the Seven before the apostles (6:5–6). While the disciples affect only the Seven, the Twelve affect both the disciples and the Seven. The Twelve as a group are participant-actors in one ergative material process affecting other people (they summon the disciples). The Twelve are participant-actors in one ergative relational process (they position their hands on the Seven). Conversely, the widows are acted on, but never act on anything or anyone else. The Hellenists are participants in one ergative verbal process (they complain about the neglect of the widows).

Summary and Conclusion

Throughout Luke-Acts widows are characterized as dependent on the narrator to report their cause, on members of their community to raise their concerns, and on the males to settle disputes concerning their welfare.[73] The episode concerning the neglected widows in the daily

---

72. Contra Spencer (*Portrait of Philip*, 198, 199) who sees no hierarchical relationship between the Seven and the Twelve, but he focuses on the democratic process of community action. See also Price (*Widow Traditions*, 213) who asserts that it is an "ideal scene constructed in order to provide the imprimatur for a practical arrangement for church governance."

73. Spencer ("Neglected Widows," 721–33) treats the Hellenist widows within a network of several episodes concerning widows in Luke-Acts. The episode involving

ministry provides opportunity for the appointment and naming of the Seven, the differentiation of the Seven from the Twelve, distinguishing of the widows from the Seven, and a reaffirmation of the role of the Twelve as the primary carriers of God's word and administrators of the *ekklēsia* in Jerusalem.

Although the Seven are named in Acts (Stephen, Phillip, Prochorus, Nikanor, Timon, Parmenas, Nicolaus, 6:5), only two, Stephen and Phillip, are ever mentioned again (6:8–7:40; 8:4–40; 11:19–21; 21:8). The presence of a list of named men (the Seven) makes the anonymity of the Hellenist women all the more salient. The narrative is centered on examining, appointing, and electing men. Similar to Sapphira and the women at Pentecost, the widows are differentiated from the men; they share the apostles and community's belief in the lordship of Jesus Christ, they inhabit the same space, but they are doubly removed from having any say in the daily ministry or in the resolution of disorder even when that disorder concerns them.

Schüssler Fiorenza argues that Luke attempts unsuccessfully to "gloss over differences among the leadership in the Jerusalem church (or churches)," including the Hellenist conflict.[74] But, in fact, Luke does not want to play down the conflict. He foregrounds it so as to privilege the Seven above the widows and to privilege the Twelve above the Seven. Luke constructs self-identity for the believing community over against others, and this othering project requires that he capitalize on conflict and the construction of difference (e.g., between table ministry and the word of God ministry). Luke inserts conflict so as to provide a solution that favors male leadership. Luke's aim is not to present a conflict-free church, but to show that through the guidance and power of God's spirit, the *ekklēsia* can withstand and resolve any obstacle or conflict. And the internal others are the foil against which an orderly communal identity is formed.

---

the Hellenist widows is the penultimate of six incidents in Luke-Acts. The first is the prophetess Anna in Luke 2; second is the widow of Nain; third is the persistent widow in Luke 18; fourth are the poor widows in Luke 21:1–4; sixth are the Hellenist widows; and seventh are the supported widows at Joppa, Acts 9:36–43.

74. Schüssler Fiorenza, *In Memory of Her*, 163.

Tabitha—Acts 9:36–42

Tabitha is the first woman of noble reputation and widespread influence to die in Acts. In light of Dorcas' contributions to the community, news of her illness and death imply that she is virtually indispensable and will be sorely missed. This creates a situation in which Tabitha is separated, by death, from the widows whom she served and whom depend on her community service.

THE PROXIMATE INTERNAL OTHER–A FEMALE DISCIPLE, FULL OF GOOD WORKS, BUT SPEECHLESS

The Greek text sets Tabitha apart from Peter and from everyone else in the episode. She is a *mathētria*, a female disciple. While this feminine descriptive is a New Testament *hapax legoumenon* (occurring only once), it is used to describe Mary Magdalene in the apocryphal *Gospel of Peter*. There Mary Magdalene is a *mathētria*, a female disciple, of the Lord.[75] The linguistic description of Tabitha as a *mathētria* and as "full of good works and alms" signifies both proximity and difference in relation to the Seven in Acts 6 who are *mathētēs* (male disciples) and "full of the holy spirit and wisdom." She is a proximate other. Dorcas' generosity toward the poor widows may indicate that she was a woman of means and possibly a widow as well. If she is a widow, her "good works" are directed toward people who are like her.

After Tabitha's death, her fellow disciples place her lifeless body in the upstairs room, which is reminiscent of the women in the upper room early in Acts (cf. 1:14). The disciples summon two men to bring Peter to Joppa, but it is not clear what they expect Peter to do. When Peter arrives, the widows are devastated. Widows line the room mourning and displaying the garments Dorcas constructed for them. Similar to when Jesus raised Jairus' daughter, Peter ushers everyone outside of the room before he resuscitates Dorcas. In the case of Jairus' daughter, Jesus cleared everyone from the room except his intimate circle, i.e., Peter, John, James, and the child's parents (Luke 8:51–55). The only witnesses to Peter's resuscitation of Tabitha are Peter, the omniscient narrator, and the reader.

---

75. *Gos. Pet.* 12:50. The term is also used for Eubula, one of Paul's disciples in *Acts Pet.* 2.9.

When Peter stretches his body over Tabitha's lifeless corpse, he commands her to stand up. Peter's imperative to her is similar to his words to the paralytic Aeneas in the immediately preceding healing story (9:32–35). In Aeneas's case, Peter says, "Jesus Christ heals you." Conversely, Peter does not use the name of Jesus when he raises Tabitha. Tabitha opens her eyes, and Peter helps her to her feet. Different from Tabitha, Aeneas is told to stand up and make up his bed (9:40; cf. 9:34), which he does. But Tabitha is rendered totally dependent on Peter. The scene does not allow for Tabitha to respond to the name of Jesus, but to the "sympathetic bond" of Peter's body on her corpse and his touch.

Noticeably, Tabitha says and does nothing after her resuscitation. After Jesus raised the widow of Nain's son, the young man spoke (Luke 7:15). But when Jesus raised Jairus' daughter from death, she said nothing (Luke 8:51–5). In Luke-Acts, when women are resurrected, they are silent and/or they get up and begin serving. But men speak. Brock has noted how Luke in his Gospel gives no commissioning of women to go and tell anyone the news of the resurrected Jesus.[76] Luke continues this pattern in Acts of not commissioning individual women to preach.

Although Peter had cleared the mourning widows from the room while he raised Tabitha, when he presents her alive, he does so in the presence of the saints *and* widows.[77] This phrase, *saints and widows* may signify a community that Tabitha has formed who now attest to the miracle. As in the case when Peter healed Aeneas, the raising of Dorcas is spread throughout Joppa resulting in many new believers (9:42).

THE REDEMPTION OF PETER?

Spencer argues that Peter redeems himself in his treatment of Tabitha and the widows whom she supported. While the apostles were less compassionate toward the Hellenist widows in 6:1–7, here Peter does not

76. Brock, *Mary Magdalene*, 35. This differs in the other three Gospels, where either Jesus or the messengers send Mary Magdalene along or with the other women to proclaim the news. This noticeable absence of the commissioning "significantly influences Mary's status as a resurrection witness."

77. Price (*Widow Traditions*, 100) argues that Peter has rescued Dorcas' clientele from a life of dependence on the church's limited resources. If the group of widows that Dorcas served (cf. 1 Tim 5:16) had had to depend on the church's dole, this dependence "would have meant a significant loss in autonomy and freedom in ministry."

neglect their practical and economic needs when he presents Tabitha alive to the widows and community who depend on her good works.[78] "Like Jesus in Nain, Peter in Joppa brings back to life the widows' most cherished supporter and restores her to them. . . . Supporting widows has been upgraded from secondary to priority status, on a par with prayer, in Peter's ministerial agenda."[79] Thus Spencer incorrectly asserts that Peter has redeemed himself and his fellow apostles "from their miscalculation in Acts 6 . . . [and has removed] all appearance of complicity in neglecting widows." Spencer views the response of the Twelve to the widows, under the leadership of Peter, as dynamic—moving from negative to positive.[80] Spencer fails to note that the works of the widows is differentiated both lexically and semantically from the ministry of the word and of the table to which Peter has devoted himself and to which he consecrated the seven Hellenist men, respectively.

The ministry and care for widows belongs to one who may be one of them; Tabitha may have been a widow, as noted above. Her good works are narrowly defined as is her constituency. Dorcas' good works do not place her among the approved intermediaries; she remains an internal other. Peter's pattern has not changed. Peter's (and the Twelve's) ministry is still distinguished from the ministry of others, especially women as the internal other. In fact, what women like Tabitha do is not even called *ministry*, but *good works*. Tabitha, like the Hellenist widows, is othered in that her activities are not called ministry and her "good works and alms" are not associated with being filled by the Spirit. She need not be full of wisdom, but it is only required that her works be good and that she be considered charitable. The widows are among the internal others, and Peter remains complicit.

TRANSITIVITY ANALYSIS

Transitivity analysis shows the disciples involved in three ergative material processes affecting other persons. The disciples wash Tabitha's body, they place the body in the upper room, and they send two men to find Peter. Peter is a participant-actor in two non-ergative material processes (i.e., kneeling, and praying) and one ergative relational clause

78. Spencer, "Neglected Widows," 731–32.
79. Ibid.
80. Ibid.

(he turned toward Tabitha). Peter is also the participant-actor in two ergative material processes affecting people (he casts all the widows out of the upper room, and he helps Tabitha to her feet).

Transitivity analysis shows that Tabitha is a participant-actor in two ergative material processes (she practiced almsgiving, she made clothing), two non-ergative material processes (she opened her eyes, she sat up), and three relational clauses (she was full of good works; she became sick; she died). Tabitha exercises agency over no individuals but over things (i.e., clothing and almsgiving); otherwise, most of her agency is reflexive. But Peter exercises transitive agency more often over an individual beyond himself, and of course, that person is Tabitha. Again, different from transitivity analysis involving charismatics or *the Jews*, Peter shows more agency in relation to women in the community than toward external others.

Summary and Conclusion

In summary, as with the Hellenist widows, Dorcas' death constitutes a narrative instability. Her death represents the death of a reputable member of the community who provided a much needed service and who may have formed a small local assembly for which she performed good works. Few people merit resuscitation in Luke-Acts or in the Gospels, but she does. Her life is worth saving for the sake of community order, but Sapphira's life was worth taking so as to restore order.

Similar to the Hellenist widows, Dorcas is described in relation to her community. As the internal other who enhances Peter's status as a community leader, performer of miraculous acts, and a restorer of community order, Tabitha plays no active part in the resolution of the instability or the impact of her restoration on the community. When Peter resurrects her, she has no voice; she is silent. This is typical of females who experience resuscitation in the New Testament.

Rhoda, Servant Girl in Mary's House—Acts 12:1–19

Rhoda is the fourth named woman (after Mary, Sapphira, and Tabitha) paired with Peter in Acts. Rhoda enters the story after Herod beheaded the apostle James and subsequently imprisoned Peter. This is the first instance that an apostle is jailed associated with the murder of

another apostle. But this is not the first time the apostles are imprisoned, nor is it the first time the angel of the Lord delivers an apostle
from prison (cf. 5:17–20). However, this is the first time the *ekklēsia*
has gathered to pray for an apostle's release from prison. Even though
the imprisonment of two apostles, Peter and John, follows the first
occurrence of the Greek word *ekklēsia* ("assembly" [of believers]) in
Acts (5:11), the *ekklēsia* did not gather to pray for their release in that
episode. Peter is alone in his incarceration when the angel of the Lord
visits him in prison (12:7). And the emergence of the praying *ekklēsia*
in Mary's house facilitates the entrance of Rhoda.

As some scholars have noted, Rhoda's story is reminiscent of the
scene where the high priest's slave girl recognizes Peter as a follower
of Jesus in Luke's Gospel (Luke 22:56). A slave girl recognizes Peter
again, but in Acts she has a name, Rhoda. Spencer notes that the setting
of both recognition scenes borders between public and private space.
Rhoda is in the private home of Mary, but she participates in a semi-
public gathering of the *ekklēsia*.

REDEEMING PETER: ANOTHER RECOGNITION SCENE

Despite a sympathetic audience (a community of believers to which she
presumably belongs), Rhoda fares no better than the slave girl in Luke's
Gospel.[81] In fact, Luke may be offering a direct parallel between Rhoda
and the slave girl in the Gospel. Both are slave girls in recognition
scenes involving Peter. Both recognize Peter before anyone else does.
In the Gospel, Peter denies the slave girl's recognition of him. In Acts,
the believers deny Rhoda's recognition as real. Luke may be redeeming
Peter's character from the negative portrayal and publicity he received
in Luke's Gospel by placing Peter in this relationship of recognition
with the slave girl Rhoda. In this way, when Peter gains entrance into
Mary's home, Rhoda's testimony is confirmed—something Peter could
not bring himself to do in the recognition scene with the high priest's
slave girl.

Paradoxically, the angel of the Lord has *freed* Peter from prison,
but the human voice he encounters at the door is that of an *enslaved*
girl. A female of slave status is the first to announce Peter's liberation to

81. Spencer, "Out of Mind," 142–44.

the *ekklēsia*. The identification of Rhoda as a slave girl makes her other than Peter in terms of gender and social status.

The voice recognition scene between a newly freed Peter and the slave girl Rhoda is preceded by another recognition scene. Peter does not realize that it was the angel of the Lord who liberated him until he finds himself outside of the city gates and the angel has disappeared (12:3, 11). Peter's appearance at Mary's house and the angel's appearance to Peter in prison both "occasion human confusion and misapprehension."[82] Although Rhoda is convinced that the voice at the door is Peter's, the believers in the house judge her to be "mad." To be diagnosed as mad is to be judged as limited in one's ability to differentiate between what is real and what is not real. But Rhoda insists that the voice belongs to Peter, for whom they have been praying. Even though Rhoda's fellow believers have not heard the voice for themselves, they rationalize that Rhoda has heard the voice of Peter's angel. Either Rhoda's fellow believers are teasing her or they consider it more likely that an angel would visit them than that Peter would have been freed. This "misidentification" of Peter, according to Spencer, further points to the "epiphanic quality" of his appearance.[83]

Hearing Peter, Silencing Rhoda

Peter's voice is the first in a succession of voices: Rhoda's voice announces Peter's re-appearance, the collective voice of the assembly declares Rhoda is mad, and Peter shares his prison ordeal in his own voice.[84] Only the male voices count. Rhoda's voice is othered as representing madness and as unreliable. Seeing is believing. In the end, it did not matter what Rhoda said. After some persistent knocking, the believers open the door. When Peter appears before the *ekklēsia*, he silences everyone in the house including Rhoda, effectively seizing "her role as witness."[85]

Spencer correctly argues that when Peter instructs the group to report all that he has told them to James and the others, he is treating

82. Weaver, *Plots of Epiphany*, 203.

83. Ibid., 205.

84 Ibid., 204.

85. Spencer, "Out of Mind," 145.

all of them, including Mary, as his messengers.[86] However, this blanket instruction precludes Rhoda from being recognized as the exceptional witness that she is. Rhoda was the first to recognize him and the only one to recognize his voice without first seeing him. Rhoda's witness is effectively subordinated. Perhaps as a slave who is charged with opening doors, she is expected to recognize the voices on the other side of the door, even though in this case she is not believed. She was simply performing the duties of a doorkeeper. In spite of her testimony, she remains other over against Peter and the larger community.

The continued subordination of Rhoda—first as a slave and then as a slave whose testimony cannot be trusted (historically, except under torture)—allows that Peter is the one who validates and commissions witnesses and testimonies. Her discernment of Peter's voice and her faith are quickly forgotten so that Peter's commissioning of the group to tell others about what the Lord has done for him is foregrounded.

Peter's encounter with Rhoda in some respects parallels Paul's encounter with Lydia and the Pythian slave girl. Both Lydia and Mary are homeowners. Both the Pythian slave girl and Rhoda are socially marginalized, but they both possess insider information. The Pythian slave girl shares information that identifies Paul and Silas as servants of the most high god; Rhoda identifies the man at the door as Peter. But the Pythian girl loiters on the outside of Lydia's house of prayer. The Pythian slave girl is stigmatized as mad in that an unclean spirit possesses her body; Rhoda is similarly and explicitly defined as mad. In both instances, the testimony of the slave girl is dismissed.

Rhoda's characterization has several functions in the episode. She functions as a "foil for highlighting the praying community's lack of faith even as they were engaged in active intercession to God."[87] Rhoda is also a "stock character" patterned after the motif of the running and mad slave found in ancient comedy.[88] According to Weaver, "the invocation of this stereotype to characterize Rhoda thus has the additional effect of portraying Peter's appearance as a supernatural or quasi-supernatural event."[89] Indeed, Peter's calm manner is contrasted with Rhoda's ecstatic demeanor. Peter patiently continues to knock at the door until someone

---

86. Ibid.
87. Martin, "Acts," 783–84.
88. Ibid.; Morton, "Acts 12:1–19," 67; Johnson, *Acts*, 218.
89. Weaver, *Plots of Epiphany*, 205.

opens it, but Rhoda's failure to open the door enhances Peter's overall miraculous appearance. Rhoda's recognition of Peter's voice does not remove the extraordinary nature of the event. "Peter's attempt to gain admittance to the house, the assembly's identification of Peter as the angel of the Lord, and Peter's concluding pronouncement of God's action" help to portray Peter's appearance as an "angelophany." [90] Rhoda is crucial to this depiction of Peter. This representation of Peter, however, diminishes Rhoda's witnessing role. Most significantly, Rhoda functions not as the keen witness she is, but as the internal other who enhances or contributes to the epiphanic nature of Peter's appearance.

Transitivity Analysis

Transitivity analysis reveals that while Rhoda is central to the narrative instability, she demonstrates less agency in grammatical structure than do the other members of the prayer group. Rhoda is the participant-actor in two ergative mental processes (she hears knocking, she recognizes Peter's voice). Rhoda is a participant-actor in two ergative material processes, but one is negated (she attended to the door, she did not open the door). Rhoda is a participant-actor in one non-ergative reflexive material process (she ran), and two ergative verbal processes (she told what she saw, she persisted in telling). Rhoda affects only an inanimate object (the door) and herself. She speaks as often as the group, but she repeats the same message.

In contrast, the disbelieving group of praying believers are participant-actors in one ergative material process (they opened the door), two ergative perception and mental processes (they saw Peter, they are amazed at Peter), two ergative verbal processes (they said you are mad, they said it is an angel). Although Rhoda is more often a participant-actor than is the group, the group is a participant-actor in verbal clauses the same number of times, but their speech varies. She is central to the narrative instability, but she is not a part of its resolution. The disbelieving group helps to resolve the narrative conflict when they open the door.

Peter is a participant-actor in two ergative material processes (twice, he knocks on the door). He is a participant-actor in one ergative

90. Ibid., 207. Peter's appearance lacks the "thaumaturgical display of the preceding prison angelophany" (208).

verbal clause (he told them) and two relational clauses (he motions with his hand, he left). Peter shows the least amount of agency, but he has the last word. Rhoda's agency as expressed in the grammar is circumscribed by her social status in the story as a female slave. Peter exercises the least transitive agency affecting no people, but this is offset by the fact that he is the object of a miraculous prison release.

SUMMARY AND CONCLUSION

In summary, similar to the other women discussed thus far, Rhoda is not a part of the resolution of the narrative instability. The narrative instability is resolved by the answering of the door, which Rhoda fails to do. Luke contrasts Rhoda's frantic demeanor with Peter's calm disposition; Peter patiently continues to knock on the door until someone opens it, but Rhoda's failure to open the door enhances Peter's overall miraculous appearance. Rhoda is the internal other witness who serves as a foil to construct Peter's miraculous appearance and his authority to commission the believers to tell his story.

Conclusion

I have argued that Luke constructs women in relation to Peter as the internal other. Women function to redeem Peter from his negative characterization in the Gospel of Luke, where he lacks spiritual discernment, lies, and is unable to be a reliable witness about his association with Jesus. The juxtaposition of named women with Peter enhances and privileges Peter's role as an apostolic witness and approved intermediary. In community settings, Peter demonstrates spiritual discernment, administrative authority, ability to resurrect the dead, and authority to commission witnesses.

Sapphira, the Hellenist widows, Tabitha, and Rhoda's speech or speech about them is foregrounded. A feature that is brought into prominence will be foregrounded only if it relates to the meaning of the text as a whole.[91] Foregrounded text invites interpretation or meaning making.[92] As internal others, these women are "largely background

---

91. Halliday, *Linguistic Studies of Text*, 98.
92. Fowler, *Linguistic Criticism*, 73–76.

material,"[93] but their actions or inactivity and their speech or silence are often foregrounded. The foregrounded part of women's characterization invites interpretation not of women's actions but of men's actions as the approved intermediaries. Most often when speech is attributed to these women in relation to Peter, their words are negated or provoke a negative response. Rhoda is told that she is mad or hallucinating, Sapphira is told she has tested God's Spirit, and Tabitha and the widows are simply rendered mute. When contrasted with Peter, these women's false, unbelievable, and muted voices serve to highlight Peter as an authentic witness, a God-inspired and Holy Spirit-filled leader, and an approved intermediary of the gospel.

93. O'Day, "Acts," 311.

4

The Construction of Women as Internal Other and Paul

WOMEN OVERWHELMINGLY CONSTITUTE THE MAJORITY IN FILLING the church's roles, and they are lauded for the talents and gifts they bring as well as for their crucial financial support. More and more women are enrolling in seminaries and divinity schools, so that they consist of fifty to sixty percent or more of ministerial students. Yet, the percentage of women allowed to occupy the role of senior pastor in our churches, particularly in African-American churches, has barely changed.[1] Women who are gifted and who desire to serve as senior pastors or pastors at all continue to be rejected and marginalized; they remain the internal other in many faith communities. Despite the special gifts (financial, intellectual, and spiritual) that many women bring to the table, it remains an unwelcoming table.

Named women that Luke pairs with Paul are gifted and share a special relationship or bond with him, and they are functionally more like him than not. Proximate others are "selflike others." "Selflike others" who can also constitute "internalized others" are "marginalized by the collective self [the larger believing community]." But internal others enjoy a special association to the othering subject.[2] Paul and Prisca are both tentmakers and are coworkers; he and Lydia are brought together through a vision and exercise leadership over some believers; and both Paul and Philip (father of the four daughters) are Hellenists, and by extension so are Philip's daughters. Paul is named as one of the prophets (and teachers) in the Antioch *ekklēsia*; Philip's daughters have the gift

1. See Carpenter, *Time for Honor*.

2. Domínguez (*People as Subject*, 184) is discussing collective Israeli Jews and other Jews.

of prophesying and Prisca is a teacher (13:1). The women Luke pairs with Paul engage in tent making, purple dyes, leading a household, and prophecy. They are a teaching wife, a single head of household, and four virgin daughters. All the women except Lydia are already members of the Jesus movement; Lydia, like Luke, is a Godfearer. All of the women are subordinate to Paul and to a third intermediary, as I demonstrate below. Thus, they experience a double marginalization from the collective self (the church) that has already selected its approved intermediaries; this may be because of their exceptional giftedness as teacher, leader of a house of prayer, and prophesying virgins.

In this chapter I employ the concept of otherness as a framework for analyzing women in relationship to the apostle Paul. Women in relation to Paul are proximate others, and Luke constructs them as internal others. Different from women paired with Paul, women coupled with Peter emerge in the context of problems of community disorder and/or order. This disorder is manifested in the breaking of community rules by Sapphira and Ananias; the temporary death of Dorcas who previously brought stability or order to the lives of widows; the disruption of *diakonia* caused by the complaining associated with the neglect of the Hellenist widows; and the disruption of the community by Peter's imprisonment and release. When women emerge in narrative instabilities with Paul the issues are diverse and do not concern community disorder and order. This is likely to do with the fact that Paul is a travelling missionary unlike Peter who is primarily a leader in the Jerusalem *ekklēsia*,[3] which is depicted as the headquarters of the Jesus movement. Paul has been sent to preach to numerous and various communities. Yet, the function of women remains the same. Women function as a foil to enhance the characterization of the apostle Paul as an approved intermediary. But women paired with Paul may be well known community leaders as revealed by their giftedness in Acts (cf. Rom 16:3; 1 Cor 16:19).[4]

---

3. Peter does travel outside of Jerusalem (see 8:14–15; chs. 10–12).

4. Schüssler Fiorenza (*In Memory of Her*, 50) asserts that Paul expresses gratitude toward women in his letters because he "had no other choice than to do so because women like Junia and Prisca already occupied leadership functions and were on his level in the Christian movement."

Lydia—Acts 16:8–16a, 39

The first named woman paired with Paul holds a leadership position. Lydia is a leader of a synagogue gathering and the head of her household. Lydia's story is linked with the story of the unnamed Pythian slave girl, a charismatic other. The episode involving Rhoda at Mary's house is the only time two named women appear in the same story in Acts. Interestingly, in both narratives we find both a female householder and a slave girl, but here, as noted, the Pythian girl is nameless. In neither case do we find an explicit mistress/slave relationship between the female householder and the female slave. Both Rhoda/Mary and Lydia/Pythia slave girl narratives are associated with imprisonments and release, one precedes the narrative and one follows.

A Linguistic Project of Othering: Them and Us

Similar to other named women analyzed thus far, Lydia is at the center of a narrative instability. However, this is an instability facilitated by a vision. In the vision, a man requests that Paul come to Macedonia to help "us." The pronoun us infers that the man in the vision is an insider and/or one who identifies himself with the people who need Paul's help. Pervo argues that whoever the man in the vision is, he speaks for the larger Macedonian community, both males and females.[5] However, this may not necessarily be the case, especially since Paul's activities are primarily confined to Lydia's people (her synagogue gathering and her household) to whom he also returns after his release.[6] The us maybe limited to Lydia's household and/or those who gather at her house of prayer. The type of help being solicited is not specified, but we can assume that the help falls within the range of Paul's previous activities as an apostle to the Gentiles. This is confirmed by the household conversions.

This evaluation of us as needing Paul's help constructs the us as other than Paul. But once Paul's assistance is accepted by the us, they become internal others. Readers are introduced to three primary characters, namely, Lydia, the Pythian slave girl, and the jailer. We have dealt

5. Pervo, Acts, 403.

6. Contra Pervo (Acts, 404), who argues that Lydia is "the host of a house church, not its explicit head."

with the Pythia slave girl as an external other in chapter 1. Here we focus on Lydia. Lydia constitutes a proximate other as a Godfearer, and she becomes an internal other after her acceptance of the gospel. Therefore, I conclude that Lydia and her people are the explicit *us* in Paul's vision. It is while visiting Lydia's synagogue that Paul meets the Pythian slave girl. And Paul's exorcism of the Pythian slave girl leads to his imprisonment, as noted in chapter 1. Lydia is referred to twice by name, once when she is introduced into the story (16:14) and once at the end of the story when the apostles are leaving Philippi (16:39).[7] This framing of events in Philippi with the mention of Lydia's name may indicate that Paul and Silas were summoned primarily to help Lydia and her household, as noted above. The Pythian girl represents the casualty of a charismatic external other, but the jailer constitutes an incidental household conversion (especially since Luke attached no household conversion to Peter's miraculous release and given Luke's tendency to create parallels between Peter and Paul narratives).

Some scholars have argued that Luke's account of the women in Philippi is likely fictitious.[8] Whether or not this is true, Luke represents this story as authentic in two says. First, Luke provides a proper name for Lydia, as well as specific personal background information. Second, Luke prefaces Paul's entrance into Macedonia with a divine vision from which Paul and Silas conclude "God has summoned *us* to preach the gospel to *them*" (16:9–10). Otherness is inscribed in this theological assertion, which discursively establishes a polarity between *us* and *them*, as noted above. And the etching of this distinction between *us* and *them* into a discursive theological framework has the force of sanctioning this paradigmatic polarity of otherness.

Significantly, immediately after the man in the vision summons Paul and Silas to help *us* at verse 16:10, the first-person plural *we* narrator emerges: "*We* immediately desired to go out to Macedonia." The *we* could include Timothy whom Paul recently picked up in Lystra (16:1–5) or the *we* could simply be inclusive of Luke.[9] In any case, this *we* stands in contrast to *us*. Already otherness is inscribed in the narrative in this juxtaposition of pronouns distinguishing between *us* and *them*.

---

7. Fitzmyer, *Acts*, 585. The name Lydia corresponds to the district in Asia Minor from which she came.

8. Abrahamsen, "Women at Philippi," 17–18.

9. Fitzmyer (*Acts*, 580) says most likely Luke includes himself; contra Haenchen, *Acts*, 430.

BORDERING CROSSING AND THE CONSTRUCTION OF OTHERNESS

The dichotomous *us* and *we* situated within the context of Paul's border crossing into Europe to help an unknown, but proximate other, reinforces Luke's project of otherness. God summons Paul and Silas to Macedonia, and they end up in Philippi. According to Acts, Philippi is a leading Macedonian province and a Roman colony. Historically, Philippi was not the capital of Macedonia.[10] Paul's entrance into Philippi (synecdochically Macedonia) marks the beginning of his ministry in Europe, and Lydia becomes the first convert in Europe.[11] Jeffrey Staley offers a post-colonial reconstruction of Paul's ministry in Macedonia, and he argues that the author constructs "Macedonia otherness and territory." He aptly notes that Paul's journey to Macedonia differs from his other journeys because it begins with a vision.[12] The vision, according to Staley, is based on an imperial ideology whereby divine authorization is given for a transfer of power, which can be seen in Paul's exorcism of the Pythonic girl whose story falls on the heels of Lydia's encounter with Paul. Exorcism in foreign territory, Staley argues, becomes an overt act connecting political oppression with accusations of demon possession. Macedonia is both foreign territory and Roman territory.[13] It is chiefly "Paul's encounter with the two women that marks the territory as a major border crossing" in Acts.[14] This account of the two women (Lydia and the Pythoness) is the only one where we discover two women on the border. These women embody "the ambiguous relationship of the colonized to the colonizer."[15] The women have no say in the type of help, let alone that they need help. When Philip crossed over into Samaria, as noted in chapter one, he also encountered two borderland males—Simon and the Ethiopian eunuch.

---

10. Fitzmyer, *Acts*, 584; Conzelmann, *Acts*, 130; Koester, *Introduction*, 108. The capital of Macedonia was Thessaloniki.

11. Schüssler Fiorenza, *In Memory of Her*, 167; also Reimer, *Women in Acts*, 71.

12. Staley, "Changing Woman," 122, 123.

13. Ibid., 124–125.

14. Ibid., 126.

15. Ibid., 127, 130.

PAUL FINDS A FEMALE GODFEARER AND LEADER OF A HOUSE OF PRAYER

Once in Philippi, Paul and Silas wait until the Sabbath day to venture outside the city gate and hike toward the river. They thought[16] that they would find a *proseuchē* somewhere near the river.[17] The uncertainty or cognition expressed by the Greek verb *nomizō* (to consider or think) signifies the contingent and limited nature of information they received from the vision. The narrative does not make an explicit link between the vision and the search for a *proseuchē*. But given Paul's pattern throughout the text, an explicit link is not necessary. Paul customarily attends a Jewish synagogue wherever he travels, and this is no exception.

The number of Jews and Godfearers living in Philippi is likely relatively few, and thus the uncertainty about the location of *proseuchē*. That the Pythian slave girls' masters accuse Paul and Silas of being Jews who are disturbing the city might signify the scarcity or even absence of Jews in the region. It may also demonstrate that any Jews that reside in the city are inconspicuous. The request for help suggests that Macedonia needed special assistance and that it had been relatively neglected territory with regard to the Gentile mission.

Historically, a *proseuchē* was known as a place of prayer, and later possibly an informal kind of synagogue. Synagogues were often built near the water for convenience of performing prescribed ritual washings.[18] Josephus mentions a decree allowing the Jews to establish their "*proseuchae*" at the seaside.[19] Luke usually refers to Jewish gatherings as synagogues, and not as a *proseuchē*, as Price notes.[20] Lydia's *proseuchē* is likely not a gathering of Jewish people, per se, but of Godfearers.

---

16. A Western textual witness, D, has *edokei*: "there *seemed* to be a *proseuchē*."

17. Ryan ("Lydia," 285–89) argues that Lydia's *proseuchē* was not a synagogue since women would not have been present in a synagogue. Similarly, Thomas ("Place of Women," 117) argues that the women at Lydia's *proseuchē* were "deprived of the systematic teaching of the law usually associated with the synagogue and because they were women they could not found a synagogue." In fact, Thomas asserts there did not appear to be any synagogue at Philippi and probably very few Jews.

18. Greeven, "*proseuchē*," *TDNT* (1968) 807–8.

19. Josephus, *Ant.* 14.10.22 (258). Josephus (*Mos.* 277) also mentions a *proseuchē* as a large edifice that had the capacity to hold a large number of people.

20. Price, *Widow Traditions*, 226. Some scholars use this single irregularity to infer the use of a source (Gerd Lüdemann, *Early Christianity*, 182).

Lydia herself is a Godfearer (*sebomenē ton theon*) from the city of Thyatira (16:14–15). She possibly learned to worship the God of Israel from Jewish persons she met while conducting her business, but otherwise the text is silent. This religious designation would not necessarily mean that Lydia was solely devoted to Judaism. As a Godfearer, Lydia is not a proselyte, namely a full convert to Judaism. Because of the "fluidity of religious belief" during the first century CE, it would not be unusual for a "Christian" (or Godfearer) to continue pagan religious practices.[21] Lydia is one of three named persons in Acts explicitly called a "Godfearer." The other two are Cornelius (10:2, 22) and Titus Justus (18:7). Nevertheless, Paul and Silas join the gathering and speak to the women about the "word of the Lord" and God's grace (cf. 13:40–4, 44; 14:3).

Lydia is also identified by her provenance and occupation. She deals in purple cloth, one of the industries for which the city of Lydia was known. In antiquity, purple cloth was often associated with luxury and wealth. Diodorus Siculus of Sicily (first-century BCE Greek historian) reports that a certain Zaleucus, a lawmaker, wrote a new system of law in order to curb the desire for "harmful luxury and wanton living." Zaleucus, as Diodorus reports, legislated that a freeborn woman was not allowed to adorn herself in gold jewelry or garments with purple borders unless she was a courtesan.[22]

Because Lydia trades in purple cloth, some scholars presume that she is a wealthy woman. Johnson argues that Lydia's trade together with her status as a homeowner "suggests that she is a woman of substantial means."[23] Schüssler Fiorenza argues that even as a dealer in purple cloth, Lydia was not necessarily a wealthy woman. She further suggests that Lydia "might have been a freedwoman, since she came from the East and sold purple goods which were luxury items. She was not necessarily, therefore, a wealthy high-born woman."[24] Historically, if Lydia were a freedwoman rather than a high-born woman, this would not have prevented her from amassing some material wealth, especially if she practiced a lucrative trade. Although most freedwomen were not wealthy, some did accumulate a great deal of wealth through their

21. Valerie Abrahamsen, "Women at Philippi," 22.

22. Diodorus of Sicily, 12.20.20–21.

23. Johnson, *Acts*, 292–93; also Ryan, "Lydia," 288; Martin, "Acts," 784.

24. Schüssler Fiorenza, *In Memory of Her*, 178.

trades.[25] Lydia probably fared pretty well economically since purple cloth was a luxury item in demand, sold primarily to upper-class persons, and was considered a sign of royalty.[26]

Schottroff argues that each element of the story betrays Lydia's power. Lydia has gained power by way of her "relationship with the God of Israel," first without knowing the gospel and then as a Christian.[27] A second way in which Lydia has attained power, Schottroff argues, is as a community leader who has united and shaped the lives of members of her community.[28] But the scuffle with the Pythian's masters in the immediately following episode where they accuse Paul and Silas of being Jews who are disturbing the city suggests that being a Godfearer or a member of the Jesus movement would *not* have been considered a position of power in that context.

"And Your Young *Men* Shall Have Visions"

According to the text, it is solely because of the vision that Paul finds himself preaching to Lydia and her people. Peter's encounter with Cornelius in chapter 10 offers an interesting comparison with Lydia and Paul's meeting. Lydia is the first European convert, and Cornelius is arguably the first Gentile convert.[29] "Lydia functions as a kind of female 'Cornelius.'" Lydia becomes the first Gentile woman to respond to Paul's preaching and this "expands an issue that originally centered on men."[30]

25. Pomeroy, *Goddesses*, 198–99. "Legislation concerning the right to bequeath property was applicable to freedwomen worth at least 100,000 sesterces, and the Emperor Claudius offered the privileges of women who had four children to freedwomen who invested in the grain market for feeding of Rome. Both of these provisions show that there were some wealthy freedwomen, and the resources of many freedwomen were obvious from the burial places they were able to construct for themselves and at times for their own slaves and freedmen. A few wealthy freedwomen are known by name. Lyde, freedwoman of the Empress Livia, owned at least four slaves, and the fictitious Fortunata of the Satiricon, who wallows in riches, is probably a caricature of real freedwomen."

26. 1 Macc 10:62–65; Josephus, *Ant.* 2.5.7; 10.11.2; 11.3.2; *J. W.* 6.8.3 (390).

27. Schottroff, *Let the Oppressed*, 135; see also Reimer, *Women in Acts*, 101–9.

28. Ibid.

29. Depending on how one views the Ethiopian eunuch, he could be considered the first Gentile convert in Acts.

30. According to Matson (*Household Conversion*, 152–53) Lydia's story falls after the Jerusalem Council and this has both theological and practical implications. Also

Similar to Cornelius (10:48b), Lydia invites the apostles to stay at her house. Matson categorizes the two stories as household conversion stories, which he reads against the mission of the Seventy-two (Luke 10:5–7). Both stories contain the *oikos* formula, namely, "with all her/his household,"[31] although in the Lydia story we have an abbreviated version: "and her house" (*kai ho oikos autēs*). In the Cornelius story, both Peter and Cornelius receive a vision. Cornelius is portrayed as worthy of the vision because God has remembered his prayers and almsgiving (10:4). The angel of God tells Cornelius to send men to Joppa and summon Peter who is at Simon's house by the sea (10:3–6). On the following day, as the men are arriving at Simon's house, a hungry Peter has a vision while praying on the roof. The vision prepares Peter to receive the visitors from Cornelius. Peter then travels to Cornelius's house where he preaches to the entire household, who subsequently receive the Holy spirit and are baptized (11:44–47).

Why does Luke not depict Lydia as receiving a vision as he does Cornelius? Unlike Cornelius, Lydia is depicted as a passive recipient of the apostles' help. She is the differentiated other, and eventually the internal other. She is not made aware of Paul or his impending visit. But Paul, similar to Peter, is made aware through a vision that somebody in Macedonia needs his help. Lydia's household does not expressly listen to Paul's words.[32] Contrary to what most often occurs, Luke does not mention a divided audience of believers and nonbelievers in response to Paul's preaching in synagogue gatherings.[33] The Lord is the only participant-actor in an ergative material process clause in this episode: the Lord "opens" Lydia's heart. Paul speaks words, and Lydia listens to his words, but it is the Lord who affects the person. Lydia and her house are baptized.[34]

Lydia's conversion results in a Jewish person entering into a Gentile's house and sitting down to eat with them.

31. Matson (*Household Conversion*, 113, 135, 147) uses the term "type-scene" for these household conversion narratives.

32. Ibid., 147.

33. Price, *Widow Traditions*, 227.

34. Thomas ("Place of Women," 118) argues that as the first candidate for baptism at Philippi "Lydia points to a new status for women, a new estimate of the value and place of woman in the purpose of God." Reimer (*Women in Acts*, 114), focusing on historical reconstruction, credits Paul with the establishing a house church in Lydia's home.

As the head of her household, Lydia invites Paul and his companions to stay at her house (16:15b). Lydia may have been a widow, which would account for her status as head of household.[35] The narrative does not explicitly state that Paul visited Lydia's house, but the narrative abruptly transitions from Lydia's request that Paul and Silas stay at her house (that is if they have found her faithful) to Paul and Silas returning to the *proseuchē* and meeting the Pythian slave girl (16:15–16). The phrase "stay at my house" likely meant the reception of hospitality and the sharing of daily fellowship at Lydia's house or at the gathering of the *proseuchē* by the riverside.[36] Lydia becomes the first person, male or female, to host Paul since his official commissioning in Acts 13.[37] Paul visited with Titus Justus, a Godfearer like Lydia, at his home next door to the synagogue (18:7).

Luke attributes the following urgent appeal to Lydia following the baptism: "If you consider me to be faithful in the Lord, remain with me. Remain and enter into my house" (16:16). This appeal reflects a woman seeking the approval of her superiors.[38] It shows that she is dependent on Paul and Silas to evaluate whether she is faithful in the Lord. Thus, Lydia is represented as appropriating as part of her own self-identity, the construction of herself as internal other within the Jesus movement.[39]

SUMMARY AND CONCLUSION

In summary, Lydia is part of a narrative tension. The author and/or narrator has made the evaluative statement that someone in Macedonia needs Paul's help. The reader does not know whom the narrator/author is specifically indicating. The tension is resolved as the story progresses. As is the case for other women in Acts, Lydia has no part in the resolution of the narrative tension. Lydia never states a need for Paul's help,

35. Ryan, "Lydia," 289.

36. Martin ("Acts," 784) argues that Lydia's *proseuchē* is in her home.

37. Matson, *Household Conversion*, 147.

38. Reimer (*Women in Acts*, 124) argues that the pressure Lydia puts on the apostles to stay at her house is a "sign of her solidarity with them. She recognizes possible hostilities the Roman authorities would have toward Jews, and she extends hospitality for their protection."

39. O'Day ("Acts," 310) argues that "Lydia's house quickly became a center of the Philippian church, but Luke does not credit [her] with any leadership role in that development."

nor is she allowed to define the parameters of the help that is offered in her behalf. *God* has sent Paul and Silas to Macedonia through a vision. Like Peter and Cornelius, it is because of a vision that Paul meets Lydia. But unlike Cornelius, Lydia has no vision of her own. If Luke's version of the Joel prophecy contradicts his portrayal of silent women in Acts, it is on target with its declaration that "your young men shall see visions." The only persons in Acts who have visions are males, namely Peter, Cornelius, and Paul (9:10, 12; 10:3, 17, 19; 11:5; 12:9; 18:9; 26:19). Lydia is the internal other. She is proximate other to Cornelius with regard to her need to hear the gospel and with respect to the conversion of her entire household. She is proximate to Cornelius in that they are both Godfearers; she proximate in that both she and Cornelius reflect boundary crossing for both Peter and Paul. She responds positively to Paul's preaching. Consequently she and her household are baptized, and she continues an association with Paul beyond her baptism. Yet, Lydia does not receive the Holy Spirit in the same way Cornelius' household does after their baptism. Lydia is still other, but after her baptism, she is the differentiated internal other.

Prisca—Acts 18:1–28

Prisca is introduced into the narrative with her husband Aquila. They practice the same tent making trade as Paul. The couple arrive in Corinth after being expelled from Italy by decree of Claudius (18:2a). The three are in Corinth together for a while, and when Paul leaves Corinth for Ephesus, he takes them with him. But when Paul departs from Ephesus, Priscilla and Aquila are left there. It is in Ephesus during Paul's absence that the couple encounter a third party named Apollos. Apollos is a Jew and native of Alexandria (18:24). Prisca and Aquila's encounter with Apollos both enhance Luke's portrait of Paul and also differentiates Prisca and Aquila from Paul.

Prisca offers some readers a welcome contrast to Luke's portrayal of Sapphira (and Ananias). Prisca's name most often occurs prior to her husband's name (18:18; 18:26; Rom 16:3; 2 Tim 4:19; Cf. 1 Cor 16:19).[40] Some scholars argue that this unique nominal prefixing signi-

---

40. D and other witnesses transpose the names, placing Prisca's name first at Acts 18:26.

fies that "she was the more active and significant of the two."[41] That the couple's names are always mentioned together with her name sometimes occurring first implies, according to O'Day, that Prisca and Aquila "were genuine partners in ministry and that Priscilla was not Aquila's subordinate."[42] Indeed, this pairing of their names and the sometimes sequential priority of her name may signal that Prisca experienced some kind of equality with her husband, but she never functions apart from him. As Beauvoir notes, "the Church expresses and serves a patriarchal civilization in which it is meet and proper for woman to remain appended to man."[43] Prisca remains appended to Aquila. Or perhaps Aquila is appended to Prisca so that she does not appear autonomous, out of place, or even perceived inappropriately as a married, yet detached woman, working with the single unattached Paul. Even in Paul's letters, they are always together, and they co-lead a church in their home (1 Cor 16:19).

THE SUBORDINATION OF PRISCA TO APOLLOS AND TO PAUL: WHO CARES ABOUT BAPTISM?

Luke does, however, subordinate Prisca and Aquila to both Paul and Apollos (and by extension Apollos to Paul) (cf. 1 Cor 1:12; 3:4–6; 22; 4:6; 16:12). Apollos is a very capable preacher of the word, knowledgeable about the Scriptures, accurate, and charismatic, but he knew (*epistamai*) only John's baptism (8:25). After Prisca and Aquila hear Apollos speak boldly in the synagogue, they initiate a private teaching session in order to explain more accurately the Way to him (8:26). Here is the second time in the Alexandrian text that Prisca's name is mentioned first. The "Western" text witness, D, places Aquila first. That manuscript witness was probably uncomfortable with the appearance of Prisca taking the lead to instruct a male. This private lesson is reminiscent of Philip and the Ethiopian eunuch. The grammar may imply that when Prisca and Aquila took Apollos aside, they brought him into their home. Or the implication may be that they simply "drew him aside." In any case, the sense is that the couple *privately* instructed Apollos. Seim argues that this means that "even Priscilla is portrayed as . . . active in instruction

41. E.g., Seim, *Double Message*, 129.
42. O'Day, "Acts," 311.
43. Beauvoir, *Second Sex*, 171.

only at home. [Similar to Philip's daughters and Lydia] [s]he is not granted any dispensation from the rule that women's activity belongs to the house."[44]

The depiction of Prisca and Aquila as more knowledgeable about the way of God than Apollos may show that he had less access to "the way," and/or he had no personal mentoring by Paul, as they had (18:26). Paul's first letter to the Corinthians infers that he had a relationship with Apollos, for Paul strongly encouraged (*polla parekalesa*) Apollos to visit the saints in Corinth, but "[Apollos] was not willing"; Apollos would visit when he has a good opportunity (*eukaireō*; 1 Cor 16:12). Prisca and Aquila are not depicted as preaching or teaching while Paul is present, only in his absence (18:4). After the couple's lesson with Apollos, it is the "brothers," and not the couple, who write to the disciples in Achaia to welcome Apollos (18:27). One might expect that Prisca and Aquila as Paul's coworkers would write such letters, which in Acts is a sign of authority (15:23; 1 Cor 16:3). So it is in the encounter with Apollos that Prisca, especially if the more frequent ordering of her name is an indication of her importance and competency, is differentiated as other; she cannot publicly teach or recommend Apollos to the brothers.

Luke tells Prisca's story "with as much restraint and decorum as possible."[45] While it is true that Luke avoids explicitly describing Apollos as full of the Spirit,[46] this is no less true of women in Acts, especially the ostensibly gifted ones such as Prisca. Luke does not fail to inform his readers that Apollos was fervent in the Spirit. Although Apollos knew only the baptism of John, after being privately instructed by Prisca and Aquila he is shown as engaging in the identical activities as Paul. "[H]e powerfully refuted the Jews in public showing by the scriptures that the Messiah is Jesus" (18:28 NRSV).

Similar to Apollos, the Ephesians in the following episode (ch. 19) had only received John's baptism; therefore, Paul baptized them in the name of the Lord Jesus. After the baptism, the Ephesians speak in tongues and prophesy, both of which at times are connected with the reception of the Holy Spirit. But after Prisca and Aquila teach Apollos, who knew only the baptism of John, they do not baptize him nor is there any manifestation of the Spirit, such as speaking in tongues or

44. Seim, *Double Message*, 130.

45. O'Day, "Acts," 311.

46. Johnson, *Acts*, 332.

prophesy. Thus, the couple have less authority than Paul and are differentiated from him as the internal others. Neither Prisca nor her husband are approved intermediaries. Philip was at least able to baptize the Samaritans to whom he preached. Prisca and Aquila rate below Philip. The couple's encounter with Apollos differentiates them from Paul who does baptize other disciples in the same city of Ephesus. But similar to Philip, Prisca and Aquila cannot lay hands on Apollos and anoint him with the Holy Spirit, even though he does not know about the baptism of the Holy Spirit (since he only knows John's baptism). Obviously, they are not approved to do so. They are subordinate to Apollos, to Philip, and to Paul. Prisca (and Aquila) are the internal others.

The question arises whether the absence of a baptism after the instruction has anything to do with the portrait of Apollos as Paul's "rival" in his first letter to the Corinthians. That letter reveals that some believers had polemically aligned themselves with different charismatic figures—Paul, Apollos, Cephas, or Christ himself—and were quarreling among themselves (1 Cor 1:12). Significantly, there Paul argues that he baptized none of them and that Christ did not send him to proclaim the gospel "by wisdom of the word" (*ouk en sophia logou*; 1 Cor 1:17). This statement may be a jab at Apollos, who is described as a learned or eloquent man (*anēr logios*) in Acts.

Summary and Conclusion

In the absence of Paul, Prisca together with her husband Aquila teach Apollos, but the grammatical priority shown Prisca does not change her image as a married woman in a patriarchal society, subordinate to her husband. Regardless of the prior mention of her name, her status as a coworker with her husband remains the same. And they both are depicted as subordinate to Paul, Apollos, and to the "brothers." In terms of transitivity, Prisca and Aquila affect another person, whereas other women (i.e., Philip's daughters and Lydia) in Acts do not. Prisca and Aquila are involved in two ergative clauses that affect another person. They both take Apollos aside and they teach him. However, like the other women in the second half of Acts, Prisca's actions enhance and exalt males as approved intermediaries, i.e., Paul and Apollos. She is differentiated from approved intermediaries as the internal other.

Philip's four Prophesying Virgin Daughters—Acts 21:9

The narrative instability into which Luke introduces Philip's four daughters concerns the predicament of whether or not Paul should go to Jerusalem. As with the other women studied thus far, they function to foreground and enhance the activity and speech of male approved intermediaries. Philip's daughters also serve as a foil to reinforce Paul's subordinate apostolic standing relative to the Jerusalem leadership and/or *ekklēsia* (which, of course, differs from how the Galatian's account positions him in relation to the Jerusalem leadership). Philip's daughters are not the focus of the narrative instability, but they are physically and dis-functionally located at the center of it. However, they serve as unassuming bystanders.

Paul receives three warnings about the dangers awaiting him in Jerusalem: from disciples in Tyre (21:3–4), from the Judean prophet Agabus, and from the *we* narrator and the people of Caesarea (18:9–12). The disciples of Tyre and the prophet Agabus warn Paul at the unction of the Holy Spirit. Yet, Paul is determined to go to Jerusalem, in spite of having received warnings through persons who claim to be motivated by the Holy Spirit. In Caesarea, Paul is staying with the Hellenist evangelist Philip (21:7–8).

Seim argues that Paul's visit to Philip's house shows a shift from the public city sphere to the more private domestic sphere.[47] This is an occasion when women's giftedness is circumscribed in the semi-private space of the home. With the presence of other disciples and the intrusion of Agabus, Philip's home is transformed from private space to semi-public space. In this semi-public or semi-private space of their father's home, the four daughters remain utterly dependent on the graciousness of males, not unlike Lydia, who must strongly impose upon Paul and Silas to deem her worthy of their acceptance of her hospitality.

The narrator introduces Philip's daughters as an extension of their father's identity: "and belonging to him were four daughters, virgins, prophesying" (21:9). They are not simply women; they are the daughters of their father, and they have never been wives of men. And the last thing we know about them is by way of a present participle tacked on to the end of the sentence. Here, Luke avoids the noun form of the finite verb meaning "to prophesy." This is similar to how Simon's activities are

47. Seim, *Double Message*, 145.

represented in chapter one; he is practicing magic; but not a magician. Luke does, however, use the feminine Greek noun *prophētis* at Luke 2:36 to describe Anna. But Anna, like the four daughters, is robbed of the opportunity to prophesy. Instead Simeon prophesies, even though he is not called a prophet, but a righteous and devout man who is anticipating the comforting of Israel (2:25). The Holy Spirit rested on and guided Simeon, and he presents an oracle (the *Nunc Dimittis*; 2:25–32). Strategically, Luke depicts the daughters not as holding the prophetic office, but only of practicing the gift. When women in Luke-Acts possess gifts associated with prophetic utterance, they utter not a word.

The women's relationship to their father and to other males is foregrounded. Luke does not want to emphasize their gift, but only their relationship to their father as daughters and to other males as virgins. While it is historically true that in the Second Temple period most daughters were identified in relationship to their fathers, as evidenced in both inscriptions and other legal documentation such as marriage contracts and deeds of sale,[48] Seim argues that the operable word here may be "daughters," which "may function as an internal reference to Acts 2:17[-21] [Joel quotation]," even though such a characterization serves to glorify their father and to evince his "spiritual capacity."[49] It is possible that Luke expects his readers to make a lexical referential connection between Philip's "daughters" and the daughters who shall prophesy in the last days. But, for them the last days have yet to arrive.

And Your Daughters Shall Not Prophesy: One Male Prophet Trumps Four Hellenist Virginal Prophesying Daughters

In contrast to Philip's daughters, Agabus is first identified as a prophet from Judea and secondly by name (21:10). This is consistent with Luke's earlier introduction of Agabus (11:27–28) as one of the prophets who had come from Jerusalem to Antioch: "One of them by the name of Agabus stood up" (11:28). While the four daughters are functionally proximate to the prophets from Jerusalem in that they are also capable

---

48. Ilan, *Jewish Women*, 55. This is also likely the case for daughters outside of Palestine.

49. Seim, *Double Message*, 180–81.

of prophesying, they are distinguished by the fact that unlike the male prophets, they, as mentioned above, do not hold the prophetic office.

Males who surround the four daughters are depicted as speaking through the Holy Spirit, while the four virginal prophesying daughters do not speak. As noted above, the disciples at Tyre, through the Spirit, forewarn Paul about going to Jerusalem. Agabus prophesies by the Spirit about what will happen to Paul should he go to Jerusalem. Just as he had previously warned *through the Spirit* about the great famine that would afflict the entire world during Claudius's reign (ch. 11). The use of the term *prophesying* in connection to the four daughters implies that they are a vehicle of the Holy Spirit, but the giftedness of the four daughters is ignored with Agabus, a male prophet, in the house.

Even though the daughters are present, Agabus travels from Judea to deliver a prophetic oracle to Paul at Philip's house (21:10). Reimer argues that the reason Agabus prophesies and not the women is because he has come directly from Judea and thus was in a better position to interpret the situation in Jerusalem.[50] When Agabus traveled from Judea to Antioch to prophesy about the famine, are we also to say that from his position in Judea he was more able than any other prophet to interpret what the situation would be throughout the world during Claudius's reign (11:17–28)? No doubt Agabus is given special consideration as a male prophet from Judea.

Agabus uses a visual prop in the deliverance of his prophetic words. He binds his own hands and feet with Paul's girdle to dramatize the fate awaiting Paul in Jerusalem (21:11; cf. Jer 13:1–8). The animated manner in which Agabus behaves highlights the still life portrait of Philip's four daughters. The daughters are inactive, while Agabus is *über*-active. Using historical imagination, Price argues that it was the four virgins who prophesied and donned the "oracular girdles" in Luke's original source. Price associates these four women with the existence of a community of widows similar to those in the *Testament of Job*. He also argues that the practice of glossalalia is linked with both Philip's and Job's daughters.[51]

50. Reimer, *Women in Acts*, 248–49. Seim (*Double Message*, 182) argues that this overshadowing of the four women by Agabus may be because of Luke's use of distinct sources. "The brief notice about Philip and his daughters is taken from the itinerary source and shows this source's special interest in those providing hospitality in various places."

51. Price, *Widow Traditions*, 66–70. Price also dates Acts closer to the time of 1

And Again Your Daughters Shall Not Prophesy:
Your Father's an Apostle and an Hellenist

Philip's daughters are attested in several extra-biblical sources. They were known of (possibly from Acts) in North Africa and among the Montanists, who highly valued prophetic revelation. In fact two well-known female prophetesses, Priscilla and Maximilla, belonged to the Montanist movement. Many of its members were females with the gift of prophetic revelation. However, in those sources the daughters belong to the *apostle* Philip. For instance, Papias (first half of the second century CE), the bishop of Hierapolis, says that the *apostle* Philip who lived in Hierapolis (not Caesarea as in Acts) with his daughters told him a wonderful story.[52] Eusebius (fourth century), the bishop of Caesarea, wrote that Proclus (the Montanist) in the *Dialogue of Gaius* (Presbyter of Rome, early third century) mentioned that Philip and his four daughters were buried in Hierapolis.[53] Similarly, Polycrates (second century), bishop of Ephesus, in a letter to Victor (late second century), bishop of Rome, says that the *apostle* Philip is buried in Hierapolis with two aged virgin daughters, and a third rests in Ephesus.[54] Clement of Alexandria (late second century) wrote that Philip married his daughters off.[55] But Luke has written that the *evangelist* Philip had four virgin daughters who prophesied. Matthews argues that the discrepancy occurred because Luke likely had access to two lists, one of the twelve apostles and one of the Seven Hellenists. And the name Philip, according to Matthews, was the only one that occurred on both lists; Luke understood this name to refer to two different individuals. But the apostle Philip and the evangelist Philip are the same person.[56]

Tim, when there is more evidence for the existence of an order of widows to which the virgins would have attached themselves.

52. Eusebius, *Eccl. Hist.* 3.39.

53. Ibid., 3.31.

54. Ibid.

55. Ibid., 3.30.

56. Matthews (*Philip*, 18–19) argues that scholars tend to give precedent to Luke's presentation of the evangelist Philip in Acts, but Papias offers a first-hand and contemporaneous witness about the apostle Philip's four daughters. "The convergence of the second-century evidence, the onomastic data, and recent projections on the Christian population at the end of the first century render plausible the hypothesis that the confusion of the 'two Philips' has its origin with Luke" (18). I do not find Matthew's onomastic argument convincing. He states that there were only seven "Philip's" men-

Interestingly, the extra-biblical sources focus on the women's sexual status as virgins rather than on any prophetic gift they might have possessed. None of the sources attribute prophetic utterance to the women. In the extra-biblical sources, Philip is elevated to apostle and the women are no longer prophetesses. Perhaps the four women are rendered silent even in extra-biblical texts so that Philip is not upstaged in his own home and certainly not by his own daughters. The promotion of Philip from evangelist to apostle and the absence of any mention of a prophetic gift associated with the daughters may constitute two sides of the same coin—the exaltation of Philip.

Philip as one of the Seven Hellenists has already been constructed as subordinated to the Twelve. He and the Seven Hellenists were entrust with the table ministry in Jerusalem before the persecution surrounding Stephen. Afterwards, Philip preached the gospel in Samaria, but he was not permitted to confer the Holy Spirit on the people of Samaria, as discussed above in chapter 1. Instead Peter and John travel down from Jerusalem to lay hands on Philip's converts. And here the prophet Agabus has traveled from Judea to Philip's home where Paul is a guest to do what Philip's daughters are not permitted to do.[57] If Philip's daughters had prophesied, it would be difficult to explain why Philip's daughters were permitted to be a medium for the Holy Spirit's utterances, but their father Philip was not permitted to confer the Holy Spirit upon his converts in the Samaritan city. Perhaps the silencing of Philip's daughters also represents the continued subordination of the Hellenists to the Twelve.

---

tioned in extant sources between 330 BCE and 200 CE, four of which come from Josephus, two from the New Testament (Mark 3:18; Acts 1:13; 6:5; 8; 21:8) and one in Eusebius. The fact that the majority of these names have "upper class associations" and given the relatively small Christian populations of the period is a basis for assuming that the Philip in Acts and in the Gospel are the same (16–18). Matthews asserts, it seems to me, that since the name occurs so few times for all extant literature, and when it does occur it is usually among the nobility, that it is impossible for two men by the same name to exist among the relatively small group of Christians. But the sample is too small to draw such a definitive conclusion. Also, in none of the texts in which the name appears was the author interested in reporting about individuals from the lower classes by name, for the most part, unless they were instigators of trouble or they stood out for some other reason.

57. Matthews (*Philip*, 18) argues that "Luke's failure to properly identify Philip is not due to any alleged bias against Hellenist traditions, but in a perceived conflict between two pieces of traditional information."

Why are Philip's daughters introduced into the narrative? What purpose do they serve? Conzelmann sees no apparent reason for their mention given their silence. But he adds their literary presence, whether resulting from Luke's sources or their historical prominence, "contributes to the mood for the following episode."[58] Price argues that Luke chose not to extricate them from his source, but he was compelled to depict the women as silent. In this way, similar to Anna in Luke's Gospel, Philip's daughters "were showcased as embodiments of the tame Christian woman who sits in silence while men speak the word of God."[59] An appeal to source criticism is an insufficient explanation. Luke could have easily edited any sources he may have used, especially given his willingness to alter Scripture, e.g., the Joel prophecy.

In fact, the only other mention of prophesying women is in Luke's appropriation of the Joel prophecy from the Septuagint (Greek translation of the Hebrew Bible). The narrator's declaration that the outpouring of the Holy Spirit at Pentecost was a fulfillment of the Joel prophecy implies that both men *and* women were prophesying. Luke's Gospel privileges Mary as a virgin who prophesies, but of course Mary is located in Judea, and she is, of course, the mother of Jesus. Maybe Luke wants to maintain Jerusalem and/or Judea not only as the headquarters of the *ekklēsia* but also as the prophetic center of the Jesus movement. The only approved intermediaries of the *ekklēsia* in Jerusalem are males, as is reinforced in the selection of Judas' replacement (1:25) who must be male. And certainly in such an important matter as Paul's journey back to Jerusalem, which ultimately leads to Rome, the prophetic word should come from the prophetic center. Agabus's prophecy is not meant to deter Paul but to reinforce the fact that what will happen in Jerusalem is a part of God's providence and to foreground Paul's continued determination to do the will of God in spite of known opposition. And the paradoxical silent, prophesying daughters function to foreground all the male activity and masculine tenacity that surrounds them.

In Luke's Gospel, three women are identified as prophets or prophesy but only one is a virgin (cf. Deborah, Judg 4:4; Huldah, 2 Kgs 22:14; Miriam, Exod 15:20; Noadiah, Neh 6:14).[60] As noted above, Mary the

---

58. Conzelmann, *Acts*, 178. Reimer (*Women in Acts*, 248–49) surmises that Philip's daughters might have been so well known that Luke was compelled to mention them.

59. Price, *Widow Traditions*, 63.

60. Rabbinic tradition adds four more prophetesses: Sarah, Hannah, Abigail, and Esther (b Meg 14a).

mother of Jesus is the only virgin in Luke's Gospel to which Luke attributes prophetic utterances (1:27, 35, 46–55).[61] Some textual witnesses attribute Mary's words in Luke's Gospel to Elisabeth (1:46), however, Elisabeth was not a virgin.[62] Luke does not call Mary a prophet, and she is not explicitly said to be full of the Spirit. However, the Spirit overshadows her, and she carries the Holy Spirit's seed. Subsequently, the Magnificat is attributed to Mary (1:46–55). Anna, on the other hand, is explicitly a prophetess (*prophētis*; 2:36), as noted above. Similar to Philip's daughters, Anna does not give an oracle. Anna, like Phillip's daughters, is co-opted by a male, namely Simeon, who is not explicitly referred to as a prophet. Both Anna and Phillip's daughters were unmarried. Anna is an elderly widow[63] and the four daughters are virgins.

The silencing of individuals whose gift is constitutive of speech marginalizes and subordinates them to others with the same gift but who are permitted to speak. Although the women are proximate to Agabus and to Paul as members of the Jesus movement and with the same gifted ability, they are rendered as internal other. Perhaps another reason for the marginalization of the four virgins, in addition to their gender, is that they are daughters of one of the Seven Hellenists. In the same way that Peter and John went down to Samaria to lay hands on those who were baptized as a result of Philip's preaching, so Agabus had to go down from Judea to prophesy to Paul.

Summary and Conclusion

In summary, Philip's four daughters are introduced into the narrative instability involving the danger awaiting Paul should he go down to Jerusalem and the necessity for a prophetic word. But like other women in Acts, they are not a part of the resolution of the instability. They have no speech or say in the resolution. The four daughters are proximate to both Paul and Agabus. But like other women who are proximate to approved intermediaries, they serve to foreground male leadership and activity. The daughters stand in contrast to Agabus' highly dramatic prophecy. Although Paul does not allow Agabus' prophecy to hinder

61. Cf. Matt 1:23; 25:1–11; 2 Cor 7:25, 28, 34; Rev 14:4; *Gos. Phil.* 17b, 73, 82, 83; *Prot. Jas.* 9.1, 10.1, 15.2, 16.1, 19.3).

62. a b 1*; Ir[arm] Or [lat mss] Nic.

63. Thurston, "Who Was Anna?"

him from going to Jerusalem, the prophecy is true nonetheless. Agabus' prophecy foregrounds the danger awaiting Paul and foregrounds Paul's determination and courage to do what God has already ordained. The women are constructed as the opposite image of all the activity and potential activity; they are passive and silent.

The theological implication is that the Holy Spirit has chosen the male prophet over the female prophets. The invited interpretation or meaning making is that men's prophetic words are more important. Women's prophetic words are not necessary, when capable men are available, even if the men have to travel from Judea to Caesarea.

Conclusion

The named women paired with Paul function to enhance his status as an approved intermediate of the gospel to the Gentiles. Paul and other males can do what gifted females cannot do. We find a different type of disorder operating among women who are situated in narrative instabilities with Paul. This disorder is manifested in the fact that the women are out of place by "conventional" norms inscribed in the text, namely, that only male approved intermediaries exercise certain gifts and authority and all others are subordinated to them. Perhaps they are ahead of their time, at least in the narrative. This disorder consists of the mention of Prisca's name prior to her husband's, the encounter of Lydia as the only female head of a house of prayer, and four virginal prophesying females among the Hellenists. They are ostensibly gifted women. Prisca and her husband Aquila are well versed in the Way, so much so that they instruct the eloquent and knowledgeable Apollos. Lydia has organized her own prayer gathering so that when Paul and Silas arrive at her house of prayer they have an attentive audience. Philip's four daughters are Hellenist virgins with prophetic gifts. Prisca teaches Apollos, but he is the one evaluated as eloquent; Lydia is a single woman, head of household, and organizer of a *proseuchē*, but she needs Paul's help and relies on Paul to count her as faithful to the Lord. Agabus, a prophet, must come all the way from Judea to prophecy for Paul even though *four* virginal women with the gift of prophecy are already in the house. All are subordinated to approved intermediaries within the community of faith even as their gifts are known. They are internal others.

Conclusion

IN THIS BOOK I HAVE EMPLOYED A THEORY OF OTHERNESS AS A FRAME-
work for examining how certain characters are constructed in the book
of Acts in relation to the apostles as the approved intermediaries of the
gospel. I have analyzed how Luke constructs other charismatic figures
and *the Jews*, who are proximate others to the apostles as the external
others. The external other poses a threat to the progress of the mission, but that threat is short-lived. The apostles, who demonstrate the
least amount of transitive agency, who are in fact quite passive acting
in the grammar, render the charismatic others impotent. The apostles'
demonstration of superior authority and power is primarily revealed in
speech acts.

I have also attempted to show that when Acts is read closely there
is no sound justification for labeling all charismatic others as magicians.
The charismatic others are functionally proximate to the apostles, and
it is this proximity that Luke attempts to overcome by constructing difference. Likewise, *the Jews* are proximate to the apostle Paul and his
traveling companions on several levels, but Luke constructs them as the
stereotypical and aggressive external other motivated by jealousy to oppose the Gentile mission.

Named women in Acts serve to enhance the leadership capabilities
and image of the apostles Peter and Paul. Women when juxtaposed with
Peter contribute to and enhance his image as the apostle who stands in
the place of God before the community, who can discern when members are lying to God, who engenders order out of disorder, and who
commissions members to tell about what God has done for him. Luke
locates women who emerge in narrative instabilities with Peter at the
center of disorder, but they are never involved in the restoration of that
order. They remain silent except to speak a lie or to demonstrate their
madness before the community. Women who are juxtaposed with Paul
are gifted women, but they constitute anomalies—a grammatically pri-
oritized male-teaching wife, a materfamilias and leader of a synagogue

group, and four virginal daughters with the gift of prophecy. In the text world of Acts, they are ahead of their time. Consequently, they constitute the marginalized, subordinated, and muted internal other.

In both fictional and nonfictional and in secular and sacred texts, character construction has a synthetic aspect. I cannot know for certain what Luke intended. He is not here for me to ask him. If he were here for me to pick his brain, there is still no guarantee I would fully comprehend or that he could (or did) perfectly articulate what he meant to accomplish in the book of Acts. But every attempt to represent a portrait of the real world is just that, a re-presentation, a mimesis. And a mimesis never constitutes an exact replica; it cannot be that which it is not. There is also the matter of human bias and fallibility that I mentioned in the introduction. When a narrative such as Acts is read and understood as being perfectly congruent with the event(s) and characters it represents, then some mimetic aspects of the text and its characterization are allowed to function as paradigmatic models for and prescriptive for social practice. GeBauer and Wulf assert the following about the reciprocal nature of representational language:

> The medium of representational language is the focus of an interplay between pressures exerted by society and counter pressure exerted by authors . . .[M]eanings of verbal expressions in literary texts . . . are ultimately citations of social practice. . . . Inversely, literary mimesis can intervene in the mimetic process of social practice. It can provide models for the latter and influence the way in which social behavior is undertaken, alter codifications, or create new ones; it can persuade empirical persons of their ability to experience the world similarly to models found in literature, if they adopt the codification models they find there. In short, literary mimesis can itself flow back into social practice.[1]

As responsible and intelligent readers and interpreters of sacred texts, we should become intentionally conscious of othering projects inherent in the text so that we do not reinscribe or imitate them in actual social practice or in public discourse. Not only must we read critically constructions of otherness in texts and contexts, but also we should be careful not to imitate the practice of othering persons whom we do not understand or whom we fear out of ignorance. We need to

1. GeBauer and Wulf, *Mimesis*, 15, 23.

resist the demonization of others even when we see evidences of it in the biblical text. Even in the biblical text otherness is polemically and politically constructed. If we believe that God has placed his image upon all humans, in spite of our fallibilities, then the other is like me and in some ways the other is a mirror image of me. "The Other has a face, and it is a sacred book in which good is recorded . . . this difference, this otherness is rich and valuable, it is a good thing. . . . Yet it remains that as I encounter the other I too am Other."[2]

2. Kapuscinski, *Other*, 35.

Bibliography

Abrahamsen, Valerie. "Women at Philippi: The Pagan and Christian Evidence." *JFSR* 3 (1987) 17–30.

Akmajian, Adrian, et al. *Linguistics: An Introduction to Language and Communication.* 4th ed. Cambridge: MIT Press, 1995.

Alexander, Loveday. *The Preface to Luke's Gospel: Literary Convention and Social Context of Luke 1:1–4 and Acts 1:1.* SNTSMS 78. Cambridge: Cambridge University, 1993.

Arator. *On the Acts of the Apostles (De Actibus Apostolorum).* Translated by Richard J. Schrader. Atlanta: Scholars, 1987.

Archer, Léonie J. *Her Price Is beyond Rubies: The Jewish Woman in Graeco-Roman Palestine.* JSOTSup 60. Sheffield: Sheffield Academic, 1990.

———. "The Role of Jewish Women in the Religion, Ritual and Cult of Graeco-Roman Palestine." In *Images of Women in Antiquity,* edited by Averil Cameron and Amelie Kuhrt, 273–87. Detroit: Wayne State University Press, 1983.

Arlandson, James Malcolm. *Women, Class, and Society in Early Christianity: Models from Luke-Acts.* Peabody, MA: Hendrickson, 1997.

Ascough, Richard S. "Benefactions Gone Wrong: The 'Sin' of Ananias and Sapphira in Context." In *Text and Artifact in the Religions of Mediterranean Antiquity: Essays in Honor of Peter Richardson,* edited by Stephen G. Wilson and Michael Desjardins, 91–110. Waterloo, ON: Wilfrid Laurier University Press, 2000.

Austin, J. L. *How to Do Things with Words.* Oxford: Oxford University Press, 1962.

Bakhtin, M. M. *The Dialogic Imagination: Four Essays.* Translated by Caryl Emerson and Michael Holquist, edited by Michael Holquist. Austin: University of Texas Press, 1981.

Barbi, Augusto. "The Use and Meaning of (*Hoi*) *Ioudaioi* in Acts." Translated by Matthew J. O'Connell. In *Luke and Acts,* edited by Gerald O'Collins and Gilberto Marconi, 123–42. Mahwah, NJ: Paulist, 1991.

Barrett, C. K. *A Critical and Exegetical Commentary on the Acts of the Apostles.* ICC. Edinburgh: T. & T. Clark, 1994–98.

———. "Light on the Holy Spirit from Simon Magus (Acts 8, 4–25)." In *Les Actes des Apôtres: Traditions, Rédaction, Théologie,* edited by J. Kremer, 281–95. Leuven: Leuven University Press, 1977.

Barth, Fredrik. "Boundaries and Connections." In *Signifying Identities: Anthropological Perspectives on Boundaries and Contested Values,* edited by Anthony P. Cohen, 17–36. London: Routledge, 2000.

Bassler, Jouette M. "The Widows' Tale: A Fresh Look at 1 Tim. 5:3–16." *JBL* 103 (1984) 23–41.

Bauckman, Richard. *Gospel Women: Studies of the Named Women in the Gospels.* Grand Rapids: Eerdmans, 2002.

————. "James, Peter, and the Gentiles." In *The Missions of James, Peter and Paul: Tensions in Early Christianity*, edited by Bruce Chilton and Craig Evans, 91–142. Novum Testamentum Supplements 115. Boston: Brill, 2005.

Beauvoir, Simone de. *The Second Sex*. New York: Knopf, 1957.

Beck, Rosalie. "The Women of Acts: Foremothers of the Christian Church." In *With Steadfast Purpose*. Waco, TX: Baylor University 1990.

Bede (The Venerable). *Commentary on the Acts of the Apostles*. Translated by Lawrence T. Martin. Cistercian Studies 117. Kalamazoo, MI: Cistercian, 1989.

Benbassa, Esther, and Jean-Christophe Attias. *The Jew and the Other*. Translated by G. M. Goshgarian. Ithaca, NY: Cornell University Press, 2004.

Bergmeier, R. "Die Gestalt des Simon Magus in Act 8 und in der simonianischen Gnosis–Aporien einer Gesamtdeutung." *ZNW* 77 (1986) 267–75.

Beyschlag, Karlmann. *Simon Magus und die christliche Gnosis*. WUNT 16. Tübingen: Mohr/Siebeck, 1974.

Blasi, Anthony J. *Making Charisma: The Social Construction of Paul's Public Image*. New Brunswick: Transaction, 1991.

Bolt, Peter G. "Mission and Witness." In *Witness to the Gospel: The Theology of Acts*, edited by I. Howard Marshall and David Peterson, 191–214. Grand Rapids: Eerdmans, 1998.

Bonz, Marianne Palmer. *The Past as Legacy: Luke-Acts and Ancient Epic*. Minneapolis: Fortress, 2000.

Booth, Wayne. *The Rhetoric of Fiction*. 2nd ed. Chicago: University of Chicago Press, 1983.

Bovon, François, editor. *The Apocryphal Acts of the Apostles*. Harvard Divinity Studies. Cambridge: Harvard University Press, 1999.

————. "L'importance des médiations dans le projet théologique de Luc." *NTS* 21 (1974) 23–39.

————. *Luke 1: A Commentary on the Gospel of Luke 1:1—9:50*. Translated by Christine M. Thomas. Hermeneia. Min-neapolis: Fortress, 2002.

————. *Luke the Theologian: Thirty-three Years of Research (1950–1983)*. Translated by Ken McKinney. Princeton Theological Monograph Series 12. Allison Park, PA: Pickwick, 1987.

————. "The Reception of the Book of Acts in Late Antiquity." In *Contemporary Studies in Acts*, edited by Thomas E. Phillips, 66–91. Macon, GA: Mercer University Press, 2009.

————. "'Schön hat der heilige Geist durch den Propheten Jesaja zu euren Vätern gesprochen' (Acts 28:25)." *ZNW* 75 (1984) 226–32.

Boyarin, Daniel. *Border Lines: The Partition of Judaeo-Christianity*. Philadelphia: University of Pennsylvania, 2004.

Boyarin, Jonathan. "The Other Within and the Other Without." In *The Other in Jewish Thought and History: Constructions of Jewish Culture and Identity*, edited by Laurence J. Silberstein and Robert L. Cohn, 424–52. New York: New York University Press, 1994.

Brawley, Robert L. *Luke-Acts and the Jews: Conflict, Apology, and Conciliation*. SBLMS 33. Atlanta: Scholars, 1987.

————. *Text to Text Pours Fourth Speech: Voices of Scripture in Luke-Acts*. Bloomington: Indiana University Press, 1995.

Brock, Ann Graham. *Mary Magdalene, the First Apostle: The Struggle for Authority.* HTS 51: Cambridge: Harvard University Press, 2003.

Brooten, Bernadette J. *Women Leaders in the Ancient Synagogue: Inscription Evidence and Background Issues.* Brown Judaic Studies 36. Chico, CA: Scholars, 1982.

Brown, Peter. "The Rise and Function of the Holy Man in Late Antiquity." *JRS* 61 (1971) 81–101.

———. "Sorcery, Demons, and the Rise of Christianity from Late Antiquity into the Middle Ages." In *Witchcraft, Confessions & Accusations*, edited by Mary Douglas, 18–34. London: Tavistock, 1970.

Bultmann, Rudolf. *The Theology of the New Testament.* New York: Scribner, 1955.

Burkert, Walter. *Greek Religion.* Translated by John Raffan. Cambridge: Harvard University Press: 1985.

Cadbury, Henry J. "Four Features of Lucan Style." In *Studies in Luke-Acts*, edited by Leander E. Keck and J. Louis Martyn, 87–102. Nashville: Abingdon, 1966.

———. *The Making of Luke-Acts.* Peabody, MA: Hendrickson, 1999.

Carpenter, Delores. *A Time for Honor: A Portrait of African American Clergywomen.* Atlanta: Chalice, 2001.

Carter, Warren. "The Crowds in Matthew's Gospel." *CBQ* 55 (2002) 54–67.

Cerfaux, L. "La gnose simonienne: Nos sources principales." *RSR* 15 (1925) 489–511.

Chariton. *Chaereas and Callirhoe.* Translated by B. P. Beardon. In *Collected Ancient Greek Novels*, edited by B. P Reardon. Berkeley: University of California Press, 1989.

Chatman, Seymour. *Story and Discourse: Narrative Structure in Fiction and Film.* Ithaca, NY: Cornell University Press, 1978.

Cohen, Charles L. "Two Biblical Models of Conversion: An Example of Puritan Hermeneutics." *ChH* 58 (1989) 182–96.

Cohen, Shaye J. D. *The Beginnings of Jewishness: Boundaries, Varieties, and Uncertainties.* Berkeley: University of California Press, 1999.

———. *From the Maccabees to the Mishnah.* Library of Early Christianity 7. Philadelphia: Westminster, 1987.

———. "Was Timothy Jewish (Acts 16:1–3)? Patristic Exegesis, Rabbinic Law, and Matrilineal Descent." *JBL* 105 (1986) 251–68.

Collins, John J. "A Symbol of Otherness: Circumcision and Salvation in the First Century." In *"To See Ourselves as Others See Us": Christians, Jews, "Others" in Late Antiquity*, edited by Jacob Neusner and Ernest S. Frerichs, 163–86. Scholars Press Studies in the Humanities Series. Chico, CA: Scholars, 1985.

Conzelmann, Hans. *Acts of the Apostles.* Translated by James Limburg et al. Hermeneia. Philadelphia: Fortress, 1987.

Cook, Michael. "The Gospel of John and the Jews." *RevExp* 84 (1987) 259–71.

———. "The Mission to the Jews in Acts: Unraveling Luke's 'Myth of the 'Myriads.'" In *Luke-Acts and the Jewish People*, edited by Joseph B. Tyson, 102–23. Minneapolis: Augsburg, 1988.

Cooper, Kate. *The Virgin and the Bride: Idealized Womanhood in Late Antiquity.* Cambridge: Harvard University Press, 1996.

Cromer, Gerald. "The Creation of Others: The Case Study of Meir Kahane and His Opponents." In *The Other in Jewish Thought and History: Constructions of Jewish Culture and Identity*, edited by Laurence J. Silberstein and Robert L. Cohn, 281–304. New York: New York University Press, 1994.

Culpepper, Jonathan. "Inferring Character From Texts: Attribution Theory and Foregrounding Theory." *Poetics* 23 (1996) 335–61.

D'Angelo, Mary Rose. "The ANHP Question in Luke-Acts: Imperial Masculinity and the Deployment of Women in the Early Second Century." In *A Feminist Companion to Luke*, edited by Amy-Jill Levine, 44–69. Sheffield: Sheffield Academic, 2002.

———. "(Re)presentations of Women in the Gospel of Matthew and Luke-Acts." In *Women & Christian Origins*, edited by Ross Shephard Kraemer and Mary Rose D'Angelo, 171–95. New York: Oxford University Press, 1999.

———. "Women in Luke-Acts: A Redactional View." *JBL* 109 (1990) 441–61.

Darr, John A. *Herod the Fox: Audience Criticism and Lukan Characterization.* Sheffield: Sheffield Academic, 1998.

———. *On Character Building: The Reader and the Rhetoric of Characterization in Luke-Acts.* Literary Currents in Biblical Interpretation. Louisville: Westminster John Knox, 1992.

Davis, Steven L. "Women in the Third Gospel and the New Testament Apocrypha." In *"Women Like This": New Perspectives on Jewish Women in the Greco-Roman World*, edited by Amy-Jill Levine. Early Judaism and Its Literature 1. Atlanta: Scholars, 1991.

Dehandschutter, B. "La persécution des chrétiens dans les Actes des Apôtres." In *Les Actes des Apôtres: Traditions, Rédaction, Théologie*, edited by J. Kremer, 541–46. Leuven: Leuven University Press, 1977.

Delebecque, Édouard. "La misaventure des fils de Scévas selon ses deux versions (Actes 19:13–20)." *RSPT* 66 (1982) 225–32.

Derrett, J. Duncan M. "Ananias, Sapphira, and the Right of Property." *DownRev* 89 (1971) 225–32.

———. "Simon Magus (Act 8 9–24)." *ZNW* 77 (1982) 52–68.

Diakité, Dianne. "The Myth of 'Voodoo': A Caribbean American Response to Representations of Haiti." *Religion Dispatches.* Online: http://www .religiondispatches.org/archive/politics/2204/the_myth_of_"voodoo"%3A_a_ caribbean_american_response_to_representations_of_haiti.

Dibelius, Martin. *Studies in the Acts of the Apostles.* Translated by Mary Ling. New York: Scribner, 1956.

Dickie, Matthew W. *Magic and Magicians in the Greco-Roman World.* New York: Routledge, 2001.

Dijk, Teun A. van. "Discourse, Power and Access." In *Texts and Practices: Readings in Critical Discourse Analysis,* edited by Carmen Rosa Caldas-Coulthard and Malcolm Courthard. London: Routledge, 1996.

Diodorus of Sicily. *The Library of Histories.* Translated by C. H. Oldfather. 12 vols. LCL. Cambridge: Harvard University Press, 1968.

Domínguez, Virginia R. *People as Subject, People as Object: Selfhood and Peoplehood in Contemporary Israel.* Madison: University of Wisconsin Press, 1989.

Dornisch, Loretta. "A Woman Reads the Gospel of Luke: Introduction and Luke 1: The Infancy Narratives." *BibRes* 42 (1997) 7–22.

Duncan, James. "Sites of Representation: Place, Time and the Discourse of the Other." In *Place Culture/Representation*, edited by James Duncan and David Ley, 39–56. New York: Routledge, 1993.

Dunn, James D. G. *The Acts of the Apostles.* Valley Forge, PA: Trinity, 1996.

Dupont, Jacques. *Nouvelles études sur les Actes des Apôtres*. Paris: Cerf, 1984.

Edwards, Douglas. "Surviving the Web of Roman Power: Religion and Politics in the Acts of the Apostles, Josephus, and Chariton's *Chaereas and Callirhoe*." In *Images of Empire* edited by Loveday Alexander, 179–201. JSOTSup 122. Sheffield: JSOT, 1991.

Ellis, E. Earle. *Prophecy and Hermeneutic in Early Christianity*. Grand Rapids: Baker, 1993.

Epp, Eldon. *The Theological Tendency of Codex Bezae Cantabrigiensis in Acts*. SNTS Monograph Series 3. 1966. Reprinted, Eugene, OR: Wipf & Stock, 2001.

Esam, Kahlil N. "Grounding in Text Structure." *AusJL* 22 (2002) 173–90.

Esler, Philip F. *Community and Gospel in Luke-Acts: The Social and Political Motivations of Lucan Theology*. SNTS Monograph Series 57. Cambridge: Cambridge University Press, 1987.

Fairclough, Norman. *Analysing Discourse: Textual Analysis for Social Research*. London: Routledge, 2003.

Fitzmyer, Joseph A. *The Acts of the Apostles*. AB 31. New York: Doubleday, 1998.

Flanagan, N. "The Position of Women in the Writings of St. Luke." *Marianum* 40 (1978) 288–304.

Fleischman, Suzanne. *Tense and Narrativity: From Medieval Performance to Modern Fiction*. Austin: University of Texas Press, 1990.

Fludernik, Monica. *Toward a 'Natural' Narratology*. London: Routledge, 1996.

Fowler, Roger. *Linguistic Criticism*. Oxford: Oxford University Press, 1986.

————. "On Critical Linguistics." In *Texts and Practices: Readings in Critical Discourse Analysis*, edited by Carmen Rosa Caldas-Coulthard and Malcolm Courthard, 3–14. London: Routledge, 1996.

Frend, W. H. C. *The Rise of Christianity*. Philadelphia: Fortress, 1984.

Freyne, Sean. "Vilifying the Other and Defining the Self: Matthew's and John's Anti-Jewish Polemic in Focus." In *"To See Ourselves as Others See Us": Christians, Jews, "Others" in Late Antiquity*, edited by Jacob Neusner and Ernest S. Frerichs, 117–43. Scholars Press Studies in the Humanities Series. Chico, CA: Scholars, 1985.

Fusco, Vittorio. "Luke-Acts and the Future of Israel." *NovT* 38 (1996) 1–17.

Gager, John G. *Curse Tablets and Binding Spells from the Ancient World*. New York: Oxford University Press, 1992.

Garrett, Susan R. *The Demise of the Devil: Magic and the Demonic in Luke's Writings*. Minneapolis: Fortress, 1989.

Gaventa, Beverly Roberts. *The Acts of the Apostles*. Abingdon New Testament Commentaries. Nashville: Abingdon, 2003.

GeBauer, Gunter, and Christoph Wulf. *Mimesis: Culture, Art, Society*. Translated by Don Reneau. Berkeley: University of California Press, 1992.

Genette, Gérard. *Narrative Discourse: An Essay in Method*. Translated by Jane E. Lewin. Ithaca, NY: Cornell University Press, 1980.

Gerrig, Richard J. "The Construction of Literary Character: A View from Cognitive Psychology." *Style* 24 (1990) 380–92.

Gilbert, Gary. "The Disappearance of the Gentiles: God-fearers and the Image of the Jews in Luke-Acts." In *Putting Body & Soul Together: Essays in Honor of Robin Scroggs*, edited by Virginia Wiles, Alexandra Brown, and Graydon F. Snyder, 172–84. Valley Forge, PA: Trinity, 1997.

Goodman, Martin. *Mission and Conversion: Proselytizing in the Religious History of the Roman Empire*. New York: Oxford University Press, 1994.

———. "Opponents of Rome: Jews and Others." In *Images of Empire*, edited by Loveday Alexander, 222–38. JSOTSup 122. Sheffield: JSOT Press, 1991.

Green, Joel B. "Internal Repetition in Luke-Acts: Contemporary Narratology and Lukan Historiography." In *History, Literature, and Society in the Book of Acts*, edited by Ben Witherington III, 283–99. Cambridge: Cambridge University Press, 1995.

Green, Joel B., and Richard B. Hays. "The Use of the Old Testament by New Testament Writers." In *Hearing the New Testament: Strategies for Interpretation*, edited by Joel B. Green, 222–38. Grand Rapids: Eerdmans, 1995.

Haar, Stephen. *Simon Magus: The First Gnostic?* BZNW 119. Berlin: de Gruyter, 2003.

Haenchen, Ernst. *The Acts of the Apostles*. Translated by Bernard Noble and Gerald Shinn. Philadelphia: Westminster, 1971.

———. "Gab es seine vorchristliche Gnosis?" *ZTK* 49 (1952) 316–49.

Hägg, Tomas. *The Novel in Antiquity*. Oxford: Blackwell, 1983.

Halliday, M. A. K. *Explorations in the Functions of Language*. London: Arnold, 1973.

———. *An Introduction to Functional Grammar*. London: Edward Arnold, 1985.

———. *Language as Social Semiotic: The Social Interpretation of Language and Meaning*. Baltimore: University Park Press, 1978.

———. *Linguistic Studies of Text and Discourse*. Collected Works of M. A. K. Halliday 2. Edited by Jonathan Webster. London: Continuum, 2002.

Halliday, M. A. K., and Christian M. I. M. Matthiessen. *Construing Experience through Meaning: A Language-Based Approach to Cognition*. London: Continuum, 2000.

Harnack, Adolf von. *The Acts of the Apostles*. Translated by J. R. Wilkinson. London: Williams & Norgate, 1909.

Harrill, Albert J. "The Dramatic Function of the Running Slave Rhoda (Acts 12.13–16) A Piece of Greco-Roman Comedy." *NTS* 46 (2000) 150–257.

———. *Slaves in the New Testament: Literary, Social and Moral Dimensions*. Minneapolis: Fortress, 2005.

Heintz, Florent. *Simon "Le Magicien". Actes 8, 5–25 et l'accusation de magie contre les prophètes thaumaturges dans l'antiquité*. Paris: J. Gabalda, 1997.

Heliodorus. *An Ethiopian Story*. Translated J. R. Morgan. In *Collected Ancient Greek Novels*, edited by B. P. Reardon. Berkeley: University of California Press, 1989.

Hemer, Colin J. *The Book of Acts in the Setting of Hellenistic History*. Tübingen: Mohr/Siebeck, 1989.

Hever, Hannan. "Territoriality and Otherness in Hebrew Literature of the War of Independence." In *The Other in Jewish Thought and History: Constructions of Jewish Culture and Identity*, edited by Laurence J. Silberstein and Robert L. Cohn, 236–57. New York: New York University Press, 1994.

Higgins, A. J. B. "The Preface to Luke and the Kerygma in Acts." In *Apostolic History and the Gospel: Biblical and Historical Essays Presented to F. F. Bruce on His 60th Birthday*, edited by W. Ward Gasque and Ralph P. Martin, 78–91. Exeter, UK: Paternoster, 1970.

Hopper, Paul J., and Sandra A. Thompson. "Transitivity in Grammar and Discourse." *Language* 56 (1980) 251–99.

Hull, John M. *Hellenistic Magic and the Synoptic Tradition*. Studies in Biblical Theology 2/28. Naperville, IL: Allenson, 1974.

Ilan, Tal. *Integrating Women into Second Temple History*. Peabody, MA: Hendrickson, 2001.

———. *Jewish Women in Greco-Roman Palestine*. Peabody, MA: Hendrickson, 1996.

Janowitz, Naomi. *Magic in the Roman World. Pagans, Jews and Christians*. New York: Routledge, 2001.

Jauss, Hans Robert. *Toward An Aesthetic of Reception*. Minneapolis: University of Minnesota Press, 1982.

Jervell, Jacob. *Die Apostelgeschichte. Übersetzt und erklärt von Jacob Jervell*. Göttingen: Vandenhoeck & Ruprecht, 1998.

———. "The Church of Jews and Godfearers." In *Luke-Acts and the Jewish People*, edited by Joseph B. Tyson, 11–20. Minneapolis: Augsburg, 1988.

———. *Luke and the People of God: A New Look at Luke-Acts*. Edited by Joseph B. Tyson. Minneapolis: Augsburg, 1972.

———. *The Unknown Paul: Essays on Luke-Acts and Early Christian History*. Minneapolis: Augsburg, 1984.

Ji, Yinglin, and Dan Shen. "Transitivity and Mental Transformation: Sheila Watson's *The Double Hook*." *LL* 13 (2004) 335–48.

Johnson, Luke Timothy. *The Acts of the Apostles*. SP 5. Collegeville, MN: Liturgical, 1992.

Juel, Donald. *Luke-Acts: The Promise of History*. Atlanta: John Knox, 1984.

Kapuściński, Ryszard. *The Other*. Translated by Antonia Lloyd-Jones. London: Verso, 2008.

Karris, R. "Women and Discipleship in Luke." *CBQ* 56 (1994) 1–20.

Käsemann, Ernst. "Paul and Nascent Catholicism." *JTC* 3 (1967) 14–27.

Kaylania, Chapman. "Earthquake in Haiti–God's Wake Up Call." Kaylania's Blog, January 13, 2010. Online: http://kaylaniachapman.com/blog/2010/01/earth quake-in-haiti-gods-wake-up-call.htm.

Keck, Leander E., and J. Louis Martyn, editors. *Studies in Luke-Acts: Essays Presented in Honor of Paul Schubert*. 2nd ed. Philadelphia: Fortress, 1980.

Kee, Howard Clark. "Defining the First-Century CE Synagogue: Problems and Progress." *NTS* 41 (1995) 481–500.

———. "The Jews in Acts." In *Diaspora Jews and Judaism: Essays in Honor of, and in Dialogue with A. Thomas Kraabel*, edited by J. Andrew Overman and Robert S. MacLennan, 183–95. Atlanta: Scholars, 1992.

Klauck, Hans-Josef. *Magic and Paganism in Early Christianity: The World of the Acts of the Apostles*. Translated by Brian McNeil. Edinburgh: T. & T. Clark, 2000.

Klawans, Jonathan. *Ritual and Moral Impurity in the Hebrew Bible and Ancient Judaism*. New York: Oxford University Press, 2000.

Klawiter, Frederick C. "The Role of Martyrdom and Persecution in Developing the Priestly Authority of Women in Early Christianity: A Case Study of Montanism." *ChH* 49 (1980) 251–61.

Klutz, Todd. *The Exorcism Stories in Luke-Acts: A Sociostylistic Reading*. SNTS Monograph Series 129. Cambridge: Cambridge University Press, 2004.

———. "Naked and Wounded: Foregrounding, Relevance and Situation in Acts 19:13–20. In *Discourse Analysis and the New Testament: Approaches and Results*, edited by Stanley E. Porter and Jeffrey T. Reed, 258–79. JSNTSup 170. Sheffield: Sheffield Academic, 1999.

Koch, Dietrich-Alex. "Geistbesitz, Geistverleihung und Wundermacht: Erwägungen zur Tradition und zur lukanischen Redaktion in Act 8 5–25." *ZNW* 77 (1986) 64–82.

Kodell, Jerome. "Luke's Use of Laos, 'People,' especially in the Jerusalem Narrative (Lk 19,28–24.53). *CBQ* 31 (1969) 327–43.

Koester, Helmut. *History and Literature of Early Christianity.* Vol. 2 of *Introduction to the New Testament.* FF. Philadelphia: Fortress, 1982.

———. *History, Culture and Religion of the Hellenistic Age.* Vol. 1 of *Introduction to the New Testament.* 2nd ed. New York: de Gruyter, 1995.

Kolenkow, Anitra Bingham. "A Problem of Power: How Miracle Doers Counter Charges of Magic in the Hellenistic World." *SBLSP* (1976) 105–10.

Kopas, J. "Jewish and Women: Luke's Gospel." *ThT* 43 (1986) 192–202.

Koperski, Veronica. "Luke 10:38–42 and Acts 6:1–7: Women and Discipleship in the Literary Context of Luke-Acts." In *The Unity of Luke-Acts,* edited by J. Verheyden. BETL 142. Leuven: Leuven University Press, 1999.

Kraabel, Thomas. "The Disappearance of the 'God-Fearers.'" In *Diaspora Jews and Judaism: Essays in Honor of and in Dialogue with A. Thomas Kraabel,* edited by J. Andrew Overman and Robert S. MacLennan. Atlanta: Scholars, 1992.

Kraemer, Ross S. *Her Share of the Blessings: Women's Religions among Pagans, Jews and Christians in the Greco-Roman World.* New York: Oxford University Press, 1992.

——— "Jewish Women and Christian Origins: Some Caveats." *Women & Christian Origins,* edited by R. Kraemer and M. D'Angelo, 35–49. New York: Oxford University Press, 1999.

———. "Jewish Women and Women's Judaism(s) at the Beginning of Christianity." *Women & Christian Origins,* edited by R. Kraemer and M. D'Angelo. New York: Oxford University Press, 1999.

———. "Monastic Jewish Women in Greco-Roman Egypt: Philo on the Therapeutrides." *Signs* 14 (1989) 342–70.

———. "The Other as Woman: An Aspect of Polemic among Pagans, Jews, and Christians in the Greco-Roman World." In *The Other in Jewish Thought and History: Constructions of Jewish Culture and Identity,* edited by Laurence J. Silberstein and Robert L. Cohn, 50–79. New York: New York University Press, 1994.

Lake, Kirsopp, and F. J. Foakes-Jackson, editors. *The Acts of the Apostles.* 5 vols. The Beginnings of Christianity pt. 1. London: Macmillan, 1920–33.

Lee, Chungmin. "Embedded Performatives." *Language* 51 (1975) 105–8.

Leeuwen, Theo van. "The Representation of Social Actors." In *Texts and Practices: Readings in Critical Discourse Analysis,* edited by Carmen Rosa Caldas-Coulthard and Malcolm Coulthard, 32–70. London: Routledge, 1996.

Levinas, Emmanuel. *Humanism of the Other.* Translated by Nidra Poller. Chicago: University of Illinois Press, 2003.

———. *Time and the Other and Additional Essays.* Translated by Richard A. Cohen. Pittsburgh: Duquesne University Press, 1987.

Levine, Amy-Jill. *A Feminist Companion to Luke.* London: Sheffield, 2002.

Levinskaya, Irina. *The Book of Acts in Its Diaspora Setting.* The Book of Acts in Its First Century Setting 5. Grand Rapids: Eerdmans, 1996.

Lüdemann, Gerd. "The Acts of the Apostles and the Beginnings of Simonian Gnosis." *NTS* 33 (1987) 420–26.

Luz, Ulrich. *Matthew in History: Interpretation, Influence, and Effects.* Minneapolis: Fortress, 1994.

Machin, David, and Theo van Leeuwen. "Global Schemas and Local Discourses in Cosmopolitan." *JSoc* 7 (2003) 493–512.

Machinist, Peter. "Outsiders and Insiders: The Biblical View of Emergent Israel and Its Contexts." In *The Other in Jewish Thought and History: Constructions of Jewish Culture and Identity,* edited by Laurence J. Silberstein and Robert L. Cohn, 35–60. New York: New York University Press, 1994.

MacLennan, R. S., and A. T. Kraabel. "The God-fearers—A Literary and Theological Invention." In *Diaspora Jews and Judaism: Essays in Honor of, and in Dialogue with A. Thomas Kraabel,* edited by J. Andrew Overman and Robert S. MacLennan, 131–43. Atlanta: Scholars, 1992.

Maddow, Rachel. "Interview with the Honorable Raymond Joseph, Haitian Ambassador to the U.S." MSNBC's *The Rachel Maddow Show,* January 13, 2010. Transcript online: http://www.msnbc.msn.com/id/34863181/ns/msnbc_tv-rachel_maddow_show/.

Malony, Linda. "The Year of Luke: A Feminist Perspective." *CTM* 21 (1994) 415–23.

Maly, Eugene H. "Women and the Gospel of Luke." *BTB* 10 (1980) 99–104.

Mandelbaum, Maurice. "History and Criticism: A Commentary." *NLH* 5 (1974) 613–18.

Margolin, Uri. "The Doer and the Deed: Action as a Basis for Characterization in Narrative." *PT* 7 (1986) 205–25.

———. "The What, the When and the How of Being a Character in Literary Narrative." *Style* 24 (1990) 453–69.

Marguerat, Daniel. "Juifs et chrétiens selon Luc-Actes." In *Le Déchirement: Juifs et chrétiens au premier siècle,* edited by Daniel Marguerat. Geneva: Labor et Fides, 1996. First published as "Juifs et chretiens selon Luc-Actes. Surmonter conflit des lectures." *Bib* 75 (1994) 126–46.

———. "La mort d'Ananias et Saphira (Ac 5.1–11) dans la stratégie narrative de Luc." *NTS* 39 (1993) 209–26.

Martin-Asensio, Gustavo. "Participant Reference and Foregrounded Syntax in the Stephen Episode." In *Discourse Analysis and the New Testament: Approaches and Results,* edited by Stanley E. Porter and Jeffrey T. Reed, 235–57. JSNTSup 70. Sheffield: Sheffield Academic, 1999.

———. *Transitivity-Based Foregrounding in the Acts of the Apostles: A Functional-Grammatical Approach to the Lukan Perspective.* JSNTSup 202. Sheffield: Sheffield Academic, 2000.

Martin, Clarice J. "The Acts of the Apostles." In *Searching the Scriptures,* edited by Elisabeth Schüssler Fiorenza, 2:763–99. New York: Crossroad, 1993–94.

Mastin, B. A. "A Note on Acts 19,14." *Bib* 9 (1978) 97–99.

———. "Scaeva the Chief Priest." *JTS* 27 (1976) 405–12.

Matthews, Christopher R. "Philip and Simon, Luke and Peter: A Lukan Sequel and Its Intertextual Success." *SBLSP* 31 (1992) 133–46.

————. *Philip, Apostle and Evangelist: Configurations of a Tradition.* Boston: Brill, 2002.

Matthews, Shelley. *First Converts: Rich Pagan Women and the Rhetoric of Mission in Early Judaism and Christianity.* Standford: Stanford University Press, 2001.

Maurizio, L. "Anthropology and Spirit Possession: A Reconsideration of the Pythia's Role at Delphi." *JHS* 115 (1995) 69–86.

Mealand, David. "The Close of Acts and Its Hellenistic Greek Vocabulary." *NTS* 36 (1990) 583–97.

Meeks, Wayne A. "Breaking Away: Three New Testament Pictures of Christianity's Separation from the Jewish Communities." In *"To See Ourselves as Others See Us": Christians, Jews, "Others" in Late Antiquity,* edited by Jacob Neusner and Ernest S. Frerichs, 93–115. Scholars Press Studies in the Humanities Series. Chico, CA: Scholars, 1985.

Meskin, Jacob. "The Other in Levinas and Derrida: Society, Philosophy, Judaism." In *The Other in Jewish Thought and History: Constructions of Jewish Culture and Identity,* edited by Laurence J. Silberstein and Robert L. Cohn, 402–23. New York: New York University Press, 1994.

Metzger, Bruce. *A Textual Commentary of the Greek New Testament.* 2nd ed. London: United Bible Societies, 1971.

Millar, Fergus. *The Crowd in Rome in the Late Republic.* Ann Arbor: University of Michigan Press, 1998.

Momigliano Arnaldo. *The Development of Greek Biography.* Cambridge: Harvard University Press, 1993.

Morton, Russell. "Acts 12:1–19: Life in the Midst of Death." *Int* 55 (2001) 67–69.

Moule, C. F. D. "Once More, Who Were the Hellenists?" *ExpT* 70 (1959) 100–102.

Moxnes, Halvor. "Meals and the New Community in Luke." *SEA* 51–52 (1986) 158–67.

Newsom, C., and S. Ringe, editors. *The Women's Bible Commentary.* Louisville: Westminster John Knox, 1992.

O'Day, Gail. "Acts." In *The Women's Bible Commentary,* edited by Carol A. Newsome and Sharon H. Ringe, 305–12. Louisville: Westminster John Knox, 1992.

Oktar, Lütfiye. "The Ideological Organization of Representational Processes in the Presentation of Us and Them." *DiscSoc* 12 (2001) 313–46.

Origen. "Homilia XVII." In *Homélies sur S. Luc. Texte Latin et Fragements Grecs.* Translation and notes by Henri Crouzel, François Fournier, and Pierre Périchon. Paris: Cerf, 1998.

O'Toole, Robert F. "'You Did Not Life to Us (Human Beings) but to God.'" *Bib* 76 (1995) 182–209.

Pagels, Elaine. *The Origin of Satan.* New York: Random House, 1995.

Parsons, Mikeal C., and Richard I. Pervo. *Rethinking the Unity of Luke and Acts.* Minneapolis: Fortress, 1993.

Pearce, Sarah. "Belonging and Not Belonging: Local Perspectives in Philo of Alexandria." In *Jewish Local Patriotism and Self-Identification in the Graeco-Roman Period,* edited by Sian Jones and Sarah Pearce, 79–105. JSPSup 31. Sheffield: Sheffield Academic, 1998.

Perry, Ben Edwin. *The Ancient Romance: A Literary Historical Account of Their Origins.* Berkeley: University of California Press, 1967.

Pervo, Richard I. *Acts.* Hermeneia Minneapolis: Fortress, 2009.

———. *Profit with Delight: The Literary Genre of the Acts of the Apostles.* Philadelphia: Fortress, 1987.

Phelan, James. "Character and Judgment in Narrative and in Lyric: Toward an Understanding of the Audience's Engagement in *The Waves*." *Style* 90 (1990) 408–22.

———. *Reading People, Reading Plots: Character, Progression, and the Interpretation of Narrative.* Chicago: University of Chicago Press, 1989.

Pippin, Tina. "'For Fear of the Jews': Lying and Truth-Telling in Translating the Gospel of John." *Semeia* 76 (1996) 81–97.

Pomeroy, Sarah B. *Goddesses, Whores, Wives, and Slaves: Women in Classical Antiquity.* New York: Schocken, 1975.

Rakotoharintsifa, Andrianjatovo. "Luke and the Internal Divisions in the Early Church." In *Luke's Literary Achievement: Collected Essays*, edited by C. M. Tuckett, 165–77. JSNTSup 116. Sheffield: Sheffield Academic, 1995.

Reimer, Andy M. *Miracle and Magic: A Study in the Acts of the Apostles and the Life of Apollonius of Tyanna.* New York: Sheffield, 2002.

Reimer, Ivoni Richter. *Women in the Acts of the Apostles: A Feminist Liberation Perspective.* Minneapolis: Fortress, 1995.

Reinhartz, Adele. "Building Skyscrapers on Toothpicks." In *Anatomies of Narrative Criticism: The Past, Present, and Futures of the Fourth Gospel as Literature*, edited by Tom Thatcher and Stephen D. Moore. SBL Resources for Biblical Study 25. Boston: Brill, 2009.

———. "'Jews' and Jews in the Fourth Gospel." In *Anti-Judaism and the Fourth Gospel*, edited by Reimund Bieringer, et al., 213–27. Louisville: Westminster John Knox, 2001.

———. "The New Testament and Anti-Judaism: A Literary-Critical Approach." *JES* 25 (1988) 1–14.

Rese, M. "The Jews in Luke-Acts. Some Second Thoughts." In *The Unity of Luke-Acts*, edited by J. Verheyden, 185–202. BETL 142. Leuven: Leuven University Press, 1999.

Ruether, Rosemary Radford. *Faith and Fratricide: The Theological Roots of Anti-Semitism.* New York: Crossroad, 1974.

Ricoeur, Paul. *Interpretation Theory: Discourse and the Surplus of Meaning.* Fort Worth: Texas Christian University Press, 1976.

Rimmon-Kenan, Shlomith. *Narrative Fiction: Contemporary Poetics.* London: Routledge, 1989.

Ryan, R. "The Women from Galilee and Discipleship in Luke." *BTB* 15 (1985) 56–59.

Salmon, Marilyn. "Insider or Outsider? Luke's Relationship with Judaism." In *Luke-Acts and the Jewish People*, edited by Joseph B. Tyson, 76–82. Minneapolis: Augsburg, 1988.

Sanders, Jack T. *Charisma, Converts, Competitors: Societal Factors in the Success of Early Christianity.* London: SCM, 2000.

———. "The Jewish People in Luke-Acts." In *Luke-Acts and the Jewish People*, edited by Joseph B. Tyson, 51–75. Minneapolis: Augsburg, 1988.

———. *The Jews in Luke-Acts.* London: SCM, 1987.

Sandmel, Samuel. *Anti-Semitism in the New Testament?* Philadelphia: Fortress, 1978.

Schaberg, J. "Luke." In *The Women's Bible Commentary*, edited by Carol A. Newsome and Sharon H. Ringe, 275–92. Louisville: Westminster John Knox, 1992.

Schottroff, Luise. *Let the Oppressed Go Free (Befreiungserfahrungen): Feminist Perspectives on the New Testament.* Translated by Annemarie S. Kidder. Louisville: Westminster John Knox, 1993.

———. *Lydia's Impatient Sisters: A Feminist Social History of Early Christianity.* Louisville: Westminster John Knox, 1995.

Schüssler Fiorenza, Elisabeth. *But She Said: Feminist Practices of Biblical Interpretation.* Boston: Beacon, 1992.

———. *In Memory of Her: A Feminist Theological Reconstruc-tion of Christian Origins.* New York: Crossroad, 1983.

———. *The Power of the Word: Scripture and the Rhetoric of Empire.* Minneapolis: Fortress, 2007.

———. *Rhetoric and Ethic: The Politics of Biblical Studies.* Minneapolis: Fortress, 1999.

———. *Searching the Scriptures.* Vol. 2: *A Feminist Commentary.* New York: Crossroad, 1994.

Schweizer, Eduard. "Concerning the Speeches in Acts." In *Studies in Luke-Acts*, edited by Leander E. Keck and J. Louis Martyn, 208–16. Nashville: Abingdon, 1966.

Scollon, Ron. "Action and Text: Towards an Integrated Understanding of the Place of Text in Social (Inter)action, Mediated Discourse analysis and the Problem of Social Action." In *Methods of Critical Discourse Analysis*, edited by Ruth Wodak and Michael Meyer, 139–83. London: Sage, 2001.

Searle, John R. *Speech Acts: An Essay in the Philosophy of Language.* Cambridge: Cambridge University Press, 1969.

Seim, Turid Karlsen. *The Double Message of Luke-Acts: Patterns of Gender in Luke-Acts.* Nashville: Abingdon, 1994.

Shelton, James B. *Mighty in Word and Deed: The Role of the Holy Spirit in Luke-Acts.* Peabody, MA: Hendrickson, 1991.

Shelton, Jo-Ann. *As the Romans Did: A Sourcebook in Roman Social History.* New York: Oxford University Press, 1988.

Shepherd, William H., Jr. *The Narrative Function of the Holy Spirit as a Character in Luke-Acts.* Atlanta: Scholars, 1994.

Sievers, Joseph. "The Role of Women in the Hasmonean Dynasty." In *Josephus, the Bible, and History*, 132–46. Detroit: Wayne State University Press, 1989.

Silberstein, Laurence J. "Others Within and Others Without: Rethinking Jewish Identity and Culture." In *The Other in Jewish Thought and History: Constructions of Jewish Culture and Identity*, edited by Laurence J. Silberstein and Robert L. Cohn, 1–34. New York: New York University Press, 1994.

Smith, Jonathan Z. "Close Encounters of Diverse Kind." In *Religion and Cultural Studies*, edited by Susan L. Mizruchi, 3–21. Princeton: Princeton University Press, 2001.

———. "Differential Equations on Construction the Other." In *Relating Religion: Essays in the Study of Religion*, edited by Jonathan Z. Smith, 230–50. Chicago: University of Chicago Press, 2004.

———. "The Temple and the Magician." In *God's Christ and His People: Studies in Honor of Nils Alstrup Dahl*, edited by Jacob Jervell and Wayne A. Meeks, 233–47. Oslo: Universitetsforlaget, 1977.

———. "Towards Interpreting Demonic Powers in Hellenistic and Roman Antiquity." *ANRW* 2.16.1 (1978) 425–39.

————. "What a Difference a Difference Makes." In *"To See Ourselves as Others See Us": Christians, Jews, "Others" in Late Antiquity,* edited by Jacob Neusner and Ernest S. Frerichs, 3–48. Scholars Press Studies in the Humanities Series. Chico, CA: Scholars, 1985.

Smith, Mitzi J. "Slavery in the Early Church." In *True to Our Native Land: An African American New Testament Commentary,* edited by Brian K. Blount. Minneapolis: Fortress, 2008.

————. "'Understand Ye a Parable!': The Acts of Peter and the Twelve Apostles as Parable Narrative." *Apocrypha* 13 (2002) 29–52.

Soards, Marion L. *The Speeches in Acts: Their Content, Context and Concerns.* Louisville: Westminster John Knox, 1994.

Spencer, F. Scott. "Neglected Widows in Acts 6:1–7. *CBQ* 56 (1994) 715–33.

————. "Out of Mind, Out of Voice: Slave-Girls and Prophetic Daughters in Luke-Acts." *BibInt* 7 (1999) 133–55.

————. *The Portrait of Philip in Acts: A Study of Roles and Relations.* JSNTSup 6. Sheffield: Sheffield Academic, 1992.

Staley, Jeffrey. "Changing Woman: Postcolonial Reflections on Acts 16:6–40." *JSNT* 73 (1990) 113–35.

————. "Reading Acts 16:6–40 on the Edges of the Navajo Reservation." *WW* 24 (2004) 296–304.

Stark, Rodney. "Reconstructing the Rise of Christianity: The Role of Women." *SocRel* 56 (1995) 229–44.

Strange, W. A. "The Sons of Sceva and the Text of Acts 19:14." *JTS* 38 (1987) 97–106.

Stratton, Kimberly B. "The Rhetoric of 'Magic' in Early Christian Discourse: Gender, Power and the Construction of 'Heresy.'" In *Mapping Gender in Ancient Religious Discourses,* edited by Todd Penner and Caroline Vander Stichele, 89–114. Biblical Interpretation Series 84. Leiden: Brill, 2006.

Strelan, Rick. "Who Was Bar Jesus (Acts 13, 6–12)?" *Bib* 85 (2004) 65–81.

Talbert, Charles H. *Literary Patterns, Theological Themes, and the Genre of Luke-Acts.* Missoula, MT: Scholars Press, 1974.

Tannehill, Robert C. "Cornelius and Tabitha Encounter Luke's Jesus. *Int* 48 (1994) 347–55.

————. "Israel in Luke-Acts: A Tragic Story." *JBL* 104 (1985) 69–85.

————. *The Narrative Unity of Luke-Acts: A Literary Interpretation.* Vol. 2: *The Acts of the Apostles.* Minneapolis: Fortress, 1990.

————. "Rejection by Jews and Turning to Gentiles: The Pattern of Paul's Mission in Acts." In *Luke-Acts and the Jewish People,* edited by Joseph B. Tyson, 83–101. Minneapolis: Augsburg, 1988.

Tavangar, Manoochehr. "Lexical Foregrounding: A Perennial Problem in Translating Literary Communication." *Babel* 49 (2003) 164–84.

Thomas, W. Derek. "The Place of Women in the Church at Philippi." *ExpT* 83 (1972) 117–20.

Thompson, Richard P. "Believers and Religious Leaders in Jerusalem: Contrasting Portraits of Jews in Acts 1–7." In *Literary Studies in Luke-Acts: Essays in Honor of Joseph B. Tyson,* edited by Richard P. Thompson and Thomas E. Phillips, 327–44. Macon, GA: Mercer University Press 1998.

Thurston, Bonnie. "Who Was Anna?: Luke 2:36–38." *PRS* 28 (2001) 47–55.

Tiede, David L. "'Glory to Thy People Israel': Luke-Acts and the Jews." In *Luke-Acts and the Jewish People*, edited by Joseph B. Tyson, 21–34. Minneapolis: Augsburg, 1988.

Trocmé, Etienne. "The Jews as Seen by Paul and Luke." In *"To See Ourselves as Others See Us": Christians, Jews, "Others" in Late Antiquity*, edited by Jacob Neusner and Ernest S. Frerichs, 145–61. Chico, CA: Scholars, 1985.

Tuckett, Christopher M. *Luke*. New Testament Guides. Sheffield: Sheffield Academic, 1996.

Turner, Max. "Jesus and the Spirit in Lukan Perspective." *TynB* 32 (1981) 3–42.

———. "Spirit Endowment in Luke-Acts: Some Linguistic Considerations," In *Biblical and Historical Essays from London Bible College*, edited by Harold H. Rowdon, 131–58. Vox evangelica 12. London: London Bible College, 1981.

Tuzlak, Ayse. "The Magician and the Heretic: The Case of Simon Magus," In *Magic and Ritual in the Ancient World*, edited by Paul Mirecki and Marvin Meyer, 416–26. Religions in the Graeco-Roman World 141. Leiden: Brill, 2002.

Tyson, Joseph B. *Images of Judaism in Luke-Acts*. Columbia: University of South Carolina Press, 1992.

———. "The Problem of Jewish Rejection in Acts." In *Luke-Acts and the Jewish People*, edited by Joseph B. Tyson, 124–37. Minneapolis: Augsburg, 1988.

Unnik, W. C. van. "Die Apostelgeschichte und die Häresien." *ZNW* 58 (1967) 240–46.

Vanhoye, Albert. "Le Juifs selon les Actes des Apôtres et les Épîtres." *Bib* 72 (1991) 69–89.

Via, E. Jane. "Women in the Gospel of Luke." In *Women in the World's Religions, Past and Present*, edited by Ursula King, 38–55. New York: Paragon, 1987.

———. "Women, the Discipleship of Service and the Early Christian Ritual Meal in the Gospel of Luke." *SLJT* 29 (1985) 37–60.

Vos, Craig S. de. "Finding a Charge that Fits: The Accusation against Paul and Silas at Philippi (Acts 16.19–21)." *JSNT* 74 (1999) 51–63.

Waitz, H. "Die Quelle der Philipusgeschichten in der Apostelgeschichte 8,5–40." *ZNW* 7 (1906) 340–55.

Wall, Robert W. "The Acts of the Apostles." In *The New Interpreters Bible*. Nashville: Abingdon, 1994.

Weaver, John B. *Plots of Epiphany: Prison-Escape in Acts of the Apostles*. Berlin: de Gruyter, 2004.

Willimon, William H. *Acts*. Interpretation. Louisville: John Knox, 1988.

Wills, Lawrence M. "The Depiction of the Jews in Acts." *JBL* 110 (1991) 631–54.

———. *Insiders and Outsiders in the Biblical World*. Lanham: Rowman & Littlefield, 2008.

———. *The Jewish Novel in the Ancient World*. Ithaca: Cornell University Press, 1995.

———. "Third Maccabees as Fiction and Non-Fiction." Paper presented in the Hellenistic Judaism and Ancient Fiction and Early Jewish and Christian Narrative Sections at the Society of Biblical Literature Annual Meeting in Nashville, November 20, 2000.

Wilson, R. McL. "Simon and Gnostic Origins." In *Les Actes des Apôtres: Traditions, Rédaction, Théologie*, edited by J. Kremer. BETL 48. Leuven: Leuven University Press, 1979.

Wilson, Stephen G. *The Gentiles and the Gentile Mission in Luke-Acts*. Cambridge: Cambridge University Press, 1973.

Winter, Bruce W., and Andrew D. Clarke, editors. *The Book of Acts in Its Ancient Literary Setting*. Grand Rapids: Eerdmans, 1993.

Witherington, Ben, III, editor. *History, Literature, and Society in the Book of Acts*. Cambridge: Cambridge University Press, 1996.

———. *Women in the Earliest Churches*. SNTSMS 59. Cambridge: Cambridge University Press, 1988.

Wodak, Ruth. "What CDA Is About—A Summary of Its History, Important Concepts, and Its Developments." In *Methods of Critical Discourse Analysis*, edited by Ruth Wodak and Michael Meyer. London: Sage, 2001.

Wodak, Ruth, et al. *The Discursive Construction of National Identity*. Edinburgh: Edinburgh University Press, 1999.

Wolfson, Elliot R. "Woman—The Feminine as Other in Theosophic Kabbalah: Some Philosophical Observations on the Divine Androgyne." In *The Other in Jewish Thought and History: Constructions of Jewish Culture and Identity*, edited by Laurence J. Silberstein and Robert L. Cohn, 166–204. New York: New York University Press, 1994.

Xenophon of Ephesus. *An Ephesian Tale*. Translated by Graham Anderson. In *Collected Ancient Greek Novels*, edited by B. P Reardon. Berkeley: University of California Press, 1989.